CASS SERIES: STUDIES IN INTELLIGENCE
(Series Editors: Christopher Andrew and Michael I. Handel)

SPY FICTION, SPY FILMS AND REAL INTELLIGENCE

Spy Fiction, Spy Films
AND
Real Intelligence

Edited by
WESLEY K. WARK

FRANK CASS

First published in 1991 in Great Britain by
FRANK CASS & CO. LTD.
Gainsborough House, Gainsborough Road,
London E11 1RS, England

and in the United States of America by
FRANK CASS
International Specialized Book Services,
5602 NE Hassalo Street, Portland OR 97213

British Library Cataloguing in Publication Data
Spy fiction, spy films and real intelligence. –
(Cass series: studies in intelligence).
1. Spy fiction in English - Critical studies
I. Wark, Wesley K.   II. Intelligence and National Security
823.0872

ISBN 0-7146-3411-5

This group of studies first appeared in a Special Issue on Spy
Fiction, Spy Films and Real Intelligence of the journal *Intelligence
and National Security*, Vol.5, No.4 (October 1990), published by
Frank Cass & Co. Ltd.

Typeset by Selectmove Ltd, London
Printed and bound in Great Britain by
Antony Rowe Ltd, Chippenham

CONTENTS

Notes on Contributors

Christine Bold is author of *Selling the Wild West: Popular Western Fiction, 1860–1960* (1987) and is currently working on the US Federal Writers' Project of the 1930s. She is Assistant Professor of English at the University of Guelph, Ontario.

Alan R. Booth is a Professor of History at Ohio University, specializing in African history. His most recent book was *Swaziland: Tradition and Change in a Southern African Kingdom* (1983). He was an Air Intelligence Officer with the Navy Heavy Attack Squadron from 1956 to 1959.

Nicholas Hiley, a Research Fellow in the Department of War Studies, King's College, London, has published numerous articles on intelligence and modern history.

Eric Homberger Reader in American Literature at the University of East Anglia, was educated at the University of California, Berkeley, and Cambridge University. He is the author of *John le Carré* (1986) and several articles on spy fiction as well as *American Writers and Radical Politics, 1900–1939* (1986) and a biography of John Reed (1990). He is currently completing a book about New York City in the mid-nineteenth century.

Keith Jeffery is a Senior Lecturer in History at the University of Ulster at Jordanstown. Among his books are *The British Army and the Crisis of Empire, 1918–1922* (1984) and (with Paul Arthur) *Northern Ireland since 1968* (1988). He is joint editor of the journal *Irish Historical Studies*.

Philip Jenkins is Professor of Criminal Justice at Pennsylvania State University. His publications include *The Making of a Ruling Class* (1983), *Crime and Justice* (1984) and *A History of Wales, 1540–1990* (forthcoming). His current research focuses on contemporary European terrorism.

J.J. MacIntosh is Professor of Philosophy at the University of Calgary. He has published articles and chapters in a number of books and philosophical journals. His current research interests include the history and philosophy of science, logic, and the philosophy of religion.

Eunan O'Halpin is a Lecturer in Government at the Dublin Business School, Dublin City University. He is the author of *The Decline of the Union: British Government in Ireland 1891–1920* (1987) and *Head of the Civil Service: A Study of Sir Warren Fisher* (1989). He is preparing books on internal security in independent Ireland and on the Irish administrative system.

Denis Smyth is Professor of History at the University of Toronto and a Fellow of the Royal Historical Society. His publications include *Spain, the EEC and Nato* (with Paul Preston) (1984) and *Diplomacy and Strategy of Survival: British Policy and Franco's Spain, 1940–41* (1986). He is currently researching the secret intelligence preparations for the D-Day landings.

John Starnes was the first civilian Director-General of the Security Service of the Royal Canadian Mounted Police from 1970 to 1973. Previously he had been Canadian Ambassador to the Federal Republic of Germany and to the United Arab Republic and the Sudan, and Assistant Under-Secretary of State for External Affairs. He was chairman of the Canadian Joint Intelligence Committee, member of the Council of the International Institute for Strategic Studies, London, and member-at-large of the executive of the Canadian Association for Security Studies, Toronto. Since retiring he has published four spy novels.

David Trotter is a Reader in the English Department of University College, London. He is the author of *The Poetry of Abraham Cowley* (1979), *The Making of the Reader: Language and Subjectivity in Modern American, English and Irish Poetry* (1984), and *Circulation: Defoe, Dickens and the Economics of the Novel* (1988). He is writing a history of the English novel, 1895–1920.

Wesley K. Wark, assistant editor of *Intelligence and National Security*, is Associate Professor in the Department of History at the University of Toronto. He has published numerous articles on intelligence and is the author of *The Ultimate Enemy: British Intelligence and Nazi Germany* (1985). His current research includes work for a biography of Field Marshall Lord Ironside.

D. Cameron Watt, Stevenson Professor of International History at the London School of Economics, served in the intelligence corps in Austria in 1947–48. His books include *Personalities and Policies* (1965), *Too Serious a Business* (1974), *Succeeding John Bull* (1984) and *How War Came: The Immediate Origins of the Second World War* (1989). He is currently finishing an official history of the central organization of defence in the United Kingdom.

Introduction: Fictions of History

WESLEY K. WARK

From the beginning, the spy novel has enjoyed a special licence to thrill. It emerged from a literary family where thrills were expected and supplied in abundance. Varieties of nineteenth-century popular fiction including the detective novel, the anarchist novel, the terrorist novel, and the American dime novel, with its engagement in the affirmation of a new nation, were all part of its inheritance.[1] Out of this genetic soup the spy novel came into its own in the years just before the First World War: years in which feverish concerns for national security, imperial strength and impending conflict provided rich material for the new literary formula-to-be.[2] Erskine Childers provided momentum by penning one great spy novel, *The Riddle of the Sands* (1903). At the opposite end of the production line, hacks like William Le Queux and E. Phillips Oppenheim produced spy fiction in profusion. What these works had in common was their effort to thrill (and as an integral part of the thrill, to warn) readers with apparently real plots of international intrigue and the rescue (or corruption) of civilization through the agency of individual spies and intelligence organizations. The attraction of spy fiction has consistently rested on its use of the artifice of apparent realism; its method has been to create an alternative or counter-history. Beguiling, worrying, plausible or believable fictions of history are on offer, often with a near irresistible double guarantee of authenticity. Not only are details of plot, character and setting designed to simulate the real world, but these are frequently underwritten by explicit authorial statements. A clever example is to be found in a passage from Graham Greene's 1943 thriller, *The Ministry of Fear*, in which the reader learns that the world has finally caught up with the spy novel:

> It sounds like a thriller, doesn't it, but the thrillers are like life – more like life than you are . . . you used to laugh at the books about spies, and murders, and violence, and wild motor car chases, but, dear, that's real life: it's what we've all made of the world since you died.[3]

William Le Queux aimed at the same effect, but used a blunter pen. He was a pioneer of the faction industry, deliberately blurring the line between fiction and fact and presenting himself in his texts as a spymaster with a personal knowledge and insight into the threat posed by German spies in Britain. The opening pages of Le Queux's *Spies of the Kaiser*, with their melodramatic claims to fearful and clandestine knowledge, are typical of his style.[4] With Le Queux, apparent realism first showed its amazing potential. His pre-1914 spy and invasion scare novels set off a panic in Britain about widespread German espionage and led the government to create a secret service to ward off the (fictional) threat.[5]

The commercial and formulaic imperatives of the genre, established as early as Le Queux's day, continue to stimulate new experiments in apparent realism. Consider the television series, 'The Prisoner', which now enjoys something of a cult status. The series was loosely based on George Markstein's novel, *The Cooler*, which itself purported to be a work of fact in the guise of fiction. *The Cooler* offered as its thriller element the story of a special prison devised in Britain during the Second World War to incarcerate British and Allied agents who could not be relied upon to maintain the secrecy of operations about which they had knowledge.[6] This was given a surreal touch in the TV version, in the shape of the 'Village', with its weird society of inmates and its high-tech devices for surveillance and control. The package was abetted by the fine performance of Patrick McGoohan as 'The Prisoner', a former secret agent whose past and security 'crime' are kept deliberately shadowy. A recent twist in this complex mutation of fact and fiction has been the announcement by the Caterham Car Company (UK) of its production of a replica of the original Lotus 7 driven by 'The Prisoner', to be authenticated by a special dashboard plaque signed by Patrick McGoohan.[7]

Many other examples of the contemporary impact of apparent realism on spy fiction could be cited, from Charles McCarry's well-wrought *Miernick Dossier*, in which the text is fashioned to resemble the contents of an intelligence file – a clever adaptation of the epistolary form – to the ways in which John le Carré's one-time work for British intelligence has been used to authenticate both his spy fiction and his utterances on the state of contemporary intelligence and the defunct Cold War.

What matters about these various strategies of apparent realism in the spy novel is not the relative success obtained in depicting historical context and political process accurately, as some earlier critics of spy fiction have suggested,[8] but the successful counterfeiting of realism as a mechanism for achieving other kinds of literary, political and psychological effects. Three new and noteworthy perspectives have emerged, all of which recognize the fundamental role of the illusion of realism. John Cawelti and Bruce Rosenberg, in their collaborative study, *The Spy Story*, discuss the nature and impact of what they call 'cycles of clandestinity' in influencing not only the structure of spy fiction, but also the historical development of espionage services and popular fantasies about intelligence and secret government. The authors see the relationship between fiction and fact in the spy novel as the product of a shared cultural environment in which espionage agencies, writers and readers all live out a mutual fantasy of clandestinity. This approach allows important claims to be made for the significance of spy fiction: the authors call the genre a 'major expressive phenomenon of modern culture', but it does little to illuminate the precise strategies and uses of realism in spy fiction.[9]

David Stafford's *The Silent Game: The Real World of Imaginary Spies*, offers a compelling account of aspects of realism in spy fiction. Stafford sees the spy novel as a highly polemical idiom, fuelled by popular, exploitable fears of imperial decline. Spy fiction, in his account, translates concern about the realities of international politics into dramas of redemption or, latterly, studied despair. Again, this approach, while it concentrates on the changing political idiom of the spy novel, does not quite solve the full riddle of the genre's use of realism.

The commentator who has devoted the most attention to the role of apparent realism in spy fiction is Michael Denning. In *Cover Stories: Narrative and Ideology in the British Spy Thriller*, Denning discusses what he calls 'feigned' realism in British spy fiction. He assesses the operation of this realism in Marxist terms, arguing that 'the intelligence community serves as a shadowy figure for the social world of late capitalism where the opacities that surround human agency are cut through by projecting an essentially marginal figure, the secret agent'.[10] The 'cover story' of realism in spy fiction is not a static device. Denning notes that changing modes of presenting reality in the fictional world of spies have often marked critical shifts in the production formula.[11] This is significant not only as a means of exploring popular attitudes to such issues as power politics and intelligence, but as an indicator of the consistency with which spy fiction has pursued its alliance with a projected realism as a central narrative strategy.

Yet there remains, despite Cawelti and Rosenberg, Stafford and Denning, a real mystery as to why spy fiction has fastened so avidly on to the device of apparent realism. Then there is the perennial issue of literary reception: how, to what extent and why have popular attitudes to a whole range of issues from the character of the individual spy, to the nature of intelligence organizations and even to issues of the conduct of international relations, been shaped by spy fiction's narrative tricks? Thirdly, there is the issue of the origins of apparent realism itself. As suggested earlier, spy fiction's reliance on this device is also a claim for the fitness of an alternative or counter-history. In offering fictions of history, spy fiction in fact works as a competitor to professional or academic history. Spy fiction is, in this respect, a variety of popular history in disguise: the disguise being the old device of 'faction'.

In seeking to pursue these questions further, it is important that analysis avoid the trap of either formalist literary criticism, with its emphasis on the internal structure of the text, or a reductive historical approach, which would seek to turn the text merely into a useful archive of popular thinking. On the issue of methodology, the work of Dominick La Capra, especially *History and Criticism* and *History, Politics and the Novel*, offers inspiration.[12] In both these studies he makes a plea for a 'hybrid genre study' combining the best features of literary and historical criticism. He further argues that such an approach should lead to new ways of assessing the sociological context in which literature is created and new ways of understanding history itself through what La Capra calls the 'contestatory voices' and 'counter discourses' of the past.[13] Spy fiction clearly has its 'counter discourse' about the past and presents tremendous opportunities for an interdisciplinary critical approach.

RETAILING HISTORY

La Capra clearly imagines that a study of fiction might well liberate the historian's understanding and ways of narrating the past. Spy fiction's 'counter-discourse', however, can only be understood in opposition to professional history and does not quite deliver this sort of enlightenment. Rather by appropriating and shaping popular attitudes and fantasies about history, the spy genre provides illumination about what sort of history is wanted by mass audiences and illustrates the degree to which wish-fulfilment is separated from reality in an understanding of the dynamics of the past.

Four broad stages can be identified in the evolution of spy fiction's own version of history. The first arrives with the pre-1914 and First World War generation of heroic espionage romances. The key contributors in the writing of this period – William Le Queux, E. Phillips Oppenheim, Erskine Childers and John Buchan – all shared a recognizable doctrine of history which they wrote into their plots.[14] The historical setting for their romances was provided by a popular social Darwinistic understanding of the roots of conflict between nations and between races.[15] The world was a dangerous place in which conflict between states was nearly inevitable, made so not least by assumed differences in national character and cultural sophistication that easily posited enemies among one's neighbours. The survival of individual civilizations was a precarious business; if sufficient will (perhaps a Nietzschean borrowing) and sufficient strength on the part of states and societies could not be found then civilization would succumb to pressures from without and from within and crack under the strain. This generation of spy fiction writers found a solution to the dilemma of brutal and grinding struggle in the individual (male) hero with his capacity for regeneration and his ability to foil plots against the state.[16] These plots were themselves depicted as dangerous forces that just might provide the dreaded momentum that would launch a society into irreversible decline or into slavery or subordination at the hands of a stronger or more ruthless civilization, state or race. Buchan's Richard Hannay, who flourishes in the trilogy of novels – *The Thirty-Nine Steps* (1915), *Greenmantle* (1916) and *Mr. Standfast* (1919) – is perhaps the exemplar of this type of hero.[17]

What gave substance to early spy fiction's use of apparent realism was an historical framework consisting of shadowy social Darwinistic forces, conspiracies against order, individual heroism and melodramatic resolution. History was violent and contained grand forces, but could be bent to human will and was subject to thrilling salvation.

The next significant development in the uses of history in the spy fiction genre comes in the late 1920s and 1930s. What is characteristic about this period and its principal British authors – Somerset Maugham, Compton Mackenzie, Eric Ambler and Graham Greene – was the attempt to shake off the familiar limits imposed by the heroic spy adventure and to provide a different and more significant kind of thrill (or 'entertainment', as Greene would have it).[18] The reconstructed formula sought to plumb more deeply the character of the spy hero and the forces of history within and against which he operated. These authors rejected the social Darwinistic outlook of their predecessors and sought instead some new understanding of threats and dangers to civilization. In doing so, they steered spy fiction towards greater verisimilitude and left-wing politics. Michael Denning notes this change as the 'central mutation' of the spy fiction plot; Ralph Harper comments that with the novels of Eric Ambler, in particular, the spy genre gained a significant 'degree of sophistication' about the 'powers of darkness'.[19] A 'merchants of death' theme, with its explicit condemnation of capitalism and the profit-motive (to be found in Ambler especially) and fear of fascism, described as an imminent and pernicious threat to society's values (a feature of the 1930s novels of Graham Greene and, of course, George Orwell), turned attention in spy fiction to the dynamics of politics within states and societies.[20] Against a contemporary historical setting of the depression and the rise of class strife, social Darwinism as a fictional mechanism for situating plot and character was obsolete. The genre escaped from its clutches and embraced a more complex landscape of domestic politics in which Machiavellism (Maugham), old-boy stupidity (satires of Mackenzie), vested interests (Ambler) and moral equivocation (Greene) were the new threats to civilization. But for all its greater sophistication, spy fiction still dealt in counter-history and apparent realism, not least because the writers of the 1930s found no adequate substitute for the old and sure framework provided by social Darwinism. In their inward turn to the politics of class and the individual, the larger historical forces of conflict became blurred. Just at this experimental moment in the genre's evolution, states such as the Third Reich and Mussolini's Italy were plotting in fact to create a social Darwinist universe of struggle and war, the real equivalent of early spy fiction's fantasies.

The 1950s saw a return to what might be called, to paraphrase Mordecai Richler, 'OK history', especially in the work of Ian Fleming.[21] Each new generation of spy fiction proved intent on propelling itself away from the sorts of historical dynamics employed by its predecessors. The Fleming generation was no exception. Just as the 1930s school rejected Buchan-like heroes and their social Darwinistic adventures, so Fleming and Co. rejected the morally complex and politically fractious atmosphere of the 1930s writers. In doing so, Fleming, via James Bond, brought the spy novel to its greatest heights of popularity.[22]

What was Fleming's 'OK history'? It was a carefully sanitized version of popular tastes, bringing apparent realism safely home after its journey into the wilds of moral ambiguity, political doubt, and a history full of inner threats to order. It consisted, in large measure, of a return to the simpler formula of the first generation, though brought up to date by reference to contemporary politics, intelligence organizations, travel, consumer goods, and sexual mores. Social Darwinism was jazzed up, and took the new guise of a competition between rival secret organizations, sometimes espionage agencies, sometimes criminal groups, but always standing as a simulacrum for the larger forces of historical struggle. Perhaps the only real change that Fleming engineered to modernize the old formula was to have history made by men in organizations rather than by freelance amateurs and individualists.[23] Bond had back-up, of a kind entirely unavailable to Hannay.

The apparent realism of Ian Fleming's novels worked especially well in opposition to the hard realities of the Cold War and the Bomb. For here was a hero, albeit an organizational man with a reverence for the powers that be, who could still prevail over the foe, travel widely in the course of his missions and, notably, have a good time. The old style of the individual hero rescuing civilization was resurrected just at the moment when the stupendous forces of ideological and military confrontation appeared to rule out any role for the individual at all. Bond and his readers escaped from history back into the adventures of an earlier day and forward into a titillating world of consumerism, sexual liberation (of sorts), and global travel. These were welcome thrills and involved an irresistible fantasy of history as a superficial game. Bond's success, helped by the arrival of mass paperback fiction and the author's own assiduous courting of publicity, was assured.[24]

Predictably, the genre's next evolutionary step involved a rejection in turn of the Bond formula. Once again the stimulus for change can be found in dissatisfaction with an increasingly irrelevant and worn-out illusion of realism, and a rediscovery of the spirit of the 1930s writers. Len Deighton and John le Carré, who spearheaded the new school in their novels of the 1960s, from the start rejected the Bond adventure and all that it echoed from the genre's past (including the 'Clubland' spy tales of the 1920s) in favour of a return to something like the atmosphere of Ambler and Greene.[25] Partly, this shift can be linked to an appreciation that the Cold War could not be mimicked in Fleming style and that a truer mimetic style would require a vision of threat and conspiracy involving the new organizational man, but with a much broader horizon. In the prototypical new thriller, John le Carré's *The Spy Who Came in from the Cold* (1962), history is being freshly shaped by ideological clashes, by combative intelligence agencies, by internal conspiracy and deception and by tests of loyalty and acts of corruption. Every possible dimension of historical force seems to be at work here: international conflict, national political strategy, individual strife. In the new spy fiction, the complex determination of events vies with the reductive. The former is contained in the startling implication, prominent in the writing of both le Carré and Graham Greene, that intelligence agencies mirror the soul of the state and reflect its structures, passions and rhetoric.[26] The reductive impulse takes the by now traditional shape of an escape from the crushing weight of historical forces and a confirmation of the formulaic device of apparent realism. Escape from history is found in the theme of the righteous man, able to hold to principles in an unprincipled age. Such a hero appears over and over again, not just in the 1960s novels of Deighton and le Carré, but in the successive works of British writers like Brian Freemantle (with his protagonist Charlie Muffin), Anthony Price (the soldier/scholar David Audley), Gavin Lyall (Major Maxim) and their American counterparts including William F. Buckley and W.T. Tyler.

With the appearance of this hero, the new fiction's balance between complexity and simplification is often decided in favour of the latter. In some ways, by dishing up yet another version of the 'great man' in history, recent spy fiction defeats its own vision of the real world. Few writers other than le Carré and Greene have proved able to hold the balance and avoid the tidiness, simplification and the endings allowed by apparent realism. Even George Smiley, who may be a somewhat unlikely-looking hero and who is dogged to an unusual degree by his past, is in his individual triumphs over history a recognizable creation of spy fiction. But the presence of change in the formula is undeniable. The ingredients of adventure and induction into a secret world offered by the first generation of spy novels have, at the least, been replaced by a more complex thrill in which the reader shares the hero's triumph over history and experiences a reordering and resolution of the complexities of the external world.

This potted history of the genre suggests a typology of alternating modes of quasi-realism in which the thrill of the adventurous romance vies for command with the politically charged narrative of societal danger.[27] Both modes are perpetually recycled. Spy fiction was launched with an act of appropriation of history and continues to rely on this element for its continuity and identity, its market niche and loyal readership.

Spy fiction's own historicism had, from the beginning, a competitive advantage over rival explanations of events. It revealed the present, simplified the past, dealt in paranoia and conspiracy and offered the chance of success in history for those positioned on the right side. Above all, it had answers to worrying questions. The engine for troubling historical change was identified as secret conspiracies against order. Controlling historical change meant unearthing and halting such threats. Popular anxiety about the powerlessness of the individual was assuaged by spy fiction's depiction of history as shaped by an endless stream of everyman heroes of many shapes, sizes and political dispositions. As Colin Watson has noticed, part of the effect generated by spy fiction derives from observing and sharing the experience of the individual exercise of secret power.[28] Spy fiction also confirmed the survival of the Eurocentric world, as the internationalization of society proceeded, and offered a generally tame version of foreign places. The map of the world remained reassuringly familiar and its history remained the province of the Caucasian male. Ian Fleming was especially adept at setting spy fiction on such journeys of non-discovery.[29]

Appropriating history, filling its blank spaces with secret agents and intelligence organizations, providing reassurance about causation, and using conspiracy and paranoia as a perpetually recyclable resource were all brilliant strokes. The formula works, its narrative 'machine' is a wonder.[30] But what of the future?

SPYING FUTURES

The spy fiction factory has long had its critics. The British Prime Minister, Gladstone, denounced the poisonous effect of Colonel Chesney's early thriller, *The Battle of Dorking*, in the House of Commons in 1871.[31] Later critics turned their attention to the genre's literary and cultural perniciousness. A broad range of charges has been levelled against spy fiction from diverse points of view. One of the more curious and vitriolic attacks came from Jacques Barzun, in an essay published in 1965.[32] Barzun disliked the popularity of spy fiction, fearing that it was beginning to contaminate his more cherished and classical genre, the detective story. But he also decried spy thrillers as childish fantasies, mirroring the decline of Western civilization and the increasing inability of individuals to accept the burdens of maturity. A somewhat similar argument was made, for different purposes, by Rebecca West in her revised *The New Meaning of Treason*. She believes that spy fiction helped trivialize the nature of espionage and the concept of treason in the minds of intellectuals and so contributed to the climate in which an upper-class elite could betray its own nation.[33]

Others have taken up this critical cue. Mordecai Richler attacked the 'sanitized racialism' of Ian Fleming and denounced spy fiction as a genre likely to feed on adolescent minds, spawning xenophobia and unrealistic attitudes towards national power.[34] More recently, the popular espionage writer Phillip Knightley has argued that an intimate and unhealthy relationship exists between the perpetuation of spy fiction and the ongoing activities of intelligence agencies. Knightley writes that spy fiction's 'search for conspiracies and our fascination with betrayal shield us from reality and dangerously simplify the world around us. And the fictional glorification of spies enables the real ones to go on playing their sordid games'.[35]

A second line of persistent criticism of the genre has to do with perceptions of its stagnation. The best known exposition of this theme has come from Julian Symons. In a book published in 1972, Symons portrayed the genre as having exhausted itself, in the wake of the writings of Fleming, le Carré and Deighton.[36] He called for a 'moratorium' on the production of spy fiction for at least a decade. Of course, no such moratorium came into being, and Symons no doubt intended a good measure of irony in his statement.

Fear of stagnation has been replaced, very recently, by a notion that the spy thriller, like other weapons in the inventory of the Cold War, has been rendered obsolete by changes in East–West relations. A slightly lugubrious New Year's cartoon for 1990 in *The Globe and Mail* depicted three men ready to leap from high office windows – a bemedalled Pentagon general, a Wall Street investment banker and a publisher of spy fiction. Some check to the popularity of such a view has been given by none other than John le Carré, whose reflections on the state of spy fiction were given extensive coverage in the North American press during a tour to publicize his espionage novel, *The Russia House*. Le Carré argued that even with the end of the Cold War, 'so long as there are nation states, trade competition and statesmen who do not quite tell the truth, spying will go on'.[37] And he and others will continue to write fiction about it.

To offset the hue and cry against spy fiction, the genre has also long enjoyed critical support. Some very high claims for the genre's power and significance have been made. Thus Ralph Harper has argued that thriller fiction 'is the one place where we are exposed to what we really are'.[38] David Stafford sees a bright future for spy fiction as it begins to grapple with the theme of the decline of the American empire.[39] But perhaps the most persuasive statement on the likely future of spy fiction comes from Michael Denning, who rebuts Julian Symons' 'moratorium' call. He does so by arguing that spy fiction enjoys much room for experiment and change in plot and structure. Denning sees likely new directions for spy fiction in the production of documentary thrillers based on counter-factual premises; left-wing thrillers also have promise, he believes.[40] In both cases writers will be able to conjure with new forms of apparent realism.

At least two other new directions might be added to Denning's list. It would be safe to predict that spy fiction will utilize more extensively in future the trappings of the historical novel, especially in cultures busy discovering their own espionage past.[41] An equally safe prediction is that there is a tremendous potential for feminist spy fiction, and for spy fiction with significant female characters written into it.[42] A new audience, long estranged from the genre, awaits such production.

Spy fiction also has a future beyond the boundaries of the formula itself. Perhaps one of the most notable developments in recent years has been the infiltration of espionage themes and characters into mainstream fiction. The pioneering efforts of Graham Greene are belatedly being carried into many types of novel writing, including Latin American 'magic realism', American fabulism, and science fiction.[43] The mainstream use of spy themes often involves a fictional return to an historical event, and a reworking of its inner history – both strategies familiar to the spy formula and perhaps borrowed from it. Recent striking examples include the British writer Ian McEwan's *The Innocent* with a plot which revolves around the Anglo-American intelligence project known as 'Operation Gold', to tap Soviet communication lines in Berlin, and the American Don Delillo's *Libra*, a brilliant recreation of the assassination of John F. Kennedy, using the plot device of a notional CIA investigation of its own role in the assassination.[44]

A generally unremarked aspect of mainstream fiction about spying concerns projections of a future espionage state. Here the literature goes well beyond the formula's alternating modes of romance and realism to depict a nightmare, a dystopian world in which all history is decidely influenced by intelligence services or those in control of the means of surveillance and terror. There is but one key text in the whole dystopian tradition that has fully explored the theme of espionage. This text is George Orwell's *Nineteen Eighty-Four*. Its impact has been enormous and has long been recognized, with the curious exception of Orwell's vision of the future of espionage.[45] Orwell not only gave us a dark dream of the failure of socialism and of the dangers of totalitarianism, he also created a world in which spying was an absolute guarantee of power and in which escape from surveillance was futile.

Espionage in 'Airstrip One', Orwell's futuristic Britain, is insidious. Its elements are total domestic surveillance, counter-intelligence, deception and propaganda. Rebel and dissident spirits are accused of being enemy agents; the government of 'Big Brother' may even go so far as to invent conspiracies against it in order to stir up public support. The 'Thought Police', the intelligence arm of the state, keep members of the inner Party and elite under close surveillance, listening and watching everything, while circulating agents among the outcast 'proles' in order to quash any signs of discontent. But Orwell's genius went beyond the sketching out of a frightening intelligence apparatus for his dystopian state, to imagining espionage as a way of life. In *Nineteen Eighty-Four* espionage is the solvent of normalcy, decency and intimacy. It divides generations and provides the popular momentum for racism. Some elements of the dystopian intelligence state are especially shocking. Children are enrolled in a special organization – 'The Spies' – to keep watch on and denounce their parents. Intimacy between men and women is nullified by mutual fear of betrayal, and sex is brutalized. Women are depicted as co-opted agents of the regime. As Winston Smith relates 'It is always the women, and above all the young ones, who are the most bigoted adherents of the Party, the swallowers of slogans, the amateur spies, and nosers out of orthodoxy'.[46] The note of misogyny is harsh, but is part of the larger strategy in the novel of stressing the cancerous effects of a regime able to destroy the ordinary bonds of love. Winston Smith can scarcely even imagine a relationship with Julia, and his first thoughts about her inevitably turn to speculations about whether she is a member of the Thought Police. When Winston attempts friendships with men, his instincts are no more reliable. His deepest empathy is engaged by O'Brien, who he thinks is a kindred rebel spirit, but who turns out to be a skilful *agent provocateur*, Winston's torturer and ultimately his confessor. He fails to see through the disguise of Mr Carrington, the antique-shop owner, who betrays Winston and Julia's secret room and proves to be a hard-faced member of the Thought Police. In this dystopia, espionage is all-pervasive, a function not only of the Thought Police and their mechanism of surveillance, but of the very dogma of the State as described in 'The Book' and explained by O'Brien, and finally of the perverted nature of surviving human relationships.

One kind of evidence for the singularity of Orwell's achievement is the quality and nature of subsequent literary dystopias. Kurt Vonnegut's *Player Piano* and Ray Bradbury's *Fahrenheit 451* were but pale imitations of *Nineteen Eighty-Four*, with a similar picture of an atomized society where security forces of one kind or another (in Bradbury's novel, the book-burning 'firemen') keep a tight control of thought and dissent.[47] More interesting is the recent treatment of the dystopian theme in Margaret Atwood's *The Handmaid's Tale*, inevitably seen as a feminist version of *Nineteen Eighty-Four*. Atwood's future society possesses an updated, customized version of the Thought Police, 'The Eye', who circulate in their ubiquitous dark vans with luminescent eyes painted on the side. The major departure in *The Handmaid's Tale* is the depiction of a totalitarian male state, in place of the regime of Big Brother and its co-opted women. Offred, the female protagonist, unlike Winston Smith, ultimately finds a way to resist, risks friendship and enjoys some hope of redemption.[48]

Orwell's *Nineteen Eighty-Four* set a possible radical departure for spy fiction, which the genre has yet to follow. The dystopian spy novel, like the anti-spy novel called for by Jack MacIntosh in his essay in this volume, has yet to make its appearance. Certainly Orwell's novel owed little to the spy fiction of the day. The identifiable roots of *Nineteen Eighty-Four* lay instead in the inspiration that Orwell derived from *Gulliver's Travels*, especially Book III, where Orwell found 'an extraordinary, clear prevision of the spy-haunted "police-state", with its endless heresy-hunts and treason trials, all really designed to neutralize popular discontent by changing it into war hysteria'.[49] There was also something in the novel of Orwell's hatred of the scientific utopias of his day, and their authors, especially H.G. Wells. Orwell saw a close parallel between Wells's call for a scientifically managed society and the reality of the Third Reich, where the instruments of modernity were 'all in the service of ideas appropriate to the stone age'.[50] Yet Orwell had his own 'extraordinary clear prevision', no less remarkable than Swift's. Orwell thought of the author of *Gulliver's Travels* as 'inferring the whole from a quite small part, for the feeble governments of his day did not give him illustrations ready made'.[51] Orwell, thirty years ahead of his time, captured a fear of the intelligence state that was to become common currency and was to serve as something of a balance to the sometimes hyperbolic effects of spy fiction's reliance on apparent realism.

It is a long way from the novels of the first generation of spy fiction to the dystopia of George Orwell. Yet there is a significant link. In their common usage of spies and espionage as signifiers of threats to valued ideals, writers as different as Le Queux and Orwell have given a special charge to the fictional treatment of intelligence. Spy stories carry the burden of historicist, psychological and political interpretations of sweeping human dramas. In this unique branch of the thriller, entertainment is crossed with didacticism. E. Phillips Oppenheim expressed his prescient faith in the genre thus: 'So long as the world lasts, its secret international history will . . . suggest the most fascinating of all material for the writing of fiction'.[52] Oppenheim's successors have helped to ensure that the genre, in its manoeuvrings through the land of apparent realism, escapes being stagnant, obsolescent or necessarily corruptive. What it offers, among its many textual messages, includes important material for the study of popular attitudes to the historical process. Understood in its own structural context, spy fiction provides students of real intelligence with a guide not to how things are, but to how things are preceived to happen.

The essays that comprise this volume take different approaches to the study of spy fiction and comment on a common theme of the uses of historical realism from a variety of persectives. They are all grounded, it is safe to say, in a shared enjoyment of the spy novel, a sense that spy fiction deserves much more critical study than it has so far enjoyed, a belief in the shaping power of spy fiction over popular images, and a notion about the usefulness of interdisciplinary approaches. Together, these essays approximate the 'hybrid genre study' method of La Capra, not least in the sense of bringing together a wide range of expertise from the fields of history, literature, politics, philosophy, law and film studies in an attempt to explore new perspectives on a popular genre.

The first four essays may be described as historical re-investigations of the spy fiction genre. Christine Bold's essay uncovers the ways in which the figure of the spy gained a precarious foothold in popular American fiction of the nineteenth century. James Fenimore Cooper's *The Spy* (1821) is thus shown to be something more than an isolated text or false start. The origins of the espionage novel, as Bold shows, are clearly delineated in popular American fiction, and claims for the uniquely British origins of the genre may need to be reconsidered. David Trotter and Nicholas Hiley, in complementary pieces, focus attention on the crucial period at the turn of the century when British spy fiction was being born. Trotter distinguishes the themes of individual and national regeneration as the means by which the early writers combined adventure and politics to fashion the new genre. Hiley seeks out the original inspiration for the spy as hero and finds it in the parallels between Edwardian popular fiction and pornography and in a Freudian interpretation of the collective wish-fulfilment of a frustrated middle class. Eric Homburger takes the historical re-investigation further forward, by considering the effectiveness of British spy fiction's response to the realities of Fascism in the 1930s. He finds it to have been decidedly wanting and argues that spy fiction contributed its mite to the popularity of appeasement.

The middle part of the collection consists of essays by historians with expertise in the study of intelligence. Keith Jeffery and Eunan O'Halpin provide a comprehensive survey of the Irish setting in spy fiction and explore the gaps between apparent realism and reality in the genre's fitful appropriations of the Irish troubles. Denis Smyth takes a case-study in fact and fiction, by looking at the espionage history that informed Graham Greene's famous spy spoof, *Our Man in Havana*. The fictional quality of many episodes in real-life espionage, and the similarities in method between the intelligencer and the writer are both notable themes in Smyth's work.

The remaining five essays in the volume address disparate and neglected aspects of the study of spy fiction and film. Alan Booth traces the evolution of the spy film and shows it to have employed apparent realism as faithfully as spy fiction, but at a slower and more imitative pace. Only in one sense did spy films range ahead of their fictional counterpart: this involved a 1920s vision of the female spy, above all in such classics as Fritz Lang's *Spione* (1928).

If Hollywood spy films failed to be innovative, Jack MacIntosh sees a deeper problem in the ethical vacuum that exists in much spy fiction. In what is the first detailed treatment of this issue to appear in print, MacIntosh argues that spy fiction writers have proved consistently unable to provide their protagonists with credible motives for action. That this does not deter the reader's (or Jack MacIntosh's) enjoyment is clear, but it adds a further dimension of puzzlement to the issue of why (and whether) we should read spy fiction. There would seem to be a clear parallel between the kinds of 'apparent ethics' employed in the works of writers such as Adam Hall, and the device of apparent realism: both are deeply satisfying substitutions for the real thing.

Philip Jenkins treats, in similar pioneering fashion, the evolution and nature of the spy/terrorist 'hybrid' novel. Jenkins confirms the suggestions frequently made that contemporary terrorism and its physical settings are likely to provide a major source of material for spy fiction in the future. But he also shows how slowly and crudely the genre has developed its caricature of the terrorist.

John Starnes, a former intelligence officer turned spy fiction writer, is a member of a class of authors frequently cited for their special role in the evolution of the genre.[53] While John Starnes may have a vested interest in proclaiming that life exists for the spy novel, he makes no special claims for the uniqueness of his position as a writer. Here is an interesting picture from the practitioner's side of the hill.

Donald Cameron Watt closes the volume with a wide-ranging epilogue, focusing on the need for tighter definitions of what constitutes the varieties of spy fiction, and a reconsideration of the stuctural components of the spy story. On the apparent moral nullity of spy fiction, Watt takes issue with Jack MacIntosh: readers can decide on the merits of these respective positions for themselves. The critical thing, as Watt reiterates, is the importance of an understanding of the ethical content of spy fiction as an aid to exploring its socio-historical significance. That there are many possible explanations for the evolution of spy fiction is confirmed by Cameron Watt's surprise ending. It may be only fitting that the volume should close on a note of conspiratorial illusion.

NOTES

1. For accounts of the origins of the spy novel, see the essays by David Trotter, Nicholas Hiley and Philip Jenkins in this volume. David Stafford, *The Silent Game: The Real World of Imaginary Spies* (Toronto, 1988) provides a useful history of the evolution of the genre.
2. David Stafford, 'Spies and Gentlemen: The Birth of the British Spy Novel, 1893–1914', *Victorian Studies* (Summer, 1981).
3. Graham Greene, *The Ministry of Fear* (Harmondsworth, 1979 ed.), p. 65.
4. William Le Queux, *Spies of the Kaiser* (London, 1909). The method was foreshadowed in *The Invasion of 1910* (London, 1906).
5. This episode is well treated in Christopher Andrew, *Her Majesty's Secret Service: The Making of the British Intelligence Community* (London and New York, 1985), Ch.2; and David French, 'Spy Fever in Britain 1900–1915', *Historical Journal*, xxi (1978).
6. George Markstein, *The Cooler* (Garden City, NY, 1974).
7. *The Independent on Sunday*, 22 July 1990.
8. Ralph Harper, *The World of the Thriller* (Cleveland, OH, 1969); Bruce Merry, *Anatomy of the Spy Thriller* (Dublin, 1977) and LeRoy Panek, *Special Branch: The British Spy Novel 1890–1980* (Bowling Green, OH 1981), all vigorously deny that spy fiction has any mimetic quality.
9. John G. Cawelti and Bruce A. Rosenberg, *The Spy Story* (Chicago, 1987), Introduction.
10. Michael Denning, *Cover Stories: Narrative and Ideology in the British Spy Thriller* (London, 1987), p.29.
11. Ibid., p.60.
12. Dominick La Capra, *History and Criticism* (Ithaca, NY, 1985), Ch.5; and *History, Politics and the Novel* (Ithaca, NY, 1987), especially the Introduction.
13. La Capra, *History and Criticism*, p.132.
14. The career of William Le Queux is well documented in Stafford, *The Silent Game*, Ch.one; Oppenheim is discussed in David Trotter's essay within; Panek, *The Special Branch* devotes chapters to Childers and Buchan; Cawelti and Rosenberg, *The Spy Story*, Ch.4, is insightful with respect to Buchan.
15. On social Darwinism as a popular doctrine before 1914 see James Joll, '1914: The Unspoken Assumptions', in H.W. Koch (ed.), *The Origins of the First World War* (London, 1972); an inspiring treatment of the impact of social Darwinism on American literature can be found in Eric Mottram, *Blood on the Nash Ambassador: Investigations in American Culture* (London, n.d.), essay 6.
16. I owe this concept of 'regeneration' to the essay by David Trotter, in this volume.
17. Harper, *The World of the Thriller*, p.61, makes the case for Buchan's notion of the fragility of civilization.
18. Helpful treatments of the spy fiction output of these writers can be found in Denning, Ch.3; Stafford, *Silent Game*, Ch.8; Julian Symons, *Bloody Murder: From the Detective Story to the Crime Novel: A History* (London, rev. ed., 1985), Ch.16.
19. Denning, *Cover Stories*, Ch.3; Harper, pp.32–3.
20. Denning, *Cover Stories*.; Stafford, *Silent Game*, Ch.8; Owen Dudley Edwards, 'The Politics of the Thriller', BBC Radio Four, 23 June 1984 and *The Listener*, 21 June 1984, pp.9–10.
21. Mordecai Richler, 'James Bond Unmasked', in Bernard Rosenberg and David Manning White (eds.), *Mass Culture Revisited* (New York, 1971).
22. Colin Watson, *Snobbery with Violence* (London, 1971), Ch.18; Denning, *Cover Stories*, Ch.4.
23. Cawelti and Rosenberg, Ch.6.
24. John Pearson, *The Life of Ian Fleming* (London, 1966), Ch. 17.
25. Richard Usborne, *Clubland Heroes* (London, 1953) is a delightful and idiosyncratic study of the 1920s fiction of Dornford Yates, John Buchan and 'Sapper'; the literatue on Deighton and especially on le Carré is already large, but useful introductions include Cawelti and Rosenberg, Chs. 6–7; Alan Bold (ed.), *The Quest for le Carré* (London,

1988); Eric Homberger, *John le Carré* (New York, 1986); Lars Ole Sauerberg, *Secret Agents in Fiction* (London, 1984); and Stafford, *Silent Game*, Ch.11.

26. This view was hotly contested in Hugh Trevor-Roper, *The Philby Affair* (London, 1968).
27. Michael Denning reaches similar conclusions from different premises in *Cover Stories*.
28. Watson, p.251.
29. Richler argues that such effects were the product of the fact that Fleming was an 'appalling writer', p.341; Kingsley Amis, *The James Bond Dossier* (London, 1965), takes the contrary view that Fleming was a gifted stylist.
30. The concept of 'narrative machine', especially in the works of Ian Fleming, is discussed in Umberto Eco and Oreste del Buone, *The Bond Affair* (London, 1966).
31. See I.F. Clarke, *Voices Prophesying War, 1763–1964*, for this, and for an extended discussion of futurist treatments of war, with some valuable comments on the changing place of the spy in such fiction.
32. Jacques Barzun, 'Meditations on the Literature of Spying', *American Scholar*, 34 (1965), pp.167–78.
33. Rebecca West, *The New Meaning of Treason* (London, 1982).
34. Richler, p.354.
35. Phillip Knightley, 'Spy Lies', *Saturday Night* (September, 1988), p.72.
36. Symons, *Bloody Murder*, Ch.16, 'A Short History of the Spy Story', p.236.
37. Interview with John le Carré, *The Globe and Mail* (Toronto), 10 June 1989; similar views were expressed by le Carré in an earlier interview with the *Washington Post*, 25 May 1989.
38. Harper, p.130.
39. Stafford, *Silent Game*, Ch.12, 'Empire Blues'.
40. Denning, *Cover Stories*, conclusion.
41. A case in point is the recent outpouring of historical novels about Canadian espionage: one turns on clandestinity in Quebec politics during the Second World War: Pierre Turgeon, *Le Bateau d'Hitler* (Montreal, 1988); two others fashion plot material from the Gouzenko defection in 1945: David Helwig, *Old Wars* (Toronto, 1989) and Heather Robertson, *Igor: A Novel of Intrigue* (Ottawa, 1989); a fourth deals with the CIA brainwashing experiments conducted in a Montreal clinic during the 1960s: William Deverell, *Mindfield* (Toronto, 1989).
42. See Patricia Craig and Mary Cadogan, *The Lady Investigates* (Oxford, 1986) for, *inter alia*, an account of the fictional female spy.
43. Manuel Puig, *Pubis Angelical* (London, 1987), Thomas Pynchon, *Slow Learner* (Boston, 1984), and Stanilas Lem, *Memoirs Found in a Bathtub* (New York, 1973), are respective examples.
44. Ian McEwan, *The Innocent* (London, 1990); Don Delillo, *Libra* (New York, 1989).
45. Orwell's biographer makes virtually no mention of this aspect of *Nineteen Eighty-Four*; see Bernard Crick, *George Orwell: A Life* (London, 1981).
46. George Orwell, *Nineteen Eighty-Four* (Harmondsworth, 1984 ed.), p.14.
47. Clarke, *Voices Prophesying War*, establishes the general point about imitations of Orwell.
48. Margaret Atwood, *The Handmaid's Tale* (Toronto, 1985).
49. George Orwell, *The Collected Essays, Journalism and Letters of George Orwell*, Vol. IV, ed. Sonia Orwell and Ian Angus (London, 1968), 'Politics vs. Literature: An Examination of Gulliver's Travels', p.213.
50. Ibid., Vol.II, 'Wells, Hitler and the World State', p.143.
51. Cited in note 49; see also the discussion in William Steinhof, 'Utopia Reconsidered: Comments on *Nineteen Eighty-Four*', in Eric S. Rabkin *et al.* (eds.), *No Place Else: Explorations in Utopian and Dystopian Fiction* (Carbondale, IL, 1983), pp.147–61.
52. Quoted in Stafford, *Silent Game*, p.37.
53. On the influence of intelligence service on spy fiction writers see Antony Masters, *Literary Agents, the Novelist as Spy* (Oxford, 1987).

Secret Negotiations: The Spy Figure in Nineteenth-century American Popular Fiction

CHRISTINE BOLD

The narrative of spy fiction most often constructed by historians, critics and theorists of the genre runs as follows: although the first spy novel in English (James Fenimore Cooper's *The Spy* of 1821) was produced in the United States, the genre failed to take root in that culture because fictions of clandestinity, subterfuge and political duplicity jarred against the Republic's self-image of democratic openness. Instead, spy fiction became quintessentially British, spurred by a late-nineteenth-century crisis of anxiety in imperialist Britain and responding to the cultural and political turmoils of that nation up to the present. The spy fiction which reappears in mid-twentieth-century America is read, consequently, as a by-product of Anglo-American relations.[1] In its erasure of the spy figure from most of nineteenth-century American culture, this 'cover story' coincides with the rhetoric of the period.[2] *Beadle's Monthly*, one of the popular magazines of the 1860s, upbraided European governments for their reliance on networks of 'invisible informers', in a lengthy article on 'The Spy System in Europe', which ended with triumphant editorializing:

> What a contrast to all this does our own Republic offer! Here each man moves as he will; he talks as his judgment dictates; he acts as he sees fit. No spy dogs his steps . . . Here, where the Government *is* the people, a spy would be an anomaly . . . Blessed Fate that cast our destiny here rather than in Europe; and O, most Providential Fate, which, through the perils of civil war, has brought forth a Nation, one and indivisible.[3]

It is true that the spy did not fit easily into the Republic's pantheon of popular heroes. But the relationship between the spy figure and the formation of America's national culture is more complex than either *Beadle's* nationalistic rhetoric or received critical opinion suggests. In the cheap story-papers which flourished in the United States from the 1840s, then in the dime novels which garnered even larger sales from the 1860s, there appear a sizeable number of stories with titles that insist on their identity as spy fiction.[4] The characteristic figures and plots of these stories are marked both by the dark, ambivalent dynamic of Cooper's creation and by the optimistic, nationalistic rhetoric adopted by the mass literature of the period. Negotiating these contradictory imperatives is a spy figure who speaks to his nation's cultural anxieties just as much as the later, more famous spies of British fiction. Indeed, in constructing their fictions of American expansionism and civil war, the authors of these spy stories adopted tactics later refined by Le Queux, Buchan *et al.*: they masculinized the 'great game', allied espionage with the frontier myth to discover heroic characteristics for the spy, and used the figure to make sense of a social order undergoing rapid change.

To read this American spy figure, it is necessary to attend to the site of his appearance, in terms of the publishing context and the historical moment. Or, in Roland Barthes's terms, it is important to consider how the spy stories' properties as 'work' affect their operation as 'text'.[5] Multiple spy adventures first appeared in the mass-market story papers: cheap, weekly compilations of serialized melodramas, didactic sketches and news digests which were shaped by the explosion in America's market economy between 1830 and 1870, and which in turn shaped a new mass reading public.[6] In two senses, these publications constituted America's first national literature: rapid strides in transport, industrialization and manufacturing technology made possible continental distribution to a mass audience for the first time; and story-paper publishers turned American writing into a paying profession for the first time when they began to pay fees (anything from $100 for a novelette to $1,600 for a novel) in a desperate attempt to fill pages. The editorial paraphernalia translated merchandising calculations of scale and popularity into the rhetoric of Manifest Destiny in these years when America was battling with Mexico and Britain in its efforts to expand its Western territories. Nationalist sentiment was stirred by iconic story-paper titles (*The Flag of Our Union, The True Flag, The Flag of the Free, Uncle Sam, The Yankee Nation, The Star-Spangled Banner*), all accompanied by flamboyant heads of eagles, flags and cameos of the founding fathers. Strident editorializing fostered xenophobia: in the 1840s and 1850s, *The Flag of Our Union* regularly berated 'the pride and arrogance of the British Lion' and other degenerate Old World regimes, while celebrating the United States 'where the school-house is free to all, intelligence is not confined to gilded rooms and large houses, but stalks abroad in green fields and highways, God be praised!'[7] And the fictional formulas bolstered what Frederick Merk calls 'the new authority of the masses . . . in national politics' by commemorating the people's triumphs in the American Revolution, the War of 1812 and the Mexican War.[8] This mixture was eagerly consumed by a huge audience (*The Flag of Our Union*, for example, sold 300,000 copies a week.)

When the publishing house of Beadle and Adams introduced the dime novel in 1860, it played on the same themes of nationalism and democracy, but it exploited further advances in the technology of printing and distribution to speed up the industrial production of cheap fiction even more and win an even larger audience.[9] Paring away the editorial miscellany, Beadle and Adams published series of complete novels in convenient, pocket-sized pamphlets of standardized packaging and price. They and other dime-novel (and, subsequently, nickel-novel) publishers also managed to standardize the writing of the fiction, by combining an early form of market analysis with directives to their stables of authors. The result was that certain successful formulas became entrenched in cheap fiction: one body of adventure tales continued to celebrate historical military triumphs (from the American Revolution to the contemporary Civil War); the largest category of dime novels, however, dealt with sensational action on the Western frontier. Inscribed in these tales is the discourse of mass-marketing and nationalist politics which the story papers articulated more overtly in their editorial commentary. The spy was one of the protagonists to appear within these multiple frameworks of fiction factory rhetoric, and his function was defined in part by them.

Beyond these specific determinants, however, lay the more general commodification of culture whose effect on literary production has been hypothesized in various ways. Theories have ranged from the Frankfurt School's condemnation of the 'culture industry' manipulating a passive public to a rather naive faith in mass literature as the spontaneous expression of modern folk culture.[10] More current and more compelling than these extreme positions is the theory of 'negotiation': agency is ascribed to the publishers, authors and readers of mass literature, all of them understood to invest the text with their own agendas, vocabularies, ideologies. Michael Denning articulates the dynamic of negotiation when he says of cheap books:

> they are best seen as a contested terrain, a field of cultural conflict where signs with wide appeal and resonance take on contradictory disguises and are spoken in contrary accents. Just as the signs of a dominant culture can be articulated in the accents of the people, so the signs of the culture of the working classes can be dispossessed in varieties of ventriloquism.[11]

A full reading of nineteenth-century American spy fiction would involve study of the political establishment, the publishing interests, the writers and the readers who together and in conflict with each other 'author' these works and contribute to the textual strategies embedded in the fiction. This preliminary enquiry adopts a much narrower focus than that, investigating only the characteristics of the fictional spy figure. But the assumptions outlined above do inform this partial study: the American spy is read as the product of material and historical forces, not as some dissociated type of escapist fantasy; and this interpretation, which attempts to decode the

messages offered by spy fiction, avoids speculating on the reception of
these stories, on the understanding that readers who appropriated spy
fiction according to their own social and individual agendas could produce
a very different narrative from that constructed here.

   The literary model for the great bulk of these story-paper and dime-novel
spy tales was James Fenimore Cooper's *The Spy*, which John Cawelti
describes as a study in liminality.[12] Set in New York State during the
Revolutionary War of 1776, the novel depicts a nation riven by strife
which divides lovers, families and generations. Cooper, in fact, terms
'this unnatural struggle' a quasi-civil war in which friends and enemies
can be indistinguishable and the loss of social order spawns a sub-class of
renegades, traitors and freebooters. The uncontrolled disorder is signalled
by the proliferation of suspected spies throughout the novel; the primary
heir to these unnatural divisions, however, is the double agent Harvey
Birch, a pedlar who is widely suspected of betraying the Republic as a
Tory spy, but who, it is revealed after his death, secretly worked directly
for Washington. Birch's profession condemns him to a life of ignominy,
equivocation and radical isolation: his home is secreted in the wilderness
of 'the neutral ground'; his sole confidant is his father, who dies in the
course of the novel; and he is resolved to remain celibate for fear of tarring
others with his infamous name. Birch's lower-class status also separates
him from the landed gentry who provide the love interest and from the
community of buffoonish servants who provide the comic relief. Cooper
makes it clear that the spy is the sacrificial victim necessitated by internecine
conflict: embodiment of the unnatural divisions and alliances caused by the
Revolution, Birch must be killed off in the 1812 War to signify the complete
healing of the nation. (The other major sign of reunification is the series of
marriages towards the end of the novel, a ritual in which the unhandsome,
unheroic Birch can have no place.) As a fictional replaying of the Republic's
birth, *The Spy* offers no easy palliatives. Exercised himself over the costs and
perils of democracy, Cooper embodied in the spy figure the dark secret of
duplicity, the sacrifice of the individual to the common good which shadowed
the Republic's triumph.

   Following Cooper, the story-paper authors also revisited formative
moments in the nation's history, explicitly intending to jog popular
memory or, in the words of Ned Buntline, most prolific of story-paper and
dime-novel authors, to 'give my own neglectful, money-loving countrymen
a "dig in the ribs".'[13] That dig, however, amounts to a reversal of Cooper's
project: these authors set out to rehabilitate forgotten national heroes,
foremost among whom was Nathan Hale, the American spy hanged by
the British during the Revolutionary War. One of the story-paper tales of
Hale's career – *The American Spy, or Freedom's Early Sacrifice* (1846) by
J.R. Simms – compares the fate of the American spy with that of Major

André, the British spy reluctantly executed by the Americans during the same war:

> The dust of Maj. André, by royal mandate, has been transported across the ocean, and given a niche in Westminster Abbey with a costly monument, . . . while Capt. Hale, equally *brave and intelligent* and more *virtuous*, sleeps without a monument, and almost unknown to his countrymen. Should this be so?[14]

Buntline berates his audience: '*Americans* – or you who *claim* to be such – tell me where is *his* – where is Nathan Hale's monument? Where is his grave? . . . Oh, shame! shame upon the false memories which forget them . . .!' (p.31). Story-paper fiction repairs that wrong by enshrining the heroics first of Nathan Hale and then of fictionalized American spies. In an era of great technological progress and the burgeoning of mass society, the heroic spy confirmed the power of the individual to shape national destiny. In contrast to Harvey Birch, this version of the spy symbolized the resolution, rather than the cost, of national struggle.

Story-paper authors manoeuvred the spy figure into the nationalist project of mass literature by simplifying both Cooper's design and historical evidence. Repeatedly, these tales rework the same period and locale as *The Spy*, emphasizing the same unnatural fractures and alliances in a house divided against itself. But where Cooper dealt in the ambivalence, the divided loyalties, the political tensions – in short, in the psychological cost – of internecine warfare, the story-paper authors translated the struggle into personal attraction, melodramatic schisms and physical absolutes. Two types of easily distinguishable spies emerge: the good spies (figures of manly bearing who put love of country before self) and the evil traitors (low-browed, shifty-eyed types who sell their country for mercenary gain). This unqualified scheme is inscribed directly in history: tales of the Revolution ritually contrast the heroic André and Hale against the villainous Benedict Arnold. A further, class distinction separates André, the British gentleman spy of noble lineage, from Hale, the sacrificial patriot plucked from the democratic ranks. This schematic design allows these authors to acknowledge the stigma conventionally attached to the spy figure: Nathan Hale 'knew the stigma which the custom of nations cast upon the conduct of a spy' (*The American Spy*, p.48); the comic Black of another tale declares, 'Cuss this spy bisniss . . . let dis spy bisness go to de debble, who was de fust one . . . dat ebber hatched it up'.[15] The unfolding of the tale, however, assigns that stigma exclusively to the traitor spy; his heroic opposite, whether historical or fictional, operates free of blemish. Clearing the arena of qualification and ambiguity was the first step in transforming the spy not just into a feasible hero but into an emblem of national pride.

Legitimizing the American spy also involved rationalizing the element of secrecy, the hidden, duplicitous character of the spy's activity which was problematic in a narrative and a publication proclaiming America's openness, liberty and democracy. Strategic, here, was the story-paper handling of disguise. A standard melodramatic device in cheap fiction, disguise became a central issue in spy fiction because it was the false costume which defined a spy and condemned him to ignominious death by hanging. Disguise symbolized the deeper duplicity of espionage. While Harvey Birch's disguise was more psychological than physical, a skill at dissembling his motives and character, in the story papers the cloak of secrecy became merely a physical appurtenance. It could be removed at any stage in the narrative to prove that the heroic spy bore no lasting kinship to the enemy whose uniform he wore and possessed no deep-seated ability to dissemble. Thus the traitor spy adopts disguise eagerly to mask his sneaky undertaking; the patriotic spy has disguise thrust upon him, accepts it unwillingly, and is inept at maintaining it. In *Arnold; or, The British Spy!* (1844) by J.H. Ingraham, Arnold forces a costume upon André who, once captured, writes to Washington: 'Thus . . . was I betrayed . . . into the vile condition of an enemy in disguise within your posts'.[16]

An even greater distance is put between the spy and secrecy in Charles Averill's *The Secret Service Ship; or, The Fall of San Juan D'Ulloa*, first published in *The Flag of Our Union* in 1849 and set in the contemporaneous Mexican War. The hero is Midshipman Rogers, also known as 'THE SPY'. As an agent of the US Secret Service, THE SPY's mission is to search out a Mexican ammunitions stronghold, so that America can weaken its foe decisively. In all the complicated tangle of plot lines, character disguises, false deaths and indigestible coincidences which ensue, one fact jumps out at the reader: THE SPY is anything but secret. Everyone he encounters in Mexico immediately recognizes him as THE SPY. And little wonder: far from camouflaging himself cunningly in the dress of his Mexican surroundings, Midshipman Rogers accoutres himself as follows:

> his right arm rear[ed] proudly aloft to the breezes of the Gulf, a superb dark blue banner, on which was embroidered in bright golden characters, the inscription 'UNITED STATES SECRET SERVICE', surrounded by a circle of thirty glittering stars, such as ever gem the Flag of our Union; while the azure sash which encircled his manly waist . . . was itself a star-spangled standard, folded into a semblance of a scarf.[17]

At a climactic moment in the plot, Rogers unfurls the US flag and drapes himself in it. Here, secrecy is sacrificed to the allegorical imperative: what has infiltrated and vanquished Mexico is the type of America, the democracy where the common man (the midshipman) is hero.

The final act in the rehabilitation of the spy is his reintegration into American society at the end of his adventure, the story papers reclaiming him from liminality in a way that Birch was not. Again, this movement was part of popular fiction's conventional imperative to produce a happy ending, but the production of happiness involves a specific balance of power in the case of the developing spy formula. The crucial relationship is between spy and woman. Harvey Birch's isolation enforced his celibacy, while his lower-class, unhandsome demeanour could attract only Katy Haynes, the comic, vulgar housekeeper who desired Birch for his accumulated wealth, not for his personal attributes. In contrast, the heroic spies of the story-papers are loved by cultured, beautiful women from established families who wait for their men throughout the war and join them in actual or metaphorical union at its close. The ending either celebrates the marriage of spy and lover or, where history prevents such a conclusion – as in the case of Nathan Hale – the author emphasizes that the fiancée dedicates her life to the memory of her man. That marriage here is simultaneously personal and national is confirmed by the spy hero of *The Ocean Martyr; or, The Hunter Spy of Virginia* by Austin C. Burdick (one of Sylvanus Cobb's many pseudonyms). The hero writes to his fiancée: 'O, rapture! what joy must then be mine. When my country is free – and you are mine!' More light-heartedly, Bob Brant – of *Bob Brant, Patriot and Spy* (1864) by Edward Willett – thinks of his beloved:

> He felt as if he would like to spy into her heart, and organize himself into a foraging party to capture her love, and then confiscate her in the name of the Union – not the 'old' Union, but the kind of Union that a minister is needed to consummate.[18]

The role assigned to woman inevitably places her at the margins of the adventurous action. Standing for home, hearth and domestic legitimacy, she is barred from the professional orbit of the spy. This placing of woman can be understood as part of the struggle for ascendancy between male and female cultures in the mid-nineteenth century, in which women were repeatedly relegated to the domestic arena and repeatedly sought to build political strength out of that 'separate sphere'. As Jane Tompkins has demonstrated, much of the rhetorical dimension of this battle was played out in popular writings.[19] Popular spy fiction goes further than the conventional separation in the degree to which its empowerment of the spy disempowers woman in the private as well as the public sphere. The male spy is consistently motivated by public and private duties (by love of country and woman or patriotism and revenge), and he appropriates the public world crossed with the privacy of secret knowledge. It is from this public-private sphere – codified by the term 'honour'– that women are excluded, because they do not appreciate the delicate balance of subterfuge and fair play ruling the spy's activities. This exclusion is acted out in ritual transgressions: repeatedly woman disgraces the heroic spy by pleading with his enemies for his life or by offering to free him from imprisonment, thus violating the spy's code of honour. The ritual serves at least two purposes: by resisting the offer, the spy further demonstrates 'the triumph of an honorable mind over an unworthy temptation'(*Arnold*, p.24); simultaneously the limitations of woman's role in the spy formula are clearly demarcated. Woman passively facilitates the spy's re-entry into public and private union while she is robbed of power in both domains. She is both scapegoat and saint, possessing no active agency. Thus did nineteenth-century spy story authors strike their own blow against women's culture and enlist the formula firmly in the cause of male dominance. (The blow is that much more telling when novelists address themselves directly to 'our fair lady readers' [*Secret Service Ship*, p.65].)

In summary, story-papers retell Cooper's narrative of American independence, radically reorienting the symbolism of the spy within that design. From *The Spy* story-paper fiction accepts the spy as a figure of America's dislocation. Indeed, this cheap fiction situates its spy heroes very specifically at historical crises: the eponymous hero of Ned Buntline's *Saul Sabberday; or, The Idiot Spy* (1858), for example, advises Washington at the crossing of the Delaware, saves Mad Anthony Wayne from a potentially fatal bullet, and is the first to suspect Benedict Arnold. But the story-paper authors insist that the spy also symbolizes America's reunification. They depart from Cooper's model to follow the trajectory of their publications' optimistic nationalism when they suggest that the role of spy brings public honour to the individual as well as the nation: Saul Sabberday's experience as a spy transforms him from simple-mindedness to sense and refashions him as his country's saviour and bringer of peace at the end of the Revolutionary War. Through a series of manoeuvres which disentangle the spy from the duplicity of espionage and make him dependent on, yet superior to, women's culture, story-paper fiction secures a place for the spy in America's pantheon of popular heroes. That this process of negotiation occurs in connection with formative moments in the nation's history clearly intensifies the significance of this nationalist myth-making and moulding of popular memory.

With the appearance of the new dime format in the 1860s, these reformulations of the spy figure were largely entrenched, and they continued to be reaffirmed for about the next 30 years, a period much in need of symbols of national integration and myths to resolve discordant memories. Dime fiction contains some ritualistic speculation about the morality of the spy, but it answers that residual doubt partly by allying the spy with the frontier hero. Also, dime-novel authors foreground disguise even more emphatically than their story-paper counterparts, thereby converting secrecy from a political problem into a narrative device. In all of this, the twists and turns of espionage figure minimally, except in contemporaneous fictions of the Civil War, an exception which suggests something of the formula's limitations.

The most obvious contribution of dime novels is their expansion of the heroic spy's adventures from the sites of historical engagements to the frontier wilderness, an arena fractured by the same familial splits, enforced marriages and captivities as proliferate in the war tales. The new location allows the elision of spy and scout, the latter already a proven hero in dime novels by the time the spy appears on the frontier. Harvey Birch exhibited proficiency in woodcraft, but the dime novel spy is often a full-blown hunter and woodsman whose forest skills enable him to infiltrate hostile Indian tribes and outlaw bands. By the time of *The Bear-Hunter; or, Davy Crockett as a Spy* (1873) by Harry Hazard, the terms 'spy' and 'scout' are interchangeable. Later still, 'spy' and 'detective' become intermittent homonyms, as in *Central Pacific Paul The Mail-Train Spy; or, Yank Yellowbird's Iron Trail* (1888) by William H. Manning.

This elision further erases the stigma attached to the subterfuge of espionage. More specifically, it introduces the opportunity for self-denomination; when a character chooses to name himself 'spy' he can be understood to take on the mantle of manhood. In *The Forest Spy* (1861) by Edward S. Ellis, Peter Jenkins changes from a cowardly buffoon to a hero through the combined experience of spying and searching for a wife. The real catalyst, however, has been his adoption of the sobriquet 'The Forest Spy', to which he then had to live up to by his exploits as both military spy and forest scout. When the aged hunter Dick Dingle praises The Forest Spy for his new-found bravery at the close of the adventure, the language of his compliment is significant: 'You've got a name that any chap might feel proud of'.[20] In the fictional world of the dime novel, spying is the new yardstick of manhood.

The spy's physical disguise becomes more elaborate and proportionately more consequential in the dime novel than in the story-paper. The distance travelled from Cooper's figure is evident in *Jabez Hawk, The Yankee Spy* (1864) by C. Dunning Clark. In an obvious reference to *The Spy*, Jabez Hawk is a pedlar spy from New England, interceding in Bacon's Rebellion in colonial Virginia. But whereas Harvey Birch must obscure his heroic achievements with his role as pedlar (and indeed he is both pedlar and spy) right up to his death, Jabez Hawk casts off his lower-class dialect, his 'queer trappings' and his 'frowsy wig' the minute he takes sword in hand to do battle. His true colours reveal him to be 'a handsome fellow', Captain James Barlow of Plymouth.[21] Disguise is now less a sign of political unease than a narrative device facilitating suspense over the issue of identity. Questions of death and disguise drive dime-novel spy fiction: will the spy be caught and executed; and who is he?

That question of identity, plus perhaps the residual liminality of the spy, ostensibly allows darker and lower-class types to cluster around the spy figure and so play a more central role than is regularly available to them in mass fiction. The spy mask is adopted by eminent members of society: the Masked Spy of the American Revolution is revealed as Elmo Mountjoy, of noble English lineage and European education; Dagon, the Hunter Spy during the same conflict, turns out to be Matthew Lincoln, last male in an aristocratic Virginia family. But the mask appears to be shared by members of less established groups: the woman spy in *Stella, the Spy* (1861), the Indian spies of *The Trail-Hunters; or, Monowano, the Shawnee Spy* (1861) and *The Red Spy* (1871), even Black spies in *The Quadroon Spy; or, The Ranger's Bride* (1870) and *The Black Spy; or, The Yellowstone Trail* (1873). Championing the common people and writing them into America's history were always part of cheap fiction's rhetoric. This spy fiction appears to develop that strategy one step further, by legitimizing marginalized types, giving them a central, heroic role in the democratic order. The illusory dimension of this process is revealed towards the close of these tales: the woman turns out not to be a spy, the Indian is a white man in disguise, the Quadroon is a pro-American Mexican. In a more complex twist on the same theme, the Black spy in the novel of that name is a spy and he is Black. However, Cuff Tompkins's power is entirely borrowed from the dominant order: his espionage skill rests on his ventriloquism, which manifests itself in perfect English, though Tompkins normally speaks in broad comic dialect; when he functions as a spy, he does not speak as or for Blacks after all. These revelations do not, of course, entirely erase the manifestation of these types' potential for heroic roles; in the era of Reconstruction it is particularly significant that Black characters are given some kind of voice. And Michael Denning's observation about ventriloquism cutting both ways should not be forgotten. Nevertheless, what seems to be offered in these fictions is a cathartic resolution: types who are threatening to, or marginalized by, the dominant order are simultaneously folded into the master narrative of spy fiction and erased from the scene. That this process should devolve upon the spy figure suggests that the radically isolated victim has mutated into a distinctive and desirable figure of American heroism.

Among all these fictional feints and ruses, the only spies who visibly busy themselves about the mechanics of espionage are those appearing in Civil War tales of the 1860s. *The Border Spy; or, The Beautiful Captive of the Rebel Camp* (1863) by Lieutenant Colonel Hazelton and *The Vicksburg Spy; or, Found and Lost* (1865) by Edward Willett develop quite complex patterns of spying, double agency, disinformation and cryptography. These means are effective only in the hands of the spies who work alone, the heroic individuals who are contrasted with the herds of ineffective, treacherous spies who cluster together. But the heroic spies of the Civil War finally remain trapped in some form of liminality at the end of their adventures: the hero of *The Vicksburg Spy* is killed by a mine set by his own side before he can marry his faithful lover; the eponymous hero of *Bob Brant* survives his contribution to the Federal cause and marries his Southern belle, but is permanently scarred by the loss of his arm in battle. These imperfect unions signal the unfinished story of the Civil War, the one narrative which the formula cannot resolve.

In the nineteenth century, the spy figure never entirely lost his problematic nature as an American icon; he never became as popular or frequently used a hero as the hunter, the scout, or the detective. It is easy to understand why his existence has been overlooked so consistently by modern critics. But the turns and twists involved in positioning the spy within mass literature are significant. Story papers and dime novels do not spin plots out of the complexities of espionage in the way that modern spy fiction does. Instead, their suspense derives from the issue of the spy's allegiance, his ability to avoid capture and the mystery of his true identity. The ways in which these questions are answered amount to a ritual of doubt and reassurance: the spy is repeatedly revealed to be Anglo-Saxon in his affiliation, a true American hero who brings about national and personal harmony. Because this ritual is located at the intersection of the periodicals' propaganda and the fiction's representation of formative historical periods, it can be read as a justification of America's national mission, one of Martin Green's 'energizing myths of empire'.[22] Cooper and his imitators present the spy as central to America's triumphs in various wars; for those victories to be unqualified, the spy must be confirmed as hero. Sold in huge numbers and presented insistently to popular memory, this negotiation of the spy's image became one of the affirmative stories America told itself.

NOTES

The author wishes to thank Trent University for funds in support of the research for this essay.

1. This analysis is typical of the standard treatments of spy fiction, such as Ralph Harper, *The World of the Thriller* (Baltimore, 1974); Bruce Merry, *Anatomy of the Spy Thriller* (Dublin, 1977); LeRoy Panek, *Special Branch: The British Spy Novel 1890–1980* (Bowling Green, OH, 1981); Michael Denning, *Cover Stories: Narrative and Ideology in the British Spy Thriller* (London, 1987); and John Cawelti and Bruce Rosenberg, *The Spy Story* (Chicago, 1987) – although Cawelti is unusual in acknowledging, briefly, the existence of the spy in American popular literature of the nineteenth century.
2. Denning applies his term to the stories spy thrillers tell about the world; it can apply equally felicitously to the stories critics tell about spy thrillers.
3. Anon., 'The Spy System in Europe', *Beadle's Monthly: A Magazine of To-Day*, I (Jan. – June 1866): 80–84.
4. The primary reading for this essay was gleaned from Lyle Wright's three bibliographies, *American Fiction 1774–1850: A Contribution toward a Bibliography* (San Marino, CA, 1969), *American Fiction 1851–1875: A Contribution toward a Bibliography*

(San Marino, CA, 1965), *American Fiction 1876–1900: A Contribution toward a Bibliography* (San Marino, CA, 1966); and from Albert Johannsen, *The House of Beadle and Adams and Its Dime and Nickel Novels: The Story of a Vanished Literature*, 3 vols. (Norman, OK, 1950; supp. 1962). A preliminary survey of these sources revealed 106 novels with the words 'spy' or 'secret service' in their titles or subtitles. While this number is only a fraction of the thousands of cheap novels available in nineteenth-century America, it is a large enough group to suggest the repeated production of a formula, especially given that many more spy stories would have been published by houses not covered by these bibliographies, and more still would be camouflaged by more opaque titles.

5. Roland Barthes, 'Myth Today', *Mythologies*, trans. Annette Lavers (London, 1973), pp.109–59.
6. See Mary Noel, *Villains Galore: The Heyday of the Popular Story Weekly* (New York, 1954); and Madeleine B. Stern (ed.), *Publishers for Mass Entertainment in Nineteenth-Century America* (Boston, 1980).
7. Anon., 'Ireland', and anon., 'Aristocracy', *The Flag of Our Union*, 13 January 1849, p.[3].
8. Frederick Merk, *Manifest Destiny and Mission in American History* (New York, 1963), p.50.
9. See Johannsen; and Christine Bold, *Selling the Wild West: Popular Western Fiction, 1860 to 1960* (Bloomington, IN, 1987).
10. See Tania Modleski, *Studies in Entertainment: Critical Approaches to Mass Culture* (Bloomington, IN, 1986).
11. Michael Denning, *Mechanic Accents: Dime Novels and Working-Class Culture in America* (London, 1987), p.3.
12. Cawelti and Rosenberg, p.36.
13. Ned Buntline, *Saul Sabberday; or, The Idiot Spy: A Tale of Men and Deeds of '76* (New York, 1858), p.31.
14. J.R. Simms, *The American Spy; or, Freedom's Early Sacrifice: A Tale of the Revolution, Founded Upon Fact* (Albany, NY, 1846), p.57.
15. Harry Halyard, *The Mexican Spy; or, The Bride of Buena Vista: A Tale of the Mexican War* (Boston, 1848), pp.30, 31.
16. J.H. Ingraham, *Arnold; or, The British Spy! A Tale of Treason and Treachery* (Boston, 1844), p.23.
17. Charles E. Averill, *The Secret Service Ship; or, The Fall of San Juan D'Ulloa: A Thrilling Tale of the Mexican War* (Boston, 1848), p.15.
18. Edward Willett, *Bob Brant, Patriot and Spy: A Tale of the War in the West* (New York, 1864), p11.
19. Jane Tompkins, *Sensational Designs: The Cultural Work of American Fiction, 1790–1860* (New York, 1985).
20. Edward S. Ellis, *The Forest Spy: A Tale of the War of 1812* (New York, 1861), p.101.
21. C. Dunning Clark, *Jabez Hawk, The Yankee Spy: A Romance of Early Virginia* (New York, 1864), p.96.
22. Martin Green, *Dreams of Adventure, Deeds of Empire* (New York, 1979).

Primary Works Consulted

This list comprises one-volume reprints of story-paper serials and original editions of dime novels.

Captain J.F.C. Adams, *The Black Spy; or, The Yellowstone Trail* (New York: Beadle and Adams, 1873).
——, *Oregon Sol; or, Nick Whiffles's Boy Spy* (New York: Beadle and Adams, 1884).
Charles E. Averill, *The Secret Service Ship; or, The Fall of San Juan D'Ulloa: A Thrilling Tale of the Mexican War* (Boston: F. Gleason, 1848).
Jos. E. Badger, Jr., *The Indian Spy; or, The Unknown Foe: A Romance of Early Kentucky*

(New York: Beadle and Co., 1870).

Ned Buntline, *Saul Sabberday; or, The Idiot Spy: A Tale of Men and Deeds of '76* (New York: Frederic A. Brady, 1858).

Austin C. Burdick, *The Ocean Martyr; or, The Hunter Spy of Virginia: A Revolutionary Story of Sea and Shore* (New York: Samuel French, n.d.).

Major Dangerfield Burr, *Buffalo Bill's Secret Service Trail; or, The Mysterious Foe: A Romance of Red-skins, Renegades and Army Rencounters* (New York: Beadle and Adams, 1887).

Major Lewis W. Carson, *Bashful Bill, The Spy; or, Double Hand, The Dark Destroyer* (New York: Beadle and Adams, 1873).

——, *The Specter Spy; or, The Wizard Canoe* (New York: Beadle and Adams, 1870).

C. Dunning Clark, *Jabez Hawk, The Yankee Spy: A Romance of Early Virginia* (New York: Beadle and Adams, 1864).

James Fenimore Cooper, *The Spy: A Tale of the Neutral Ground* (Philadelphia: Lea & Carey, 1821).

Edward S. Ellis, *The Forest Spy: A Tale of the War of 1812* (New York: Beadle and Co., 1861).

——, *Ruth the Betrayer; or, The Female Spy* (London: John Dicks, 1863).

——, *The Trail-Hunters; or, Monowano, the Shawnee Spy* (New York: Beadle and Co., 1861).

Harry Halyard, *The Mexican Spy; or, The Bride of Buena Vista: A Tale of the Mexican War* (Boston: F. Gleason, 1848).

W.J. Hamilton, *The Quadroon Spy; or, The Ranger's Bride* (New York: Beadle and Co., 1870).

T.C. Harbaugh, *Nicko' the Night; or, The Boy Spy of '76* (New York: Beadle and Adams, 1877).

Harry Hazard, *The Bearhunter; or, Davy Crockett as a Spy* (New York: Beadle and Adams, 1873).

Lieutenant Colonel Hazeltine, *The Border Spy; or, The Beautiful Captive of the Rebel Camp: A Story of the War* (New York: Sinclair Tousey, 1863).

Professor J.H. Ingraham, *Arnold; or, The British Spy! A Tale of Treason and Treachery* (Boston: The 'Yankee' Office, 1844).

Colonel Prentiss Ingraham, *Conrad the Sailor Spy; or, The True Hearts of '76: An Afloat and Ashore Romance of Revolutionary Days* (New York: Beadle and Adams, 1890).

——, *Dick Doom's Destiny; or, The River Blacklegs' Terror: A Romance of the Realities of the Secret Service* (New York: Beadle and Adams, 1892).

——, *The Masked Spy; or, The Wild Rider of the Hills: A Romance of the Ramapo* (New York: Beadle and Adams, 1873).

N.C. Iron, *Stella, The Spy: A Tale of the War of '76* (New York: Beadle and Adams, 1861).

Wm. H. Manning, *Central Pacific Paul, The Mail-Train Spy; or, Yank Yellowbird's Iron Trail* (New York: Beadle and Adams, 1888).

P. Hamilton Myers, *The Red Spy: A Tale of the Mohawk in 1777* (New York: Beadle and Adams, 1871).

Dr J.H. Robinson, *The Rebel Spy; or, The King's Volunteers: A Romance of the Siege of Boston* (Boston: F. Gleason, 1852).

J.R. Simms, *The American Spy; or, Freedom's Early Sacrifice: A Tale of the Revolution, Founded Upon Fact* (Albany, New York: J. Munsell, 1846).

Roger Starbuck, *The Blue Clipper; or, The Smuggler Spy* (New York: Beadle and Co., 1870).

Captain Frederick Whittaker, *Double-Death; or, The Spy Queen of Wyoming* (New York: Beadle and Adams, 1890).

Edward Willett, *Bob Brant, Patriot and Spy: A Tale of the War in the West* (New York: Sinclair Tousey, 1864).

——, *The Vicksburg Spy; or, Found and Lost* (New York: Sinclair Tousey, 1865).

The Politics of Adventure in the Early British Spy Novel

DAVID TROTTER

REAL INTELLIGENCE – CARICATURE INTELLIGENCE

In Chapter 4 of John Buchan's *Greenmantle* (1916), the hero, Richard Hannay, encounters his implacable adversary, the ruthless Colonel Stumm. 'I had struck something I had been looking for for a long time, and till that moment I wasn't sure that it existed. Here was the German of caricature, the real German, the fellow we were up against. He was as hideous as a hippopotamus, but effective.'[1] In popular fiction, and this is the source both of the pleasure it gives to ordinary readers and of the interest it retains for historians, the real invariably *is* the caricature. Popular fiction is peopled by caricatures; but those caricatures can be mistaken for real because the anxieties they encounter or express are real anxieties. Colonel Stumm, with his pyramidal head and suspiciously effeminate habits, is a caricature – but one which Buchan's readers had, in 1916, good cause to fear.

They might, perhaps, have feared the reality of Colonel Stumm even more if they had not been prepared for it by a whole series of caricatures. The years between 1900 and 1914 saw the establishment, not at all coincidentally, of the British spy novel and the British Secret Service. Before 1907 espionage was largely passive, based on amateur agents and casual informants. In that year the appointment of Lieutenant-Colonel James Edmonds as head of MO5, the Secret Services section of the directorate of military operations, marked a change of emphasis. By the end of 1910, a more active and professional system was in place: a Secret Services bureau with a Foreign Section and a Home Section (subsequently known as MI6 and MI5). The new professionalism, however, depended very much on old assumptions, as Nicholas Hiley has shown. The bureau assumed, erroneously, that Germany was preparing to invade Britain, assisted by an army of spies and saboteurs. Any information which appeared to confirm this assumption was regarded as true, any information which appeared to contradict it as false. During the Agadir crisis of 1911, the bureau's networks 'were so geared to uncovering secret preparations for surprise attack that this combined with the inherent Germanophobia of the agents to produce reports that such an attack was imminent. Despite impressive activity the secret service did not supply accurate intelligence, but slowly reinforced prejudice'. In 1912, the uncovering of a modest network of German agents only convinced the director of the Home Section that he

had hitherto under- rather than over-estimated their presence: those agents
as yet undiscovered must of course be 'the cleverest and most adroit' – the
ones entrusted with sabotage after the outbreak of war.[2] The British Secret
Service, like the British spy novel, invested in fantasy.

Indeed, they invested in the same fantasy. When Edmonds took over
at MO5, the files contained a few papers relating to the South African
War, and some relating to France and Russia, but nothing about the new
opponent, Germany. He badly needed evidence to confirm his suspicions
about Germany, which were not shared by the Secretary of State for
War, Richard Haldane. Fortunately literature came to his aid. In 1909,
the sensational novelist William Le Queux published *Spies for the Kaiser.
Plotting the Downfall of England*, in which two lawyers expose 'the vast
army of German spies spread over our smiling land of England'. His aim
was to kindle in his readers a conviction that German agents were hard at
work everywhere, reconnoitring beaches and preparing acts of sabotage.
He wanted to reinforce Germanophobia. When the novel was serialized in
the *Weekly News*, the paper appointed a Spy Editor, and ran the headlines
'FOREIGN SPIES IN BRITAIN. / £10 Given For Information. / Have
You Seen a Spy?' Le Queux received a large number of letters which
denounced perfectly innocent people for swearing in German or sporting
a wig. He passed them on to Edmonds, who used them to persuade the
Committee of Imperial Defence to set up a new Secret Services bureau.
As late as July 1908, Haldane had remained sceptical about the extent
of German espionage. Edmonds's new 'evidence', nearly all of it fantasy
rather than fact, seems to have changed his mind.[3] In Edwardian Britain,
real intelligence *was* caricature intelligence.

If literature coloured politics, politics also coloured literature. Edwardian
spy novels were, as David Stafford has pointed out, unashamedly didactic:
a political response to the erosion of Britain's status and prestige in a
period marked by relative economic decline, armaments races and crisis
diplomacy. 'At every turn,' wailed *The Pall Mall Gazette* in 1885, 'we are
confronted with the gunboats, the sea lairs, or the colonies of jealous and
eager rivals . . . The world is filling up around us.' America and Germany
were challenging Britain's industrial and commercial supremacy, while the
inexhaustible Russian and Chinese masses pressed in on Britain's most
valued possession, India. 'Now,' Lord Salisbury declared in May 1898,
in a speech which alarmed and offended foreign governments, 'with the
whole earth occupied and the movements of expansion continuing, she
will have to fight to the death against successive rivals.'[4] Stafford argues
that the 'stereotyped figure' of the incorruptible and upright British agent
was conceived as a weapon in this fight to the death against internal and
external rivals. Distinguished by his Britishness from unreliable foreigners,
and by his gentlemanliness from working-class agitators and delinquents,

the secret agent became a 'symbol of stability' in a changing world. 'These men belong to the society of clubland heroes, and there can be no fear in the mind of the reader that they will be tempted by the lures of city vice or socialism, or be other than deeply loyal to class, country, and king.' Stafford identifies the politics of this representation with a mood which, following Samuel Hynes, he terms 'Tory pessimism': a widespread anxiety that the British Empire, like the Roman, would deteriorate internally to the point where it could no longer resist external pressures. He points out that many spy novels were 'attuned' to the propaganda of militant organizations like the National Service League, which argued that national service alone would revitalize and discipline the race. Le Queux worked closely with the League's moving spirit and second president, Lord Roberts, who added spectacular fuel to invasion fantasies when he claimed in the House of Lords in November 1908 that there were already 80,000 fully trained German soldiers in Britain. Roberts wrote the preface to Le Queux's most successful melodrama, *The Invasion of 1910* (1906), and provided technical assistance on military matters.[5] The politics of the Edwardian spy novel implicate the real (that is to say, the caricature) English gentleman in a fight to the death against national and class enemies.

My aim here is to extend and deepen Stafford's analysis, and so clarify the mutual reinforcement of narrative and politics in espionage fiction. One feature of 'Tory pessimism' was a suspicion that the English gentleman was not all that he might be, an anxiety that the rot which had already destroyed the working classes might also be reaching the upper and middle classes. The emphasis of its propaganda lay not so much on preserving intact the classes which had made Britain great, but on regenerating them so that they would once again become worthy of their forefathers; not so much on stability in a world of flux as on the flux which, however painful, would create a more stable world. Popular fiction echoed this propaganda by offering heroes who must endure flux in order to achieve a properly founded stability. In one of the most daring Edwardian bestsellers, Elinor Glyn's *Three Weeks* (1907), a stolid young Englishman is awakened not only to the reality of desire, but to the responsibilities of his class, by his 'episode' involving tiger-skin rugs and a mysterious East European princess. The adventures of the secret agent, like those of any other hero, do not simply confirm what he already is: they regenerate him, physically, morally and, most important of all, politically. I shall argue that spy novels are at their most effective, both in literary and in political terms, when they explore the instability of their protagonists. For it was only by dramatizing such individual regenerations that the propagandists could hope to convey the urgency and the glamour of the collective regeneration they had in mind. Joining the National Service League was one thing; becoming a man, on a tiger-skin rug, or in pursuit of the Kaiser's spies, another.

If we are to understand that the gentleman-spy does not emerge fully-formed on the first page, but is rather generated or regenerated by his adventures, then we must recognize that the genre of spy fiction did not emerge fully-formed on the first day of the century, but was rather produced in competition with and adjustment to other popular genres.[6] The narrative and political conventions of the genre can best be understood, I believe, in relation to those of its immediate predecessor, the Terrorist Novel of the 1890s.

TERRORISTS

Bestselling literature often sells because it addresses the anxieties aroused by real events. The sensation novels of the 1860s fed off scandals involving bigamy and the forcible incarceration of the sane in lunatic asylums. The 1880s provided real events in the shape of terrorism. The British public felt most immediately threatened by the Fenian bombing campaign of 1884–85; but it would also have been aware of the assassination of Tsar Alexander II on 13 March 1880, and of the attempt to blow up Kaiser Wilhelm I on 28 September 1883. Terrorism was international in scope; it reminded people, or could be used to remind people, that Britain did not in fact enjoy a splendid isolation, but belonged to a large and threatening world. On 24 November 1883, when 'infernal machines' intended for the German embassy were found in a London lodging-house, *The Times* remarked that 'All Europe is bound together by a wide network of railways and steamers and telegraph lines, and a blow struck at any one part diffuses itself over all the rest, and is felt, in its degree, by all'.[7] By the early 1890s, assassinations and explosions had become regular events, particularly in France and Spain; on 15 February 1892, Martial Bourdin, a French anarchist, blew himself up in Greenwich Park, thus providing among other things the germ of Conrad's *The Secret Agent* (1907). Terrorism had international connections. The Fenian campaigns were planned and financed in America, by the Clan na Gael and O'Donovan Rossa's Skirmishers. On 4 February 1885, the *Pall Mall Gazette* carried an interview with the 'head of the Irish Dynamite School in Brooklyn', who displayed sketches of 'some of the weapons with which the dynamite party hope to terrify England into granting Ireland her independence'. These included dynamite flasks, explosive cigars and explosive walking-sticks.[8]

The appeal of the new scandal lay in its production of enigma: 'the sense', as Hyacinth Robinson puts it in James's *The Princess Casamassima* (1886), 'vividly kindled and never quenched, that the forces secretly arrayed against the present social order were pervasive and universal, in the air one breathed, in the ground one trod, in the hand of an acquaintance that one might touch or the eye of a stranger that might rest a moment on one's own'.[9] Dynamiters were even more secretive than bigamists. They made a point, a ceremony – paradoxically, a display – of secrecy. Initiation into the secret societies of terror was attended by the most bloodcurdling oaths and pledges. Once inside the mystery, you could never get out, as Robinson discovers. The dynamiter did not conceal a secret, like the bigamist; he or she *became* a secret. To stop being that secret was to stop being; traitors met a sudden and inevitable death. Terrorism was a machine for the production of enigma. In the popular imagination, that enigma had no outside, no end.

Writers and publishers were quick to exploit the commercial possibilities of secrets kept for ever. The publishers of Edgar Wallace's *The Four Just Men* (1905) offered substantial prizes to the readers who could explain most convincingly how the terrorists had murdered a British Cabinet minister – something the novel itself had not disclosed. But the enigma produced by terrorism was more than a opportunity to sell books. It was the product of an anxiety raw enough to be exploited for political as well as commercial ends. In Robert Cromie's *The Crack of Doom* (1895), Herbert Brande, a crazed anarcho-scientist, invents a kind of atom bomb. 'The agent I will employ has cost me all life to discover,' he murmurs. 'It will release the vast stores of etheric energy locked up in the huge atomic warehouse of this planet.' He means to detonate two bombs simultaneously, one in Labrador, one in the South Seas. The hero manages to attach himself to the South Seas expedition, and sabotage it. The Labrador expedition, Cromie notes in a preface, 'has not returned, nor has it ever been definitely traced'.[10] The thought that terrorism's expeditions have not yet been traced, and that etheric energies may yet be unlocked, demands a political response; the openness of the narrative is intended to open political assumptions.

Terrorism politicized mystery and mystified politics. People who married bigamously, or committed their best friends to asylums, usually had a perfectly intelligible, if criminal, motive. Dynamiters did not. In the first place, most of them were foreign. Their grievances and aspirations had been generated by archaic and thus barely intelligible political systems. Anarchism and Nihilism arose in societies where there was no possibility of resistance through debate or collective action. In the second place, dynamiters were motivated, more often than not, by obscure personal insults and injuries. They killed for revenge, out of hatred or perverted pride. Their motives were as elaborately and enigmatically coded as their pledges, a private suffering which would only be made intelligible by the equally private suffering of those who had tormented them. Terror was political, but also foreign and private.

Sensation novelists went to great lengths to preserve these qualities. They did not write about Fenians, whose political motive was not at all hard to understand.[11] They wrote about obscurely injured foreigners, and notably about foreign women, whose politics were always likely to remain inscrutable. The heroine of Joseph Hatton's *By Order of the Czar* (1890), Anna Klosstock, starts life in a Jewish village in Russia. She is raped by the governor of the district, General Petronovitch, and then brutally flogged. She becomes a Nihilist, marries a rich sympathizer, and inherits his wealth. Moving now in the highest society, she seduces and murders Petronovitch. When Philip Forsyth, a young English painter who has fallen in love with her, joins the secret society, she finally reveals her past and demonstrates her right to vengeance. Asked to provide a motive, she answers with her body.

> As she spoke she tore open her dress, exhibiting a lovely white arm and part of a beautiful bust, turning at the same time with swift rapidity to exhibit her right shoulder and her neck, no further than is considered correct by ladies of fashion at balls and in the opera stalls, but sufficient to thrill iron men who had themselves been witnesses of the worst of Russian tortures. Red and blue, deep ridges and welts crossed and recrossed each other, with intervals of angry patches of red, and weird daubs of grey that blurred and blotted out all remains and tokens of the beautiful form with which nature had endowed one of its loveliest creatures.[12]

Anna Klosstock's secret has been inscribed on her body; she will live with it, or in it, until the day she dies. It is a disfiguring secret, one which has blotted the tokens of a woman's beauty, and replaced them by the tokens of political commitment. Anna's body is her politics, and it demands the most intimate of responses. Her gesture has the ability to 'thrill' iron men who have seen everything (not to mention iron readers who have read everything). Instead of being interpreted and resolved, it is absorbed back into the enigma out of which it arose. Anna and her colleagues return to Russia, where they have work to do. But the police are waiting for them; they are arrested and banished to Siberia.

    Hatton, a competent journalist, researched his novel carefully and meant it to have a political impact. He was proud that it had been banned in Russia. Yet its most potent symbol, Anna's disfigured back, is by no means unambiguously political. The back thrills. But it is a hieroglyph rather than a manifesto; the injury condensed in its ruin will never enter fully into political process. Disfigurement is too mysterious an emblem to sway senates or rally crowds. Hatton has created an extremely potent enigma, but he does not really know what to do with it. He cannot see how it might be incorporated either into political process or into his narrative. For the hero, Philip Forsyth, appears to be made of rubber rather than iron. When Anna bares her back, he faints. At the end of the novel, he is arrested with the other conspirators, but released through the agency of an English friend. Instead of accompanying Anna to Siberia, he returns to London and a miserably diminished existence; though his painting of a group of exiles, including Anna, does win the Royal Academy's Gold Medal. Hatton, in short, can incorporate Anna's face into his narrative, by way of the Gold Medal painting, but not her back. He cannot marry her to Philip. In Britain in the 1890s, the disfigured figure of the terrorist could be neither ignored nor assimilated.

At the beginning of L.T.Meade's *The Siren* (1898), a respectable English bachelor, Colonel Nugent, sits down to a respectable English breakfast with his widowed sister, Lady O'Brien, his niece, Wilmot O'Brien, and his nephew, Frank Norreys, 'one of the best-looking men in the Coldstream Guards'. He receives a letter informing him that he has a daughter. As a young man he had been in the diplomatic service in St Petersburg, and fallen in love with the beautiful Countess Chrisanto. They had supposed that her husband was dead. In fact, he has been putting her to the test, and exacts his revenge by betraying her to the secret police. Her daughter by Nugent, Vera, is born in Siberia. Count Chrisanto, a Nihilist masquerading as a servant of the Tsar, has Vera stripped and flogged in public in order to ensure her commitment to Nihilism. He means her to be the instrument both of revolution and of his own revenge. She will go to England, secure Nugent's fortune for the cause, and then assassinate Nugent and the Tsar with bouquets of poisoned roses.

Vera is immensely desirable, and wreaks havoc among the respectable English, both men and women. Wilmot shares Vera's bed on the night before she is due to marry the now reluctant Frank, who has become Vera's plaything. Lady O'Brien is hostile at first, but soon won over ('That kiss thrilled through the widow almost as if it had been bestowed by a lover').[13] But the siren is tormented by the memory of the flogging in Siberia. Her beauty has been disfigured, her politics inscribed on her body. Meade, like Hatton, has created a potent symbol which cannot be incorporated fully into the narrative. Vera learns to love her English father, and longs to exchange her Russian magnetism for English respectability. But the trauma of the flogging – the secret inscription – keeps her loyal to the cause. There can be no compromise between the two ways of life, between a daughter's love for her father and a terrorist's eroticized dedication to the Russian people. Vera commits suicide rather than carry out her vow to assassinate Nugent and the Tsar.

These novels are political. But the prominence they give to women, and to women's bodies, in the end deflects them from politics into sado-masochism. Other novelists, however, did try to incorporate terrorism fully into their narratives and into political process. In *Angel of the Revolution* (1893), George Griffith forged a startling alliance between Russian terrorists and his hero, a proto-Wellsian engineer called Richard

Arnold. After his design for a new kind of airship is rejected by the British government, Arnold joins the Brotherhood, 'an international secret society underlying and directing the operations of the various bodies known as Nihilists, Anarchists, Socialists – in fact, all those organisations which have for their object the reform or destruction, by peaceful or violent means, of Society as it is at present constituted'. The Brotherhood is led by Natas, a Russian Jew who has suffered terribly at the hands of the Tsarist police. Its council chamber contains vivid paintings of scenes of exile and torture. Colston, the Englishman who recruits Arnold, has himself been flogged for coming to the aid of a defenceless woman ('That is the sign-manual of Russian tyranny – the mark of the knout!').[14] The outcome of this alliance is that Arnold builds airships for the Brotherhood, which uses them to foment and regulate a world war between Britain, Germany and Austria, on one hand, and France, Russia and Italy, on the other. Although in theory neutral, the Brotherhood brings America into the war on the side of Britain and Germany, and thus ensures their triumph. Arnold marries Natas's daughter (her back seems to have escaped damage).

Without airships, Britain and Germany would have been defeated; without the Brotherhood, there would have been no airships. Griffith uses terrorism's violation of the British way of doing things to suggest that the British way is outmoded, and that Britain will not survive into the twentieth century (the novel is set in 1904) unless it adopts a new and much harsher political creed. 'It was not now a question of nation against nation, but of race against race. The fierce flood of war had swept away all smaller distinctions. It was necessary to rise to the altitude of the problem of the Government not of nations, but of the world. Was the genius of the East or of the West to shape the future destinies of the human race?'[15] From the altitude of Arnold's airships, the world looks like an arena for the disposition of empires and races rather than nations. If the British are to survive in it, they must stop thinking of themselves as the most democratic of trading nations, and start thinking of themselves as the most powerful of empires, head of an Anglo-Saxon Federation. The last battle the Federation wins is against Muslim hordes pouring out of the East. Griffith thought that Britain was in decline, and quite incapable of regenerating itself; no amount of argument or exhortation would make any difference. So he enlisted the potent enigma of terrorism as a catalyst. The Brotherhood takes Arnold seriously; he in turn is fortified by its dedication and ruthlessness. This political awakening is as crucial a part of his adventure, and of our enjoyment of his adventure, as the expeditions and battles. Hatton and Meade had broached the subject of politics, but did not really know what to do with it. Griffith incorporated it fully into his narrative.

In *Angel of the Revolution*, Griffith set a political agenda: the awakening, by any means possible, of a sluggish and complacent ruling class. Writers in another genre were also proposing rude awakenings for polite people. In May 1871, *Blackwood's Magazine* had published a cautionary tale by an army officer at the Royal Indian Civil Engineering College in Staines, Lieutenant-Colonel George Chesney. The narrator of the story recalls, 50 years after the event, how the Germans invaded Britain. The army is in Ireland, crushing the Fenians, and the navy scattered throughout the world. Landing at Brighton, the Germans push the few remaining defenders back to the ridge between Guildford and Dorking, and wipe them out. Demoralized by greed and political reform, the population offers no further resistance. 'A nation too selfish to defend its liberty,' the narrator concludes, 'could not have been fit to retain it.' Chesney became a Tory Member of Parliament in 1892.16

Within a month, *The Battle of Dorking* had been reprinted as a sixpenny pamphlet, of which 80,000 copies were sold. It was translated into French, German, Dutch and Italian. Gladstone denounced it as alarmist, but invasion-fantasies became immensely popular, with the identity of the invader varying according to political circumstances. The visit of the Russian fleet to Toulon in 1893 inspired the Franco-Russian alliances of *Angel of the Revolution* and William Le Queux's *The Great War in England in 1897*, which went through 16 editions after it had been endorsed by Lord Roberts, Britain's most famous military strategist. In the latter, the French land on the South Coast, while in Birmingham Russian troops impale babies on their bayonets. Outside the National Gallery the mob makes a bonfire of paintings and conducts 'wild reckless orgies' around it. However, a 'feeling of thankfulness' soon spreads through the land as Germany and Italy come to the rescue.17 Ten years later, Roberts and Le Queux collaborated on *The Invasion of 1910*. Now it is the Germans who impale babies until finally baffled by the British genius for guerrilla warfare. The story was serialized in the *Daily Mail*, and Le Queux was encouraged to adjust the route taken by the invaders so that it passed through towns where the paper sold well.

The problem with Chesney's formula was that it was altogether too cautionary. It allowed, at best, for last-minute revivals of fighting spirit, eleventh-hour awakenings in the rubble that had once been the capital of empire; whereas the political agenda called for a regeneration which would *precede*, and thus avert, the total destruction of British society. Fortunately, however, there were preliminaries to invasion. Military and literary strategists of the time agreed that the success of an attack would depend on surprise and secret preparation.18 Invading armies had to be trained and assembled secretly. They would only get ashore if they knew exactly where the enemy was weakest, and if key installations had been destroyed in advance by sabotage. There would be no invasion without spies.

In the early years of the century, spy fever superseded Hyacinth Robinson's terrorist fever. The menace lurking 'in the hand of an acquaintance that one might touch or the eye of a stranger that might rest a moment on one's own' was now likely to be sponsored by the Kaiser. 'How little the public knows,' Le Queux complained, 'of the stealthy treacherous ways of modern diplomacy, of the armies of spies seeking always to plot and counter plot, of the base subterfuges of certain foreign diplomatists.' He made it his business, in novel after novel, to let the public know. 'Nations, jealous of our prosperity, are ever plotting our downfall; known spies flock into England and yet we receive them; great armies are drilling daily in expectation of a struggle with us, and in every foreign navy yard, swift ships, destroyers and submarines, are being built for one purpose – to some day overthrow our naval supremacy.' Before the war, he lamented in 1916, German spies had 'swarmed in all cities, and in every village; her agents ranked among the leaders of social and commercial life, and among the sweepings and outcasts of great communities' – some of them had even been, horror of horrors, 'on golfing terms with the rulers of Great Britain'.[19] Paranoia was Le Queux's most effective political and literary technique.

Suspicion that menace lurks in the hand of an acquaintance or the eye of a stranger motivates the narrator of one of the earliest thrillers, Headon Hill's *The Spies of the Wight* (1899). Philip Monckton, a journalist, is holidaying with his mother on the Isle of Wight when he notices something odd in the hand of an old acquaintance, Arthur Doring, an artillery officer, and in the eye of a mysterious stranger, the bloated and wheelchair-bound Mr Campion. A missing cuff-link reveals Doring's implication in a conspiracy to steal the plans of some new forts guarding Portsmouth. He has been enmeshed by Campion's daughter, whose androgynous beauty recalls that of the terrorist sirens. Campion himself is only pretending to be a fat cripple, and soon sprints nimbly away from his wheelchair; he is in fact the Baron von Holtzman, German master-spy. The Campions maintain an appearance of unruffled English domesticity. It takes supreme vigilance and enterprise on Monckton's part to spot the flaws in their disguise: his inquisitiveness, her troubling sexuality, both profoundly unEnglish.

But there is also, from the political point of view, a flaw in Hill's narrative, namely Monckton's motivation. Monckton is a journalist, who wants above all to secure a scoop for his paper. 'At the same time, in the interests of justice and of patriotism, I felt that I must so arrange that the "boom" in the paper was followed by prompt action on the part of the authorities in arresting the culprits; it would do even such a strong journal as ours more harm than good if its premature exploitation of the affair acted as a warning, and enabled the miscreants to escape.' Patriotism and justice come a poor second to the scoop. It is in these terms that his editor congratulates him, after a boatload of spies has been blown out of the water. "'You have done your work pretty thoroughly, Monckton," said my editor, as he shook my hand again; "exposed the spies first, and then sent them to the bottom of the sea. A neat bit of up-to-date journalism"' – but not, apparently, a neat bit of up-to-date patriotism.[20] Politics and adventure both feature in *The Spies of the Wight*, but they remain separate; the hero's adventures do not include a political awakening.

If the spy-novel was to fulfil the political agenda sketched by Griffith, it had to generate a different kind of hero: one who would be changed in every way by his experiences. It found that hero in the amateur agent or accidental spy, the sleepy young Englishman whose lassitude and political complacency are shattered when he stumbles across some fiendish plot. Outlawed by society, since no-one takes him seriously, he must learn to believe in himself; regenerated by adventure, he will save the nation. We can define the characteristics of this new hero if we compare the narrator of *The Spies of the Wight* with the narrator of Erskine Childers's *The Riddle of the Sands* (1903).

At the beginning of the novel, Carruthers – 'a young man of condition and fashion', who knows the right people, belongs to the right clubs, and has 'a safe, possibly a brilliant, future in the Foreign Office' – is finding it hard to endure the emptiness of London in September. Despite giving the appearance of personal and professional stability, he feels that he is wasting his life; his job bores him, and he cannot quite believe that his friends miss him as badly as they say they do. All is not well with this particular member of the ruling class. Then he receives a letter from his college friend, Davies, who invites him for a spot of yachting and duck-shooting in the Baltic. 'Yachting in the Baltic in September! The very idea made one shudder.'[21] Still, he decides to accept.

He begins to benefit from his decision almost immediately. 'An irresistible sense of peace and detachment, combined with that delicious physical awakening that pulses through the nerve-sick townsman when city airs and bald routines are left behind him, combined to provide me, however thankless a subject, with a solid background of resignation.' He needs all the resignation he can muster when the spartan Davies introduces him to the tiny yacht on which they will spend the next few weeks. Even so, an early-morning swim removes 'yet another crust of discontent and self-conceit', as does his subsequent initiation into the mysteries of sailing and navigation. Childers describes these events in intricate detail because, although there is not yet a storm or a Hun in sight, the real adventure – the regeneration of Carruthers – has begun. The weeks which follow constitute a 'passage' in his life, 'short, but pregnant with moulding force, through stress and strain'.[22]

Davies teaches Carruthers the art of roughing it, and so transforms him from a 'peevish dandy' into a hardy and self-reliant outdoorsman. But he possesses another kind of wisdom as well. In him, 'devotion to the sea' is wedded to 'a fire of pent-up patriotism struggling incessantly for an outlet in strenuous physical expression'. His patriotism has produced a 'theory'. Davies believes that Germany is preparing for war with Britain, and that British apathy and conceit may well ensure German triumph. 'It's not the people's fault. We've been safe so long, and grown so rich, that we've forgotten what we owe it to. But there's no excuse for those blockheads of statesmen, as they call themselves, who are paid to see things as they are.' Government, in fact the entire ruling class, is too complacent to recognize the danger; 'and it's only when kicked and punched by civilian agitators, a mere handful of men who get sneered at for their pains, that they wake up, do some work, point proudly to it, and go to sleep again, till they get another kick'. Davies, like Richard Arnold, demands a radical change of attitude, a gigantic effort to revitalize the Empire. 'By Jove! we want a man like this Kaiser, who doesn't wait to be kicked, but works like a nigger for his country, and sees ahead.' 'We're improving, aren't we?' Carruthers pleads, but without much conviction.[23]

Davies's theory is sponsored by Tory pessimism and long since incorporated into sensational fiction. What is important about it is that it provokes a second transformation in Carruthers. Carruthers begins to believe it. Just as the peevish dandy had been transformed into an outdoorsman, so the civil servant joins the civilian agitators. The narrative turns as much on the second as on the first of these transformations. When the amateur spies discover the identity of the treacherous Dollman, Carruthers suggests that he should at once travel to England and inform the Admiralty or Scotland Yard. 'It would be strange if between them they couldn't dislodge him, and, incidentally, draw such attention to this bit of coast as to make further secrecy impossible.' Carruthers, the civil servant, wants to hand over to the authorities. Davies, the civilian agitator, believes that the authorities will do nothing, and that the matter must be resolved by the men on the spot. When Carruthers realizes that Davies is right – 'London was utterly impossible' – he experiences an awakening as fundamental as his rejection of dandyism.[24] He is freed to play his full part in uncovering a German plan to invade England. This political awakening represents, more vividly than any escapade, his adventure – and our adventure, as readers. It is an experience denied to the scoop-happy Philip Monckton.

The elision of politics and adventure distinguishes the spy novel from the terrorist novel and establishes it as a genre in its own right. 'This, however, is a narrative, not a criticism', insists the narrator of Le Queux's *Secrets of the Foreign Office* (1903), after launching a savage attack on British apathy and conceit.[25] But in the Edwardian spy novel, the criticism *is* the narrative. The story works as a story if it awakens the reader politically. In Mrs Braddon's best-selling bigamy novel, *Lady Audley's Secret* (1862), a young lawyer, Robert Audley, is revitalized and given a purpose in life by his efforts to discover the truth about his mysterious aunt, Lucy Graham. In Dickens's *Our Mutual Friend* (1865), two more young lawyers are similarly reinvigorated by their efforts to discover the truth about the mysterious John Harmon. But the enigma which regenerates the two young lawyers in Le Queux's *Spies of the Kaiser* is political in origin and effect. Politics alone will arouse the latent energies of future rulers.

The figure of the amateur agent, in some way unstable at the outset, but grounded and strengthened by adventure, allowed readers to experience, rather than merely learn about, the political and moral regeneration which seemed necessary if Britain was to survive world-conflict. However, the imminence of that conflict also generated an institution, the secret service bureau, and with it a new figure, the professional agent. Captain Jack Jardine, the Man from Downing Street, arrived to assist the lawyers and yachtsmen. The Richard Hannay of *The Thirty-Nine Steps* (1915) is an amateur, the Richard Hannay of *Greenmantle* (1916) a professional. The professional agent is already secure both in his expertise and in his political commitment; he does not need to be grounded and strengthened by adventure. And yet so compelling was the theme of regeneration that it survived into the world of the professional agent, who more often than not gets a little rusty, a little complacent, between assignments. At the beginning of *Greenmantle*, Hannay is kicking his heels in London, every bit as peevish as Carruthers; then he too receives his summons to adventure. At the beginning of Ian Fleming's *From Russia, with Love* (1957), Bond kicks *his* heels. 'The blubbery arms of the soft life had Bond round the neck and they were slowly strangling him. He was a man of war and when, for a long period, there was no war, his spirit went into a decline.'[26] Just for a moment we can identify with these men in their blubberiness; then the adventure begins, and the blubber melts away. But we have been reminded that physical and political commitment must constantly be renewed.

OPPENHEIM

One way to understand the establishment of the spy-novel as a distinct genre with its own literary and political conventions is to follow the careers of its major exponents. The major, if by no means the most accomplished, exponents of the genre during the Edwardian period were William Le Queux and E. Phillips Oppenheim. They set the tone and reaped the rewards. Since David Stafford has said most of what needs to be said about Le Queux, I shall concentrate here on Oppenheim.[27]

Oppenheim was born in London in 1866, the son of a leather merchant who later moved to Leicester. In 1882, he followed his father into the leather business, and published his first novel, *Expiation* (1882) at his own expense. It was well received, and led to a contract to write six serials for the *Sheffield Weekly Telegraph*. But it was *The Mysterious Mr Sabin* (1898) which established his supremely successful formula of intrigue in high and luxurious places. *The Mysterious Mr Sabin*, sometimes described as the first spy-novel, still relies heavily on the potency of terrorism. Lord Deringham, a retired admiral, writes feverishly, day and night, in his study. He is generally considered crazy but harmless, until various criminal masterminds start to show an interest in his work, which turns out to include a detailed survey of Britain's coastal defences. Mr Sabin, a sinister cosmopolitan who walks with the aid of a jewelled stick, succeeds in stealing Deringham's papers. He will hand them over to the Germans in exchange for help with his plan to restore the French monarchy. He is stopped not by the British, who prove completely ineffectual, but by a secret society, to which he once belonged, and which still exercises over him an authority greater even than that of the Kaiser. Britain is the only country in Europe which grants asylum to Nihilists, and so must be preserved – and preserved it is, not by a great political awakening, but by the symbol of international terrorism: a small red sign, between a cross and a star, on Mr Sabin's wall. Oppenheim was clearly aware of the German threat. 'A war between Germany and England,' one character declares, 'is only a matter of time – of a few short years, perhaps even months.'[28] But he was as yet unable to imagine how the threat might be used to stimulate moral and political regeneration.

International secret societies continued to fascinate Oppenheim. Mr Sabin reappears, in more benevolent guise, in *The Yellow Crayon* (1903), where he is obliged to rescue his wife from a secret society which has become the vehicle of one man's revenge. That man is a German prince, but Sabin defeats him by appealing over his head to the Kaiser, who is presented as an admirably idealistic and hard-working chap. In *The Double Four* (1911), another secret society, once criminal in its aims but now political, wields more power than the British government. Peter Ruff is recalled, Bond-like, from 'the ignominy of peace' – which seems to mean a country estate and an unhealthy obsession with golf – to become head of operations in London. He manages to outwit and defeat a sinister German spymaster. As in *Angel of the Revolution* or *The Mysterious Mr Sabin*, it is the secret society alone which has the means both to avert war and to regenerate individual members of the ruling class.

Oppenheim's fantasy allegiance clearly lay with the French aristocracy: Mr Sabin is in fact the Duc de Souspennier; the Order of the Double Four is run by the Marquis de Sogrange. The leather merchant from Leicester could only set the world to rights by adopting the jewelled sticks and limpid conservatism of an ancient but indisputably foreign race. No wonder he became a fixture on the French Riviera. However, the alignments in his novels began to shift as his perception of the German threat sharpened, and with it his sense of the need for a political awakening. In 'An Accidental Spy', the opening chapter of *A Maker of History* (1905), Guy Stanton – 'just a good-looking, clean-minded, high-spirited young fellow, full of beans, and needing the bit every now and then'[29] – stumbles across a secret meeting between the Kaiser and the Tsar in a forest on the German border. A page of secret treaty, which floats out of a window and lands close to his hiding-place, reveals that they are co-ordinating an attack on Britain. Stanton, who can't speak the lingo, and is in any case too full of beans to be interested in politics, becomes the focus of deadly intrigue. The French get hold of him before the Germans, but won't admit it to anyone. Sir George Duncombe, a friend of a friend, who has fallen in love with a photograph of his sister, herself a captive by this time, eventually tracks him down. The fatal page persuades the French government to ally itself with Britain rather than Russia, and the new alliance proves strong enough to avert war.

   A Maker of History alludes to history, to real events like the Russian navy's attack on a British fishing fleet. The Anglo-French alliance of 1904, another real event, enabled Oppenheim to write a different kind of narrative, one based not on the intervention of a secret society, but on a widespread political awakening. What connects the protagonists is not membership of an Order or clan, but their status as amateurs. They are *all* 'accidental spies'. Stanton, the callow tourist, receives a political education. Sir George Duncombe, galvanized by the photograph, undergoes a rite of passage. 'His days of calm animal enjoyment were over. Sorrow or joy was to be his. He had passed into the shadows of the complex life.' Duncombe's assistant, a journalist called Spencer, learns how to reconcile patriotism with the desire for a scoop. Meanwhile a similar regeneration takes place among their French counterparts. The kidnappers belong to an aristocratic brotherhood. One of them, 'a drug-sodden degenerate of a family whose nobles had made gay the scaffolds of the Place de la République', betrays the brotherhood. But another, who poses as a 'decadent' – 'The joy of Paris to one who understands is the exquisite refinement, the unsurpassed culture of its abysmal wickedness' – turns out to have the right stuff. The adventure makes men out of boys; it also awakens members of the British and French ruling classes to the gravity of their political responsibilities. The leader of the brotherhood (a Marquis, of course) concludes that 'We amateurs have justified our existence'.[30]

   In *The Secret* (1907), a British amateur justifies his own existence without any help from the French. J. Hardross Courage, man of leisure and accomplished cricketer, gets implicated in an attempt on the life of Leslie Guest, alias Wortley Foote, who possesses The Secret: yet another scheme to restore the French monarchy, this time backed innocently by some American millionaires whose wives want to become titled ladies, and less innocently by the Germans, who plan to invade Britain after the forts protecting London have been put out of action by a fifth column masquerading as the German Waiters' Union. Courage, who had previously found life 'a tame thing', is transformed by his encounter with Guest, and with the equally enigmatic Adele Van Hoyt, who is attempting to detach herself from the conspirators. 'A few yards behind me,' he muses as he stares out over ancestral acres, pipe in hand, 'in the room which I had just quitted, a man was looking death in the face; a man, the passionate, half-told fragments of whose life kindled in me a whole world of new desires.' The desires thus kindled are not likely to be quenched by the inflammatory presence of Miss Van Hoyt. 'The excitement of his appeal was perhaps more directly potent; yet there was something far more subtle, far stranger, in my thoughts of her.'[31] Sexual and political appeals combine to regenerate Courage. He infiltrates the Waiters' Union and discovers the invasion-plan. But, like Carruthers, he cannot simply pass the information on to the authorities. The Prime Minister, a politician of the old school who despises Secret Service work, refuses to believe him. The political system remains locked into archaic complacency; it is up to the amateur, the civilian agitator, to save his country. Courage forms an alliance with the scaremongering press, the main platform for those who felt that the politicians would continue to ignore their warnings.[32] He takes his story to the editor of the *Daily Oracle*, who decides to print it, even though his office is under siege by heavily armed German waiters. The British have at last found the Courage of their convictions.

Oppenheim continued to use the dilemma of the accidental spy to engage his readers in adventure and in political awakening.[33] In his most elaborate thriller, *The Great Impersonation* (1920), Major-General Baron Leopold von Ragastein encounters in Africa an Englishman, Everard Dominey, whom domestic tragedy has reduced to a drunken wreck. Noticing a distinct physical resemblance, von Ragastein decides to kill Dominey and take his place in English society, in order to gather information about the mentality of the ruling classes. Dominey, however, is not so drunk that he fails to notice what's going on. Getting his retaliation in first, he disposes of his would-be attacker, and from then on impersonates von Ragastein impersonating himself. This causes immense confusion both to his English wife, Rosamund, whom he won't sleep with because he's pretending to be von Ragastein, and to von Ragastein's voluptuous Hungarian mistress, whom he won't sleep with because he's not von Ragastein. However, the Germans think he's their man and, on the outbreak of war, entrust him with their invasion-plans. He passes these on to the authorities, who have by this time apparently learnt to respect amateurs.

The Great Impersonation embeds a spy-novel in a domestic drama which might easily have been written by Mrs Braddon. Ten years before his encounter with von Ragastein, Dominey had been attacked by Roger Unthank, a rival for Rosamund's hand, and had apparently killed him. Unthank, however, lives on, in a loathsome pestilential thicket at the bottom of their garden, emerging every night to terrorize Rosamund by hallooing outside her window. But the Everard Dominey who returns from Africa is a different man; he has assimilated the discipline and resolution of his Prussian opponent. The regenerated Everard catches Unthank and razes the thicket to the ground. His marriage and his ancestral estate have both been purged (or will be once he no longer has to impersonate von Ragastein impersonating himself). Espionage produces moral and social, as well as political, regeneration. It would seem that you have to become a Prussian in order to become an Englishman.

FRONTIERSMEN

Chapter 11 of *The Riddle of the Sands*, in which Davies and Carruthers begin their exploration of the Frisian coast, is entitled 'The Pathfinders'. Davies is the real Pathfinder, a nautical version of Cooper's Natty Bumppo. 'He had, too, that intuition which is independent of acquired skill, and is at the root of all genius; which, to take cases analogous to his own, is the last quality of the perfect guide or scout. I believe he could *smell* sand where he could not see or touch it.'[34] The allusion to Cooper reminds us that in the Edwardian era spying was often regarded as an extension of scouting by other means. The frontier-myth which had made heroes out of scouts could also be used to make heroes out of spies.

In a lecture delivered at Oxford in 1907, Lord Curzon defined the frontier of Empire as the site of individual and collective regeneration. Curzon had recently been Viceroy of India, responsible for 5,700 miles of sensitive border, and was fully aware both of the strategic significance of such boundaries, and of their 'peculiar fascination'. The lecture consists largely of a discussion of frontier policy in recent history, with much reference to buffer states, protectorates and spheres of influence. But its tone changes towards the end, when Curzon launches into some fervent remarks about the effect of 'Frontier expansion' upon 'national character'. American historians, he pointed out, had recently devoted themselves with 'patriotic ardour' to 'tracing the evolution of national character as determined by its westward march across the continent'. Their labours demonstrated that the American nation had been born in the forests and on the trails of the frontier, 'amid the savagery of conflict'. Were the frontiers of Empire witnessing the rebirth of the British nation? Curzon thought so. 'I am one of those,' he concluded, 'who hold that in this larger atmosphere, on the outskirts of Empire, where the machine is relatively impotent and the individual is strong, is to be found an ennobling and invigorating stimulus for our youth, saving them alike from the corroding ease and the morbid excitements of Western civilization.' The larger atmosphere would transform the national character by regenerating young men and women. 'The Frontiers of Empire continue to beckon.'[35]

The leader of the school of historians to which Curzon referred was Frederick Jackson Turner, who delivered his famous paper on 'The Significance of the Frontier in American History' in Chicago on 12 July 1893. Turner thought that the frontier had shaped the national character more profoundly than institutions or constitutions. 'American social development has been continually beginning over again on the frontier. This perennial rebirth, this fluidity of American life, this expansion westward with its new opportunities, its continuous touch with the simplicity of primitive society, furnish the forces dominating American character.' The pioneer pushes beyond the line of settlement into a wilderness which forces him to return to fundamentals, to begin all over again. 'It strips off the garments of civilization and arrays him in the hunting shirt and the moccasin.' The corroding ease and morbid excitements of civilization are stripped off along with its garments. The pioneer learns to plough with a sharp stick and take the scalp. He becomes an Indian in order to become an authentic American. The sum of these reinvigorations will be a stalwart and rugged race.[36]

Such, at any rate, was the hope of one of Turner's most enthusiastic and influential admirers, Theodore Roosevelt. Roosevelt had himself been reinvigorated during the years he spent ranching in Dakota after the deaths of his wife and his mother in 1884, and the subsequent thwarting of his political ambitions. When he reentered politics in 1886, he brought with him a frontier-myth, the doctrine of the 'strenuous life'. Between 1885 and 1895, he published three books about his experiences as a rancher and hunter, and several volumes of an ambitious historical survey, *The Winning of the West*. He believed that the strenuous life would regenerate the ruling class: young men like him who had been brought up in luxury and ease, and had gone soft. Close friendships with diplomats like James Bryce and Cecil Spring Rice and popular writers like Rudyard Kipling and Rider Haggard ensured that his views found an echo in Britain. On 22 May 1918, Haggard wrote in his diary: 'There are two men left living in the world with whom I am in supreme sympathy, Theodore Roosevelt and Rudyard Kipling'.[37]

The strenuous life was mythologized most effectively by Roosevelt's friend since Harvard days, Owen Wister. Wister's essay on 'The Evolution of the Cow-Puncher' (1895) describes the fate of an English lord who has somehow found his way to Texas. The frontier awakens the 'slumbering untamed Saxon' in him, and he is regenerated, soon winning the hearts of his cowboy companions. In *The Virginian* (1902), the archetypal cowboy tale, the greenhorn narrator and the gentle schoolmarm undergo similar regenerations 'amid the savagery of conflict'. Meanwhile, the essential gentility of the Virginian himself, descendant of Natty Bumppo, has been nurtured by education and marriage; he ends up as proud possessor of a ranch and member of a new Western aristocracy. Like Roosevelt, Wister advocated a reinvigorating alliance between high-born and low-born, between innate gentility and frontier environment. No wonder Childers thought he was writing a Western. For if Davies is Natty Bumppo, then Carruthers is the greenhorn Easterner, the English lord who discovers in himself the 'slumbering untamed Saxon'.

It was one thing to celebrate the strenuous life in fiction, quite another to introduce it into political process. Roosevelt, of course, succeeded. His British allies did not. They campaigned long and hard for measures which would strengthen the Empire economically and militarily, for tariff reform and national service. Curzon's election to the Chancellorship of Oxford University and Kipling's Nobel Prize were signs that the message was getting through, as were the growth of empire youth movements and the establishment of an Empire Day. But the imperialists never succeeded in altering government policy, and they lost their political leader when Joseph Chamberlain suffered a stroke in 1906.[38] The strenuous life would have to be pursued outside the political system, perhaps in defiance of it.

On Christmas Eve 1904, Roger Pocock wrote to ten newspapers announcing the formation of a Legion of Frontiersmen. Pocock had led an adventurous life in the colonies, and celebrated the adventurous life in novels like *Curly. A Tale of the Arizona Desert*, in which a cowpuncher forms an alliance with another peripatetic aristocrat ('Being thoroughbred stock, this British lord and his son didn't need to put on side, or make themselves out to be better than common folks like me').[39] East meets West when the son marries an outlaw's daughter. Pocock had firm views about the corroding ease and morbid excitements of civilization, which he expressed in *Rottenness. A Study of America and England* (1896). Since the political system was rotten to the core, regeneration could only come from outside, through the creation of a Kiplingesque 'Lost Legion':

> There's a Legion that never was 'listed,
>   That carries no colours or crest,
> But, split in a thousand detachments,
>   Is breaking the road for the rest.[40]

The Legion was intended to serve as the eyes and ears of Empire, Pocock recalled in his autobiography. 'Many men were awake, manning the outposts and the frontiers, whose training in war, in wild countries and at sea had made them vigilant. Scattered throughout the planet, to the margin of exploration and beyond, nothing on earth escaped their attention.' The Legion carried no political colours or crest. 'Royalists and Imperialists to a man, we cared nothing for local or party politics, but we loved everything mellow and sound in the Old Country.' Pocock's description of the recruitment of legionnaires recalls Roosevelt's description of the recruitment of Rough Riders for the war in Cuba. Like Roosevelt, he wanted to combine physical with political awakening, the strenuous life with imperialism.[41]

But there was a quite specific focus to Pocock's patriotism: the German threat. He was convinced that the Germans meant to attack Britain, and appalled by British complacency. The only solution was to train his scouts to spy. 'And underneath that mask of the visible Legion there grew unseen a little hidden Corps, the Legion invisible. It was limited to very few members, engaged in counter-espionage, watching the steady growth of the German Menace.' The Legion's Intelligence Branch specialized in unearthing German invasion-plans. But the information it collected would appear to have been supplied by the fertile brains of two of its members, Erskine Childers and William Le Queux. Of the two invasion-plans Pocock mentions, one derives from *The Riddle of the Sands*, while the other was written up as *The Invasion of 1910*.[42] Like their heroes, Childers and Le Queux reckoned that they would have to fight the German menace on their own, without any help from government or police. The only political home they could find was among patriots who had renounced party politics.

Pocock was ousted from the Legion in 1909, but his departure did not lead to any change of emphasis. The Legion's Official Gazette, *The Frontiersman*, relaunched in 1910, continued to stress the German menace. 'Frontiersmen have created the Empire,' the Commandant-General announced in the first issue, 'and to Frontiersmen must the Empire now turn for assistance in an emergency.' The most important assistance they could offer was in the field of intelligence, 'the dominating Power that maintains peace and assures victory over every foe'. United by bonds of brotherhood rather than by dogma or self-interest, the Frontiersmen would inspire a new patriotism. 'We have escaped the notice of politicians, having worked and fought for no political party – only for the Empire.' The front cover provided a glimpse of the strenuous life in the shape of an advertisement for the Imperial School of Colonial Instruction at Shepperton-on-Thames, complete with pictures of lasso-practice.[43]

Subsequent issues kept up the pressure with allusions to the fate of other empires ('The Frontiersmen of Rome were recalled too late to save their country') and the announcement of the formation of an English Waiters' Union ('We do not want official England overrun by foreigners to the prejudice of national and Imperial prosperity'). Equally significant was the support tendered to Baden-Powell's Boy Scout movement, which by 1910 had successfully elided scouting and spying. Baden-Powell based the kind of training given by the movement on the expertise of 'frontiersmen', 'real *men* in every sense of the word, and thoroughly up in scout craft'. But his models tended to the war-like: a young Indian brave in Cooper's *Pathfinder*, or Kipling's Kim, skilled in the Great Game played on the frontiers of Empire. He, too, made reference to Rome, and to 'wishy-washy slackers without any go or patriotism in them'. 'Your forefathers worked hard, fought hard, and died hard, to make this Empire for you. Don't let them look down from heaven, and see you loafing about with hands in your pockets, doing nothing to keep it up.'[44] Hands removed from pockets could usefully be fastened around tent-pegs and triggers. The front cover of *Scouting for Boys* shows a scout observing from behind some rocks as an invasion-party lands. In the exercises of the Scouts, as in those of the Legion, there was no more distance between physical and political regeneration than there is in the crises of a spy-novel. In his memoir, *My Adventures as a Spy* (1915), Baden-Powell celebrated spying as an extension of scouting by other means, and as the best possible form of regeneration. 'For anyone who is tired of life, the thrilling life of the spy should be the very finest recuperator!'[45]

THE THIRTY-NINE STEPS

Someone who certainly finds spying a fine recuperator is the most famous of all the amateur agents, Richard Hannay. Published in 1915, and concerned with events leading up to the outbreak of war, *The Thirty-Nine Steps*, like Oppenheim's *The Double Traitor*, is a vindication of the scaremongering politics of adventure which had shaped the spy novel. Indeed, Buchan's literary sophistication turned his first espionage 'shocker' into a brilliant recapitulation of the short history of the genre.

When he made that effort, he was very much under Oppenheim's influence. But he had already laid the foundation for his own politics of adventure in a novel of Empire, *The Half-Hearted* (1900). The hero of this novel is physically and politically supine, 'over-cultured' and 'enervated'. But he is persuaded to use his knowledge of the Indian frontier to help foil a Russian invasion, and this new role unlocks hidden reserves of energy and commitment. 'Life was quick in his sinews, his brain was a weathercock, his strength was tireless . . . he was in a fair way to taste the world's iron and salt, and he exulted at the prospect.' He dies defending a pass against the Russian Army, whole-hearted at last.[46]

Hannay's heart is never anything less than whole, of course. But the opening chapter of *The Thirty-Nine Steps* finds him back in London, having made his 'pile' in South Africa, living among the distinctly over-cultured and enervated. 'The weather made me liverish, the talk of the ordinary Englishman made me sick, I couldn't get enough exercise, and the amusements of London seemed as flat as soda-water that has been standing in the sun.'[47] The race meetings and the dinner parties bore him. Hannay himself has been reinvigorated by the frontier; but the class he belongs to is sliding rapidly into metropolitan torpor and frivolity. His complaints about society have a political edge to them. They recall the 'restlessness' and 'distaste' Buchan himself felt on returning to England from South Africa, where he had held the responsible post of private secretary to Lord Milner, in 1903. 'South Africa had completely unsettled me. I did not want to make money or a reputation at home; I wanted a particular kind of work which was denied me.' He felt that the work was being denied to him by political complacency. 'I was distressed by British politics, for it seemed to me that both the great parties were blind to the true meaning of empire.' Political distress combined with horror at the 'vulgar display of wealth' to create an apocalyptic mood. 'I began to have an ugly fear that the Empire might decay at the heart.'[48] Hannay is no stranger to that fear, though he doesn't express it so forcefully.

Then Franklin P. Scudder waylays him and enlists him in the cause. After Scudder's death, his first thought is to find the nearest frontier. 'My notion was to get off to some wild district, where my veldcraft would be of some use to me, for I would be like a trapped rat in a city.' Once in the wild, he experiences, like Carruthers, a delicious physical awakening, as the crust of discontent and self-conceit disappear. His awakening differs, though, in that it is literary as well as physical. It tells him what kind of novel he is in. Carruthers has a dip, Hannay has a hike across the heather, followed by 'The Adventure of the Literary Innkeeper'. The literary innkeeper wants to write like Kipling and Conrad, and it doesn't take him long to place Hannay's yarn. ' "By God!" he whispered, drawing his breath in sharply. "It is all pure Rider Haggard and Conan Doyle." ' The fact that the yarn is 'pure' romance – that it defies the conventions of domestic realism, and the comfortable view of the world they sustain – makes it all the more credible to the innkeeper. 'He was very young, but he was the man for my money.'[49] The reader for Buchan's money will be the one who has enough imagination to take Hannay at his word – that is, to accept an unauthorized, unofficial version of events. In a complacent world, literary romance is political truth.

Hannay's second generic awakening is as much political as literary. It occurs during 'The Adventure of the Radical Candidate', when he deciphers Scudder's notebook. Scudder had originally told Hannay that an international anarchist conspiracy, backed by Jewish financiers, was fomenting revolution. In his paranoid fantasy, 'the Jew' is 'the man who is ruling the world just now', and the Jew 'has his knife in the Empire of the Tzar, because his aunt was outraged and his father flogged in some one-horse location on the Volga'. Listening to Scudder's yarn, Hannay could have been forgiven for thinking that he was in a terrorist novel. The notebook, however, tells a different tale, about a German plot to provoke war with Britain. 'While we were talking about the goodwill and good intentions of Germany our coast would be silently ringed with mines, and submarines would be waiting for every battleship.'[50] The notebook makes it clear that Hannay is in a spy-novel; the switch of genres alerts us to his political awakening. The knowledge he has gained enables him to refute the Radical candidate's claim that the 'German menace' is a Tory invention. This is a turning-point in the narrative. Sir Harry, the Radical candidate, may be in even greater need of awakening, but once awoken he brings Hannay in from the cold by introducing him to Sir Walter Bullivant, Permanent Secretary at the Foreign Office. The accidental spy now has a direct route to the heart of the political system.

But Buchan never forgets that Hannay is a frontiersman, and that frontiersmen are forever excluded from the political system, and the cosy bourgeois world it protects. The final scene of *The Thirty-Nine Steps*, where Hannay tracks the German spies down in the heart of the cosy bourgeois world, is not only a brilliant *dénouement*, but a poignant reminder of his status as an outsider. Buchan's spies, like Headon Hill's,[51] occupy a villa on the coast, a 'decent commonplace dwelling'. They have merged imperceptibly into the life of 'ordinary, game-playing, suburban Englishmen, wearisome, if you like, but sordidly innocent.' Their apparent innocence terrifies Hannay, who is at home with the upper and lower classes, but not with the middle: 'what fellows like me don't understand is the great comfortable, satisfied middle-class world, the folk that live in villas and suburbs. He doesn't know how they look at things, he doesn't understand their conventions, and he is as shy of them as of a black mamba'.[52] The conventions, sustained perfectly by the spies, momentarily destroy his self-belief. Perhaps he is imagining it all. The frontiersman's instincts, always at odds with those of bourgeois society, are interrogated mercilessly and then, at the last moment, vindicated. A tiny gesture betrays the spies.

No wonder Theodore Roosevelt was so enthusiastic about *The Thirty-Nine Steps*. If Carruthers is the most memorable of the 'Easterners' who go 'West' to regenerate themselves through espionage, Hannay is the most memorable of the 'Westerners' who go 'East'. Like the Virginian, Hannay has been shaped by experience rather than by convention. He is nomadic, protean, occasionally violent, a symbol not so much of stability as of the instability needed to revitalize a society which is too stable, too rigid in its conformity. He upholds the law, without himself being protected or defined by it. Like the Virginian, unlike Natty Bumppo or Davies, he has one final change in store, a social evolution. He civilizes himself, becoming an insider, a member of a new aristocracy. His social evolution begins in *The Thirty-Nine Steps* when he abandons the lands (the veld, the frontier) and travels south to meet Sir Walter Bullivant in the heart of rural Berkshire, 'a land of lush water-meadows and slow reedy streams'. By the time of the fourth Hannay novel, *The Three Hostages* (1924), the rough colonial has become a pillar of the establishment: Sir Richard Hannay, DSO, CB, gentleman-farmer and squire of Fosse Manor in the Cotswolds. Now, at last, he can be regarded as a symbol of stability. But it is the process by which stability has been achieved which constitutes the political message of the novels, and the process by which the symbol has been created which keeps us reading.

NOTES

1. John Buchan, *Greenmantle* (Harmondsworth, 1956 ed.), p.50.
2. Nicholas Hiley, 'The Failure of British Espionage against Germany, 1907–1914', *Historical Journal*, 26 (1983), p.883; idem, 'The Failure of British Counter-Espionage against Germany, 1907–1914', *Historical Journal*, 28 (1985), p.855.
3. Hiley, 'Counter-Espionage', pp.843–4. See David French, 'Spy Fever in Britain, 1900–1915', *Historical Journal*, 21 (1978); Christopher Andrew, *Secret Service. The Making of the British Intelligence Community* (London, 1985). Hiley points out that Haldane may well have considered the alarmists more of a threat than the spies they claimed to expose. Even so, Edmonds got his bureau.
4. Both quotations from Bernard Porter, *The Lion's Share. A Short History of British Imperialism* (London, 1975), pp.117 and 126.
5. David Stafford, 'Spies and Gentlemen: The Birth of the British Spy Novel, 1893–1914', *Victorian Studies*, 24 (1981), pp.491, 503, 500, 505.
6. Most historians of spy fiction seem reluctant to discuss it in relation to other contemporary genres. See Bruce Merry, *Anatomy of the Spy Thriller* (Montreal, 1977); John Atkins, *The British Spy Novel* (London, 1984); Michael Denning, *Cover Stories. Narrative and Ideology in the British Spy Thriller* (London, 1987); John G. Cawelti and Bruce A. Rosenberg, *The Spy Story* (Chicago, 1987).
7. *The Times*, 24 November 1883.
8. Quoted by Barbara Melchiori, *Terrorism in the Late Victorian Novel* (London, 1985), p.31. For the political response to terrorism, see Bernard Porter, *The Origins of the Vigilant State* (London, 1987).
9. Henry James, *The Princess Casamassima* (London, 1977), p.436.
10. Robert Cromie, *The Crack of Doom*, 2nd edition (London, 1895), p.121.
11. An exception is Coulson Kernahan's sprightly *Captain Shannon* (London, 1897), based on Fenian 'outrages'. Even here, though, the villain is not a Fenian, but a member of an international terrorist conspiracy which aims to liberate Ireland first, and then Russia.
12. Joseph Hatton, *By Order of the Czar* (New York: John Lovell, 1890), p.357.
13. L.T. Meade, *The Siren* (London, 1898), p.137.
14. George Griffith, *Angel of the Revolution. A Tale of the Coming Terror* (London, 1893), pp.32, 14.
15. Ibid., p.307.
16. George Chesney, *The Battle of Dorking* (Edinburgh, 1871), p.64. See I.F. Clarke, *Voices Prophesying War, 1763–1984* (London, 1966).

17. *The Great War in England in 1897* (London, 1894), pp.46–7, 54–5.
18. John Gooch, *The Prospect of War* (London, 1981), Chapter One.
19. William Le Queux, *Her Majesty's Minister* (London, 1901), p.7; idem, *The Man from Downing Street* (London, 1904), pp.151–2; idem, *Number 70, Berlin. A Story of Britain's Peril* (London, 1916), pp.106, 189.
20. Headon Hill, *The Spies of the Wight* (London, 1899), pp.81–2, 279.
21. Erskine Childers, *The Riddle of the Sands* (Harmondsworth, 1978), pp.27, 32.
22. Ibid., pp.37, 47, 50.
23. Ibid., pp.115, 118, 119.
24. Ibid., pp.210, 277.
25. William Le Queux, *Secrets of the Foreign Office* (London, 1903), p.72.
26. Ian Fleming, *From Russia, with Love* (London, 1977 ed.), p.78.
27. David Stafford, 'Conspiracy and Xenophobia: the Spy Novels of William Le Queux, 1893–1914', *Europa*, 3 (1982).
28. E. Phillips Oppenheim, *The Mysterious Mr Sabin* (London, 1898), p.64. Oppenheim was slower than Le Queux to single out Germany as the enemy. As late as *The Betrayal* (London, 1904), it is still the French who are after the plans of the coastal defences.
29. E. Phillips Oppenheim, *A Maker of History* (London, 1905), p.40.
30. Ibid., pp.251, 272, 195, 313.
31. E. Phillips Oppenheim, *The Secret* (London, 1907), p.88.
32. A.J.A. Morris, *Scaremongers. The Advocacy of War and Rearmament, 1896–1914* (London, 1984).
33. In *The Double Traitor* (Boston, 1915), a young diplomat accidentally overhears a German spymaster briefing a subordinate; once again, an incriminating piece of paper comes to hand. Unable to convince the police or the government of the German threat, he has to go it alone, pretending to enlist as a German spy.
34. Childers, *Riddle of the Sands*, p.143.
35. Lord Curzon, *Frontiers* (Oxford, 1907), pp.3, 7, 55–8.
36. F.J. Turner, *The Frontier in American History* (New York, 1921), pp.2–5.
37. Morton Cohen (ed.), *Rudyard Kipling to Rider Haggard. The Record of a Friendship* (Rutherford, 1963), p.99.
38. For a succinct account of their position, see Bernard Porter, 'The Edwardians and their Empire', in Donald Read (ed.), *Edwardian England* (London, 1982).
39. Roger Pocock, *Curly* (London, 1904), p.16.
40. *Kipling's Verse. The Definitive Edition* (London, 1940), p.195.
41. Roger Pocock, *Chorus to Adventurers* (London, 1931), pp.23, 32. See Theodore Roosevelt, *The Rough Riders* (1899), Volume XI of the National Edition of the *Works* (New York, 1926), pp.8–20.
42. Ibid., pp.50, 61–3. The Legion receives honourable mention in *The Invasion of 1910*. Childers contributed a section on 'Boat Sailing' to Roger Pocock (ed.), *The Frontiersman's Pocket Book* (London, 1909). Other writers known to have been members of the Legion include Rider Haggard, Edgar Wallace and Conan Doyle.
43. *The Frontiersman*, n.s., 1, January 1910, pp.1–2.
44. R. Baden-Powell *Scouting for Boys* (London, 1908), pp.9–10.
45. R. Baden-Powell *My Adventures as a Spy* (London, 1915), p.45.
46. John Buchan, *The Half-Hearted* (London, 1900), p.299.
47. John Buchan, *The Thirty-Nine Steps* (London, 1946 ed.), p.8.
48. John Buchan, *Memory Hold-the-Door* (London, 1940), pp.126–8.
49. *The Thirty-Nine Steps*, pp.24, 39.
50. Ibid., pp.12, 45.
51. There are parallels between the two novels. In both, the German spies submerge themselves in English domesticity. In both, the amateur agents take a look at their getaway yachts, and encounter an officer or crew-member who doesn't speak English like a native.
52. *The Thirty-Nine Steps*, pp.123, 126, 129.

Decoding German Spies:
British Spy Fiction 1908–18

NICHOLAS HILEY

Between 1908 and 1918 Britain was invaded by an army of fictional spies. They landed in their thousands on bookstalls and in bookshops. They used the short story to establish themselves in hundreds of newspapers and magazines, successfully infiltrated dozens of popular stage plays, and were even spotted in cinemas and on the pages of children's comics.

Yet no one seemed to know where they came from. The spy, explained a writer in *The Graphic* in 1914, 'is always conceived of as a tremendously romantic type of villain by the unromantic average person who has never set eyes on him':

> To make up for this he has read all about him, and has seen him repeatedly on the stage, only, as it happens, neither the playwright nor the novelist is any better informed than the rest, which accounts for the extraordinary likeness between all the spies of the literary imagination. They are all faithful replicas of each other, all copies of the same type, originated by goodness knows whom, goodness knows when.[1]

But where did they come from, these dark villains 'with shifty eyes and an unpardonably bad pronunciation of English', and their female counterparts, whose seductive costumes were 'always a tremendous asset'?[2] What was the origin of the stock fictional foreigner, living quietly somewhere in eastern England, who, on one inevitable and preordained morning, 'boldly throws off the mask and appears before his fiancée in the hated garb of our Teutonic invaders'.[3]

The most popular explanation is that these fictional characters were rooted in international politics, and took their nourishment from national decline. Spy and invasion stories, I.F. Clarke observed, belong to the literature of patriotism, for their subject 'is not the behaviour of recognisable individuals, as it is in the novel; it is the nation, the enemies of the nation, the new instruments of war, and the future greatness of the fatherland'.[4] Spy fiction, adds David Stafford, is a literature of 'national passions and phobias', for its genesis was 'inextricably linked with the crisis of confidence in British power and security that obsessed the Edwardian age'. Early British spy fiction formed 'propaganda for a conservative cause . . . designed not only to thrill and entertain but also to instruct and educate, delivering messages alerting their audience to dangers threatening the nation'.[5] The spy novel, Christopher Andrew explains, was born in Edwardian Britain from 'a new sense of imperial frailty'.[6]

The spy story indeed had a mythical quality. I.F. Clarke observed how early tales of spies and imaginary wars describe 'a myth-world created out of animosities and anxieties', and formed 'popular epics for a period of universal literacy'.[7] A number of writers have noted this parallel between folk myths and spy novels, but, despite their epic quality, spy stories are not in fact myths but urban legends, a recognized form of modern folk-narrative.[8] Urban legends borrow elements from myth and from fairy-tale, but unlike those forms they tell of recent events and the actions of normal people. Spy stories indeed obey Jan Brunvand's criteria for urban legends, for they are always related as true, 'there is usually no geographical or generational gap between teller and event', and in almost all cases they 'gain credibility from specific details of time and place or from references to source authorities'. Again, whether or not we believe their details, both spy stories and urban legends serve an underlying need 'to know about and to try to understand bizarre, frightening, and potentially dangerous or embarrassing events that *may* have happened'.[9]

Spies were employed in many fictional contexts. They were grafted on to Edwardian science fiction, as in L.J. Beeston's story *A Star Fell*, and on to detective fiction – E.S Turner noting how often in the *Union Jack* Sexton Blake defeated enemy spies, or uncovered plans for the invasion of Britain.[10] Dashing heroes such as Lieutenant Daring of the Royal Navy – strangely reminiscent of Commander Bond of the Royal Navy – could really show their mettle when pitted against enemy agents. In October 1912 the British and Colonial Film Company previewed its forthcoming film *Lieut. Daring and the Plans of the 'Mine Fields'*, and got an excellent write-up in the trade magazine *The Bioscope*:

> In this, the latest 'Daring' film, the Lieutenant has to deal with a brace of crafty foreign spies. He first meets them on Mr. and Mrs. Chas. Austin's houseboat on the Thames, where they are posing as an artist and his model. Later, in his own home, they bind and gag him, after the plans of the Mine Fields have been copied on to the shoulders of the female spy. Daring is freed by his wonderful dog 'Nero', and then begins a thrilling chase across country . . . At Brooklands, Daring appeals to . . . Lieut. E.H. Hotchkiss for the loan of the latter's monoplane . . . At Folkestone the young officer hires a motor-boat, and catches up and boards the Channel steamer in mid-ocean. Locating his quarry, he keeps them in sight until France is reached . . . ending with the arrest of the miscreants in the streets of Boulogne.[11]

Yet alongside this analysis of the spy story as heroic myth there has recently developed a new critique, based on the influence of actual intelligence operations over the genre. Donald McCormick has commented on the 'astonishingly long list of authors who have actually been involved at some time or other in intelligence work'.[12] David Stafford has confirmed that many famous spy writers 'have been professional or amateur players in "the silent game" of intelligence', and noted how 'the lines between fact and fiction have often been blurred'.[13] The idea is attractive, and the 1920s and 1930s may indeed have seen the increasing contribution of fact to fiction, but in these early years the flow was entirely the other way, for most British intelligence officers took the greater part of their ideas of secret service directly from fictional sources.

In April 1907, for instance, Major Ernest Swinton published the short story 'An Eddy of War', describing an imagined German invasion of Britain. As one character explains, it almost succeeded, for the Germans resident in Britain formed part of a worldwide conspiracy:

> It's all run by the Hunnish General Staff under the title of 'Die Götterdämmerung Gesellschaft,' or the Company of the Twilight of the Gods. In London the Gesellschaft has sub-branches in the 'Allgemeine Panhunsche Kellnerverein' – that's the Universal Pan-Hunnish Waiters' League – and the 'Blutwurst Bund', consisting of clerks chiefly.

These clerks and waiters were trained in sabotage, and assisted the invaders by cutting telegraph and telephone lines, and blowing up bridges and gasometers.[14]

Swinton's paranoid fantasy was utter nonsense, but it nevertheless fired the imaginations of keen military officers. In May 1907 a Lieutenant in the Volunteer Artillery wrote to the press confirming that these dangers were real, for 'I know at this moment the house in which is the headquarters of the organising staff of the German army, resident in a suburb of London'.[15] In 1908 Lieutenant-Colonel James Edmonds, the newly-appointed head of MO5, the War Office 'Special Section', confidently included organized sabotage in his secret analysis of the German danger. An invading army, he declared, would undoubtedly get help from resident German aliens:

> They have made arrangements for cutting the submarine cables in case of war, and know where to effect all the railway demolitions they deem necessary to impede our mobilization and concentration, and they know all about our difficulties in case of mobilization . . . They have a German officers' club in London with German servants, where military matters concerning England can be discussed with perfect security, and German hospitals where even in delirium no secrets could be revealed to British subjects.[16]

London's German clubs were more likely full of lonely young men seeking comradeship, cheap food, and possible employment,[17] but Edmonds always liked his fact well spiced with fiction. By the time he compiled this assessment he was already logging reports of suspicious foreigners and peculiar occurrences, and in 1909 obtained a crop of new sightings from the popular novelist William Le Queux. Le Queux's postbag was bursting with letters following the publication of his latest novel *Spies of the Kaiser*, but Edmonds gaily disregarded their doubtful value as evidence. However, many of these stories had reached Le Queux through the *Weekly News*, which owned the serial rights to *Spies of the Kaiser* and was running it alongside a prize competition for readers' letters describing how they had met a spy. As the specially appointed 'Spy Editor' explained helpfully, 'readers may have discovered some of these spies at work, and may have had adventures with them, may have seen the photographs, charts, and plans they are preparing'. Le Queux forwarded the resulting fantasies to Edmonds, and he swallowed them whole.[18]

Edmonds was not the only military officer seduced by fiction, for Captain Vernon Kell, appointed as the first head of MI5 in 1909 on Edmonds' recommendation, shared his mentor's slippery grasp of reality. In *Spies of the Kaiser* Le Queux's hero Ray Raymond had uncovered German plans for landing at Weybourne in north Norfolk, and on visiting the area had found German agents already at work. In 1914, determined not to be outdone and convinced that war was imminent, Captain Kell took his summer holiday on precisely this section of coast, in order to see 'if there were any German activities going on'.[19] Even during the war his attitude to secret service owed much to fiction. John Dancy, posted to the London headquarters of MI5 late in 1915, discovered that 'Kell's Boys' were recruited from many different backgrounds:

> But among them I could sense, if not the influence of counter-espionage serials in the *Boy's Own Paper*, at least the gay abandon of Dornford Yates and John Buchan. They hankered after disguises, after suspense and after danger. They had that urge to be placed on test and show their worth.[20]

Kell was indeed addicted to romance and mystification. As his wife later admitted, he might list his hobbies in *Who's Who* as 'fishing and croquet' but this was just a part of the great deception, for 'croquet was a harmless bluff: he couldn't play it at all'.[21]

The saga of Erskine Childers' novel *The Riddle of the Sands* shows well the close relationship between fact and fiction. Childers' thrilling tale of two British gentlemen who uncover a planned German invasion appeared in May 1903, and immediately fascinated both military and naval officers.

The Director of Military Operations dispatched 'a couple of experts' to Germany to see if a force might really be embarked in barges from the Frisian islands, but they reported against it:

> The want of railways and roads, the shallowness of the water, the configuration of the coast, not to mention the terrific amount of preparation of wharves, landing-places, causeways, sheds and what-not besides, would have rendered a secret embarkation impossible.[22]

The Director of Naval Intelligence was likewise instructed to purchase the novel and 'have it examined most thoroughly and by an officer on whose judgment you can absolutely rely', but he also judged that the plan was impossible.[23]

Yet despite its obvious faults *The Riddle of the Sands* held pride of place on patriotic bookshelves, and the admiration of British officers grew as their fear of Germany mounted. By 1910 the book had become essential reading for British agents visiting Germany, and Lieutenant Vivian Brandon, caught in 1910 during a secret survey of the German North Sea coast, informed his captors that he had read the book three times. Another agent sent to complete this work the following year also showed himself to be familiar with all its details.[24] In 1912, when the War Office produced a secret guide to the German Army, it warned soberly of German agents preparing for invasion, and was careful to praise 'the brilliant imagination of the author of "The Riddle of the Sands".'[25]

By 1914 fact indeed ran close on the heels of fiction. As one official report noted, the popular image of the spy at that time came from Le Queux, and showed him as 'something between a bandit and a detective . . . a desperate fellow with a shady past a lurid future'. Yet this was merely 'an exaggeration of the official conception'. To the British government in 1914 spying was a romantic form of 'underhand warfare':

> Instead of fighting your enemy in the field or at sea, you circulated false bank notes in his country. You blew up his factories and his bridges. You slipped incriminating documents into the coat pockets of his most trusted officials. You sold him spurious information and set booby-traps of all descriptions in his path.

Even after August 1914, the report continued, British intelligence officers relished 'a certain shilling-shocker element in Secret Service work', and had always 'a tendency "to bring off a coup" . . . and to brandish individual documents or scraps of information of a superficially thrilling nature, without regard for their ultimate value'.[26] The secret agent, another writer confessed, still welcomed the chance 'to strike a heroic posture after the day's work is over'.[27]

Mansfield Cumming, first head of the British Secret Service, certainly showed an incurable love of secrecy, disguise and dramatic poses. He lived for the thrill of false moustaches and faked codebooks, and on one occasion, as a friend recalled, produced 'a photograph of a heavily-built German-looking individual in most unmistakably German clothes and was entranced when I failed to recognise the party in question – it was himself, disguised for the purposes of a certain delicate mission he once undertook on the continent before the war'.[28] Cumming had apparently visited Germany late in July 1914 to urge his agents to stay in position if war was declared, and later admitted 'that's when this business was really amusing . . . capital sport'.[29] His enthusiasm was barely dampened by the realities of modern warfare, and one old friend who bumped into Cumming in 1915 found himself immediately recruited for a secret undercover operation. Rigged out as a London taxi-driver, he was shown a special cab with 'a miniature microphone . . . concealed in the roof', and then dispatched to pick up a couple of suspects. The operation was a complete flop, but it nevertheless proved great fun, and Cumming 'appeared perfectly satisfied'.[30]

Much of Cumming's melodrama was indeed complete bluff. Francis Toye, recruited for a mission to Italy early in 1915, found the whole business rather farcical, but recalled how Cumming wrapped it 'in mysterious and awful trappings', and 'went out of his way to make you feel like a character in a spy novel'.[31] Fact and fiction sat close together in Cumming's intelligence classes, where John Millais, a sportsman roped in for an operation in Norway in August 1915, learned how to spot the numerous German agents he would encounter:

> In many instances they were invalided soldiers, or men incapable of serving in the army owing to defective eyesight, and in consequence it was easy to detect them, because (1) nearly all wore glasses or pince-nez; (2) nearly all carried a German book under their arm to read at dull moments; (3) all, almost without exception, wore German boots and clothes, which are easily recognised by their cut.

However, noted Millais, what really gave them away was that they travelled in pairs and 'had a way of standing about aimlessly or whispering in corners much after the manner of spies in the cinematograph'. Nature was indeed imitating art.[3]

Nicholas Everitt, recruited into the Secret Service late in 1914, found its theatricality a definite handicap. Despite the fact that Cumming 'never wasted a shilling where he could personally see a way of saving it', and habitually kept his agents in financial difficulties, it was still painfully apparent that 'if a big amount was wanted for some exceedingly doubtful purpose no limit seemed to be made; the wherewithal was almost certain to be forthcoming to meet the demand'.[33] The regular agents might feel neglected and abandoned, but Cumming's casual employees received lavish treatment. Frederick de Valda, recruited for a hare-brained mission to Switzerland in 1916, saw Cumming briefly and was then handed £100 in cash, without signing a receipt. Leaving Whitehall Court in a daze he did the only sensible thing – walked straight to a nearby hotel, cashed one of the £5 notes and bought himself a drink.[34]

Yet the most obvious manifestation of Cumming's passion for secrecy and melodrama came in his futile attempts at concealing his identity. Throughout the war his headquarters at Whitehall Court were codenamed 'Captain Spencer's Flat', but German Intelligence had seen through this feeble deception as early as 1915.[35] Wartime visitors to his London office were also kept in ignorance of his real name, and often left the building knowing only that he was an officer in naval uniform whose subordinates called him 'C' or 'The Chief'. Yet anyone wishing to identify this mysterious figure had only to thumb through the *London Post Office Directory*, where the tenant of 2 Whitehall Court was plainly and accurately listed as 'Commander Mansfield G. Smith-Cumming, C.B'.

In truth Cumming showed only one example of self-restraint in the face of romance. In 1914 E. Phillips Oppenheim, Le Queux's main rival in popular spy fiction, decided he could best serve his country by joining the Secret Service, and in 'repeated calls and letters' offered his services – begging for work 'which I pleaded I ought to know something about after having written nearly a dozen spy stories'. Mercifully the offer was turned down flat.[36]

It is vital to realize that in Britain during this period the majority of the images of espionage came from fiction. Spy novels, plays and films were so common, and the actual threat from foreign espionage was so slight, that even those officers employed on counter-espionage had little opportunity of testing fiction against reality. By 1918, after nine years' work, Vernon Kell's MI5 held the records of over 100,000 aliens in its Registry, with tens of thousands of dossiers on other suspects, and a card index of more than a million entries. By the mid 1920s British officials had spent years examining the records of hundreds of thousands of suspects, and yet, according to Kell himself, only a few per cent had been 'accepted by us as having been definitely connected with foreign Secret Service work'.[37]

It has to be understood that the principal function of MI5 was not to chase spies but to catalogue suspects, most of whom were entirely harmless. Few MI5 officers would have considered themselves secret agents, and May Cannan, an MI5 filing clerk at the Bureau Central Interallié in Paris during the war, recalled how even there a real spy remained a strange novelty. On one occasion an officer of the 'Espionage' section asked if she would like to see a German agent:

'If you do, take some papers and go along into "Trade" but for God's
sake don't look self-conscious.' I went. A little old man sat in the
corridor, our eyes did not meet and I did not linger, but I had seen
him.[38]

This was a once-in-a-lifetime encounter, for in truth the vast majority of
those working for British intelligence before 1918 were employed on routine
filing, and, like the general public, derived their images of the spy world
almost entirely from fictional sources. Even those recruited for missions
abroad retained romantic ideas of what it would be like. As Lieutenant
Brandon wrote sadly from Leipzig prison in 1910:

Looking back on the light-hearted way in which I drifted into this
adventure, I recognise that I am somewhat of a Peter Pan, in that
I have never really grown up. Unfortunately I have not got Peter's
talent for flying through windows, or I should not be here now![39]

Yet if fact was imitating fiction, we have still to find the original source
for the images in our urban legends. We can, however, get a little closer by
going on a literary excursion. First let us join Eveline L, heroine of the 1904
novel *The Modern Eveline*, on her walk through the streets of London:

I turned a corner. I found myself in a better thoroughfare. I stopped
before a well-lighted pastrycook's shop. I read an announcement,
'Afternoon Tea'. I entered . . . Behind the shop was the tea-room.
Behind that again a smaller room, also with small tables for tea. I
traversed all. I sat down . . . I glanced around. In one corner was a
tiny iron spiral staircase.

Eveline asks the waitress where this strange staircase leads, and is taken
up to 'a small but beautifully-furnished room', with a bed, 'a cosy sofa,
a toilet table, marble washstand, etc., several pretty chairs, and some
framed oleographs from the illustrated papers on the walls'. 'Suddenly,'
writes Eveline, 'the explanation came to me.'[40]

Yet before we learn the purpose of this room, let us jump forward three
years to walk with Hubert Hutton, hero of *The Great Plot* of 1907, on his way
to another peculiar rendezvous. Hutton pauses in Fleet Street, then enters a
small cycle shop, where the female assistant tries to sell him something:

He lingered over choosing a bell from several varieties which she
showed him, and made good use of the time in taking in the shop
and its contents. The latter were not very extensive . . . At the back
of the shop was a door, and while he was making his purchase that
door opened and a man peered out inquisitively, but finding nothing
suspicious in Hutton's appearance, quickly closed the door again.[41]

Hubert had a shrewd idea of what lay behind that door, but before we investigate let us shift to yet another part of London, and join Hardross Courage and his friend Leslie Guest, heroes of the 1907 novel *The Secret*:

> We turned northwards again towards Soho, and entered presently a small restaurant of foreign appearance. The outside, which had once been painted white, was now more than a little dingy . . . A short dark man, with black moustache and urbane smile, greeted us at the door, and led us to a table.

This establishment is the 'Café Suisse', an apparently innocuous restaurant once again concealing a mysterious back room, this time behind a locked door. On a later occasion Hardross Courage returns to the restaurant, hoping to see inside:

> There were a good many people dining there, but towards ten o'clock the place was almost empty . . . before I had been there five minutes the door of the inner room was opened, and Mr. Hirsch appeared upon the threshold. He caught my eye and beckoned to me solemnly. I crossed the room, ascended the steps, and found myself in what the waiters called the club-room.[42]

There we must leave Hardross Courage, and make our final journey with Conan Doyle's hero Dr Watson, 'speeding eastward in a hansom' to an address in London's docklands:

> Upper Swandam Lane is a vile alley lurking behind the high wharves which line the north side of the river to the east of London Bridge. Between a slop shop and a gin shop, approached by a steep flight of steps leading down to a black gap like the mouth of a cave, I found the den of which I was in search. Ordering my cab to wait, I passed down the steps . . . and by the light of a flickering oil lamp above the door I found the latch and made my way into a long, low room.[43]

There is an interesting similarity between these images. Each writer is inviting his readers to believe that somewhere in London, at the very heart of the Empire, lies a secret room, hidden perhaps in the docklands, or concealed within an ordinary shop or restaurant. This room is mysterious and strange, and yet, if one can locate it, is waiting for all those who will step aside from the well-lit streets and comfortable houses, and search for the short flight of stairs leading to its door.

The overwhelming sensation is one of great strangeness and danger concealed within the familiar, and yet the purpose of the secret room is quite different in each story. Eveline is the central character of a pornographic novel, and has here penetrated into the sexual underworld, to discover the house of assignation where she will later enjoy 'a constant whirl of copulation' with her groom.[44] Hubert Hutton, on the other hand, is attempting to foil an anarchist assassination plot, and his secret door leads to the basement of the cycle shop, from which a tunnel runs under the street, dug 'by six of the most dangerous of the Terrorists' and packed full of explosive.[45] Hardross Courage, however, is the central character of a spy novel, who has traced a network of German agents plotting the invasion of Britain, and has learned how 'in that room at the Café Suisse will be woven the final threads of the great scheme'.[46] Finally, Dr Watson's adventure is a detective story, and here he is visiting an opium den to rescue an Englishman fallen victim to this filthy foreign habit, and now entirely subjugated by 'the vile, stupefying fumes of the drug'.[47]

The four hidden rooms are thus quite different, yet all have a common function, for, like modern versions of Pandora's box, each serves to contain a serious threat to the established order of late Victorian and Edwardian society. The first holds the danger of uncontrolled sexuality, the second political chaos, while inside the third is the menace of foreign rivalry, and within the fourth is the spectre of moral decay. Each room is thus the focus of far wider tensions and frustrations. As Virginia Berridge and Griffith Edwards point out, the presentation of opium dens in late Victorian fiction displays 'an increasing tone of racial and cultural hostility' totally unrelated to their actual minor role in illegal drug-taking. Indeed, like the German spy in the novels of Le Queux and Oppenheim, 'the myth of the opium den was in the wider sense a domestic result of imperialism and the reaction to economic uncertainty,' and thus formed an image of British weakness in the face of a subtle foreign threat.[48] The danger, as Terry Parssinen observes, came from 'an alien institution . . . in the heart of London'.[49] An identical insecurity lay behind the Edwardian anarchist novel. As Graham Holderness observes, anarchist dramas 'echo the outraged prejudices of a society challenged by the widespread radical movements of the period, and anxious to pin as much blame as possible on a political group already demonised into a mythological nightmare'.[50]

Yet if the spies' inner sanctum in *The Secret* rivals Le Queux's anarchists' headquarters and Conan Doyle's opium den as a subtle threat to the British society, its outward characteristics are closer to those of Eveline's teashop. Indeed, the physical settings for late Victorian and Edwardian pornography bear an uncanny resemblance to those of contemporary spy fiction. As Steven Marcus notes of Victorian erotic fiction, its location was 'the secluded country estate, set in the middle of a large park and surrounded by insurmountable walls, the mysterious town house in London or Paris, the carefully furnished and elaborately equipped set of apartments . . . the deserted cove at the seaside, or the solitary cottage atop the cliffs'.[51] Yet, as anyone familiar with Le Queux and Oppenheim will recognize, this was also the world of the Edwardian spy. If we follow the adventurous hero of the 1902 novel *'Frank' and I*, we thus find him in a hansom cab with his friend Ford, travelling to 'Blank-street Kensington', in London's West End:

> When we reached the corner of the street, I stopped the cab . . . and we walked the rest of the way to the house. I touched the electric bell, and . . . a smartly-dressed maid-servant . . . preceded us into the house and ushered us into a large, brilliantly-lighted drawing-room . . . handsomely furnished in a most tasteful style . . . At one end of the apartment, there was a deep, broad recess, apparently opening into another room; but I could not be certain, as the place was screened by heavy curtains of dark crimson velvet.[52]

Yet if we now accompany Rupert Manton, hero of Le Queux's 1914 novel *The German Spy*, travelling in his friend's 'fine, grey Rolls-Royce' we will arrive in Clarges Street, just a stone's throw from the same house. Here the car:

> pulled up . . . before a big, dark, old-fashioned but highly respectable house, the door of which fell open as we ascended the steps, and a grave, rather sallow foreign man-servant bowed as we crossed the threshold. The hall was plainly yet solidly furnished; the Eastern carpet so thick that our feet fell noiselessly . . . Upon the green-painted walls were many shields of ancient Eastern arms, while across the centre of the place, where commenced the stairs, was a fine Cairene screen of sweet-smelling sandalwood.[53]

Only the detail of each novel would reveal that the screen in Clarges Street concealed 'the clearing-house of the espionage of the European Powers', while the curtain in Blank-street hid one of London's foremost brothels, and not vice-versa.

Indeed, the imagery of spy fiction and pornography was interchangeable. In January 1918 the right-wing *Imperialist* gave an absurd analysis of the moral danger from German espionage which employed all the clichés of the Edwardian pornographer. The author, apparently one Captain Harold Spencer, claimed to have obtained through a British Secret Service officer details of an enormous system of 'corruption and blackmail' operated by German spies in Britain. The German Secret Service, he could reveal, had even compiled a special volume 'from the reports of German agents who have infested this country for the past twenty years':

> In the beginning of the book is a precis of general instructions regarding the propagation of evils which all decent men thought had perished in Sodom and Lesbia . . . Then more than a thousand pages are filled with the names mentioned by German agents in their reports. There are the names of forty-seven thousand English men and women.

As Spencer revealed, this network of sexual blackmail was so perfect that 'no one in the social scale was exempted from contamination':

> As an example of the thoroughness with which the German agent works, lists of public houses and bars were given which had been successfully demoralised . . . To secure those whose social standing would suffer from frequenting public places, comfortable flats were taken and furnished in an erotic manner. Paphian photographs were distributed . . . Wives of men in supreme position were entangled. In Lesbian ecstasy the most sacred secrets of State were betrayed. The sexual peculiarities of members of the peerage were used as a leverage to open fruitful fields for espionage.

This nonsense was presented as fact, and proved so attractive a myth among right-wing readers that it had to be reprinted as a pamphlet, yet its imagery came straight from erotic fiction.[54]

Conversely, elements of the spy story appear in Edwardian pornography. The erotic novels *Pleasure-Bound Afloat* and *Pleasure-Bound Ashore*, dating from 1908–9, have a sub-plot involving the preparation of a German invasion of Britain. The German Navy, we are informed, had fooled the British by constructing twelve battleships at a secret base in the Pacific, and only awaited the delivery of their guns from Krupp's. These ships were 'immensely in advance of anything known', and 'when the armament was complete it was proposed to launch a blow on the British navy which should make Germany not only ruler of the seas, but of Great Britain and her colonies'. The heroes, a group of hedonists led by an old Etonian, decide to capture these guns and ammunition and seize the ships for the Royal Navy, placing it thereby 'in a position of unapproachable supremacy'. The author, apparently a Fleet Street hack, promised to reveal in a subsequent volume how his athletic heroes foiled this dastardly plot and won 'the freedom of the British Empire and the approval of Society', but, mercifully and inevitably, his stamina gave out long before theirs did.[55]

Indeed, like spy fiction, much late Victorian and Edwardian pornography reveals the deep-seated fear of its middle-class readers that their world was threatened both from within and from without. As Harold Dyos and Michael Wolff have noted, the basic structure of late nineteenth century pornography 'assumed that all servants, shop girls, and labourers were inexhaustibly libidinous', and presented them as offering the 'respectable classes' access to a world free from prudery and restraint. Yet by treating the working classes purely in terms of animal instinct, such literature inevitably reinforced that 'blend of contempt, fear, hate, and physical revulsion' found in much middle-class social observation, and therefore, paradoxically, strengthened the very constraints it appeared to condemn.[56] In *The Modern Eveline*, a pornographic novel from 1904, Inspector Walker of the Special Branch can thus at one moment praise the heroine for having 'flung from you the unnatural restraints which society pretends . . . to cast around you', and yet immediately afterwards confess his fear of imminent social collapse. As the Inspector explains, his undercover investigations had led him to 'the irresistible conviction that society in London was rotten to the core', and that lack of proper restraint among the nobility was leading to problems with 'the middle and lower classes'.[57] The speech loses some of its conviction when spoken by a man with no trousers, but reveals the essential fact that Edwardian pornographers, like contemporary writers of spy stories, were growing to fear the contents of their locked rooms. It is no coincidence that the publication of British pornography wilted as middle-class confidence declined, and that 'by 1910 it had virtually ceased'.[58]

The motif of the locked room, in which the readers' fears or fantasies were made concrete and real, was of great significance both to late Victorian and Edwardian pornography and to spy fiction. Indeed, it has an obvious psychological function. As Steven Marcus notes of Victorian pornography, the true location of its events is 'behind our eyes, within our heads', and without doubt its hidden rooms are areas of the unconscious mind ordinarily repressed and concealed. It is no coincidence that those pornographic novels most committed to this narrative device, such as *The Yellow Room* (London, 1891) or *The Way of a Man with a Maid* (London, c. 1895), are also those which employ the most disturbing imagery. Thus in *The Yellow Room*, as Donald Thomas notes, 'the code of the nursery is incongruously adapted to the fantasies of the brothel'.[59]

Yet the most important link between pornography and spy fiction lies not simply in the motif of the locked room, but in the concept of a whole hidden world, for both these types of literature present the reader with a complete new world of experience, in which almost anything is possible. If one can only give the correct sign at the right time then doors will open to this parallel existence, and, as with some hallucinogenic drug, one will have access to a more vivid reality. 'It made me feel alien to the throng', confesses the narrator of John Ferguson's 1919 novel *Stealthy Terror*, on the run from German spies:

> Outside on the pavement the miscellaneous throng of people in their bright summer clothes passed and repassed . . . In the midst of all that kaleidoscope of colour and buzz of talk I had a sense of being separate and aloof. The smooth bituminous paths that ran along the greensward and encircled the bandstand seemed to be but the thin, hardened surface that hid the burning lava on which a symbolic England moved unconcernedly. I had been through this surface, and knew what lay beneath.[60]

To contemporaries this image of a parallel world, where chaos lay so close to order, was both tantalizing and exciting. As Kay Sloan notes of the rash of films about enforced prostitution, produced during 1913 and 1914, 'the notion that at any moment everyday life could be shattered in a single brush with a drug-bearing white slaver was a titillating one'.[61] 'You think that a wall as solid as the earth separates civilisation from barbarism,' echoes the villain of John Buchan's spy story *The Power-House*, first published in 1913, 'I tell you the division is a thread, a sheet of glass'.[62]

The dangerous worlds of prostitutes and spies provided vicarious thrills for jaded readers, but it is wrong to think that spy fiction serves only to demonstrate the triumph of good amid such evil. The origin of this analysis was the detective story, which, in the words of Julian Symons, appears to confirm prevailing order through 'the inevitability with which wrongdoing is punished'. Between the 1890s and the 1940s crime literature thus 'offered to its readers . . . a reassuring world in which those who tried to disturb the established order were always discovered'.[63] The same analysis was readily applied to espionage fiction, and David Stafford argues that the evil spy functioned as 'a means of highlighting and reaffirming accepted values':

> Values are affirmed . . . by contrasting them with a set of opposing values held by others outside the group . . . The character and behaviour of enemy spies in Edwardian fiction, therefore, is of importance in helping to establish and emphasise the value and legitimacy of the gentleman secret agent.[64]

Yet ultimately this analysis fails to satisfy, for in neither detective nor spy fiction is morality more than superficial, and in neither is the resolution of the dilemma more attractive than the dilemma itself. Indeed, the thrill enjoyed by readers comes not from the battle of good and evil, nor the inevitable triumph of order, but rather from the prospect of joining the detective, the criminal, and the spy, in a world free from both law and conventional morality. The parallel world of the fictional spy is as seductively attractive as the parallel world of pornography.

The most notable feature of these hidden worlds was indeed the eagerness with which ordinary people sought entrance. On 28 August 1914 the driver of the midnight train from Euston found the signal against him at Tring, and on going to the signalbox found the signalman insensible, 'the furniture disarranged, and the telephone damaged'. The signalman later told police:

> I made an entry in my book at 12.36 a.m. then poked the fire, when the door suddenly opened, a man entered and attacked me with a knife. He tried to stab me in the groin, cutting through my trousers and shirt: I was wearing a truss which prevented me being wounded.

The signalman struck out with the poker, but his attacker 'gave a low whistle' and a second man entered, knocking him unconscious. As the signalman later confided to a reporter, the two men were almost certainly spies, and their accents 'led him to believe they were German'.[65]

In 1915 Scotland Yard was similarly informed that a German master spy had approached and threatened a 16-year-old domestic servant. When questioned, the girl told in detail of how she had been forced to work for an agent named Eric Herfranz Mullard, who trained her to operate a signalling machine called the 'Maxione':

> She said that she was in terror of her life, that the spy would come and tap at the kitchen window, that he had a powerful green motor-car waiting round the corner in which he would whisk her off to operate the 'Maxione' and the red lights, without which the submarines lying in wait in the Bristol Channel would not be able to do their fell work.[66]

Young people seemed particularly vulnerable. Another teenage domestic servant was brought to London from Bath to tell the authorities 'in great and credible detail' of how 'through her pretended love for a foreigner she had discovered that he was in nightly communication with Berlin'.[67] In June 1915 a Sea Scout messenger at Penzance similarly reported the approach of a suspicious man on a bicycle, who offered 'to buy secret or confidential letters'. He was plainly a spy, for he was dark and had a close pointed beard, so his description was quickly circulated by military intelligence.[68]

All these stories were investigated and found to be pure invention – the signalman was 'suffering from a nervous breakdown', the servant girls were fantasizing, and the Sea Scout 'admitted that he made the story up himself'.[69] The police were forced to admit that they could not confirm any of the numerous stories of 'conspiracies to commit outrage', yet the attraction of the hidden world was so strong that the fantasies themselves were made proof of its existence.[70] As one writer explained at the end of 1914, a section of the army of German agents had obviously been charged with spreading rumours 'which it was fondly supposed would create such panic in Britain that the Government would be compelled to recall the British Expeditionary Force':

> In the early days of the war there appeared to be secret agents of this description in every train, in every public-house bar, and even in good clubs, and false news spread like wildfire. The scheme was so well organised that every day brought a new rumour, which spread simultaneously from a hundred different centres . . . Letters were even sent to the papers, professedly from relatives of wounded men, complaining of Governmental suppression of facts, which proved on investigation to consist of a tissue of falsehoods, and to come from addresses which did not exist.[71]

There was no escaping the danger: if the rumours of spies were true then the country was in the grip of a huge conspiracy, and if they were false it only proved how subtle and terrible that conspiracy was.

The prevailing message of early spy literature was not in fact that spies were dangerous. Seldom in fiction or in reality do their schemes succeed, and in most spy stories, as I.F. Clarke comments, 'there is . . . no real cause for alarm, since our own agents know what is going on'.[72] More strongly conveyed is the message that spies are totally unlike ourselves. Thus in May 1915 the Winchester police became suspicious of a stranger in uniform, on the grounds that he had the 'appearance of a spy both in manner and in speech'.[73] As John Buchan noted of one character in *The Thirty-Nine Steps* that same year, he might speak 'in very good English', but nevertheless 'his close-cropped head and the cut of his collar and tie never came out of England'.[74]

The key to locating the hidden world indeed lay in detecting such small inconsistencies – holes in the fabric of the natural order through which one might glimpse the chaotic logic beneath. Lieutenant-General Robert Baden-Powell, founder of the Scout Movement, advised soldiers in 1914 that 'if you want practice at detecting spies . . . they are not uncommon, and you need not go out of England to find them'. Spies, he explained, could be discovered by noting the 'small peculiarities and details of passers-by':

> Get to know the view and action from behind of anyone you suspect – then if you come across the same back a few days later with an entirely different face you may consider him worth further attention. I have had the pleasure of arresting four foreign European spies at different times in peace time in England, and have casually detected others abroad – one an officer passing as an hotel waiter, another as a tourist, the third was a lady, and so on . . . Certain foreign governesses could tell you a good deal about our Army.[75]

This detection of incongruity, rather than any overt act of espionage, became the key to locating spies both in fiction and reality. Most of the reports logged by Colonel Edmonds in 1908 and 1909 were accounts of strange occurrences rather than of actual spies. Strangers who were 'too absorbed and businesslike for ordinary tourists', a cyclist who 'swore in German', and a barber's assistant 'discovered by accident to wear a wig over his own thick head of hair', were thus condemned by the peculiar logic of their behaviour.[76] Anything counter to the natural order was indeed thought to belong to the hidden world. In August 1914 a party of three men and a woman were reported to the Scottish police as behaving suspiciously. Travelling in a car, they spoke convincing English, and claimed to be Government Surveyors, but their behaviour at the Dalwhinnie Hotel was strangely disturbing. As the police report noted, although one of them 'dressed like a chauffeur' he nevertheless 'appeared to be one of the party from the familiar way in which he was mixing with the others and it was he who paid for the drink'.[77] Such cynical disregard for class distinction immediately marked them down as spies.

The search for incongruity reached fever-pitch in October 1914, when military intelligence ordered the investigation of any building which might have been constructed to aid an invading enemy. Local commanding officers, weaned on the fiction of Oppenheim and Le Queux, eagerly set to work. On 15 October Colonel F.J.S. Cleeve visited the Diesel works in Ipswich, and reported triumphantly that 'the block of offices would be ideal for transacting the staff and administrative work of a large army'. Furthermore, 'the water tower would have certain uses and machine guns could be mounted thereon to overawe the town and command adjacent country'. The situation in London was even worse. On 17 October Colonel F. Busche visited the Danish Butter Syndicate's works at Erith, and to his alarm discovered 'a large wooden structure about 150 feet high' just inside the entrance: 'At first sight,' he reported, 'it appeared to be a wireless installation.' Busche was shown that it was not, but even then added darkly 'it could very easily be converted into one within a couple of hours'. Finding some hollow containers under construction, the Colonel immediately realized that these 'could be easily turned into very strong platforms by filling the centre with concrete'. As he noted in his report, he cautiously asked their function 'and the Manager told me to store monkey-nuts'. It was an answer he richly deserved.[78]

Yet even if one located the secret world, how might one gain entrance? Well, one could always burst in, like Pontifex Shrewd and his faithful assistant Feng Wo, in a story from the comic *Lot-O'-Fun* in 1914:

> With a cry of rage the man sitting at the table, his ears covered with earflaps of a telephone receiver, sprang to his feet and faced them. Shrewd was halfway through the trap door when, without warning, the occupant of the room fired. The bullet snicked a piece from Shrewd's finger, and then with a lightning movement the detective's hand flashed up, and the other's weapon dropped.
>
> 'Well, Dr. Reinhans,' said Shrewd, coolly, as he sprang into the room, 'the game is up. This is a pretty little secret wireless installation you've got here, only you've rather overdone the wires outside. I spotted those aerials of yours this morning'.[79]

However, the division between the hidden world and reality was so thin that access might come through the simplest of actions, at the least expected time. A secret sign could be enough, for if one knew how spies communicated one could use this knowledge to enter their world. In 1914, recalled the head of the Special Branch, a British war correspondent reported from Belgium 'that the enamelled iron advertisements for "Maggi Soup," which were to be seen attached to every hoarding and telegraph post, were unscrewed by the German officers, in order to read the information about the local resources . . . painted in German on the back'. Readers became so fired with enthusiasm that 'screwdriver parties' were formed in the London suburbs, to tear down suspect advertisements and find their hidden messages.[80]

Another familiar method of entry was by password, the magical possibilities of which fascinated British officers. Major Fitzroy Gardner, Assistant Provost Marshal of the Thames and Medway Garrison in 1915, remembered being given the secret code word which British agents in disguise would use to identify themselves if they needed help. When uttered 'to any officer in staff uniform' this signal guaranteed the agent 'immediate facilities for communicating with the War Office through the nearest military telephone', and Major Gardner, with his theatrical background, longed for the day when it would be used to him:

> I was sure that the moment had arrived when one day in a Chatham street a man in civilian dress, with a beard such as the spy of the illustrated magazine story would use as a disguise, stopped me and politely asked whether he might speak to me privately. I took him down a side-street and waited for the magic word, but he merely said that he was an ex-officer, had been in trouble . . . and asked for the loan of half a crown.[81]

Sydney Horler was equally bowled over when entrusted with a key to the secret world in 1918. On one occasion, as a Second Lieutenant in Air Intelligence, he became night duty officer in charge of the Air Ministry building, and reported to the chief secretary for secret instructions. That official 'leaned forward and whispered, in a style worthy of the best melodrama, a telephone number . . . Mayfair 034251X'. 'I didn't know what the devil it meant,' Horler later confessed, 'I was nearly sick.' Luckily for him the night passed without incident.[82]

As so many people were eager to gain access, it is also worth considering what they thought the hidden world was like. In his consideration of late Victorian pornography, Donald Thomas noted how its imaginary world seemed a mirror-image of reality, using incest and orgy in a grotesque parody of conventional morality and social relations.[83] The world of the Edwardian spy shows an equally bizarre reversal of the natural order. Gender distinctions, for example, are strangely blurred. Men consistently break the strongest cultural taboos by dressing as women, as in the urban legend recorded by the Rev. Andrew Clark in 1916:

> In Braintree was a cook, who went out as a cook, but dined at the White Hart Hotel. 'She' was dressed as a woman, but had very large feet, and was probably a man dressed as a woman. 'She' disappeared hurriedly. Before 'she' went 'she' prophesied that, after 'she' had gone Zeppelins would come to Braintree, and also go to Scotland. It has all turned out as 'she' said. 'She' was certainly a spy. Anyone with such large feet must have been a spy.[84]

David Stafford has also pointed out how 'the attribution of femininity to male enemy spies' forms a recurring theme of early spy fiction – as in John Buchan's *Greenmantle* of 1916.[85] Similarly, Phillip Knightley has noted the sexual indetermination of these stories:

> The heroines were all female chaps, clubland heroes with longer hair. Again and again the heroine is likened to an adolescent male: she has slim hips, clean white limbs, an athlete's grace and 'but for the gentle swell of her bosom, one might have taken her for a boy'.[86]

The hidden world indeed contains many homoerotic elements, and in all the early stories, David Stafford observes, 'the life of the secret agent is reserved essentially for single men'.[87] The breakdown of gender stereotypes, and the close friendships of masculine heroes, surreptitiously offered readers a freedom they were denied in reality. Baden-Powell, founder of the Boy Scout movement, suffered from a morbid fear of his own sexuality, and could only find satisfaction in his dreams, in his fantasies about scouts and spies, and in his passion for James Barrie's *Peter Pan*. In real life all temptation was sternly suppressed: 'at manoeuvres,' he warned in 1914, 'it will often be useful practice to employ a few scouts in disguise, but it is not desirable that they should ever be dressed as women'.[88]

Yet gender distinction was not the only rule that changed as one entered the hidden world. The laws of probability altered, so that coincidence was commonplace, and important discoveries came easily by accident. Absurd situations and strange incongruities appeared natural, while bizarre transformations of people and objects were solid good sense. In November 1914 Barker Motion Photography thus produced the film *By The Kaiser's Orders*, in which German spies try to steal the secret ray machine of British inventor John Carlton. The *Kinematograph Weekly* described the climax to the film, where the spies attack the inventor's house:

Carlton, who is busy in his workroom, is interrupted by the sound of
voices proceeding from the hall. A quick glance over the bannisters
shows him the spies. Going back into the room, he locks the door,
but the enemy commence to batter it down. Realising the door will
not hold out under such measures he endeavours to drag the cupboard
. . . to form a barricade.

However, unknown to Carlton the audience has already seen a strange
sub-plot in which Carlton's house was burgled by Bob Saunders, 'a British
workman' made unemployed by the war. Saunders is now hiding in this
cupboard, but to Carlton the discovery is quite natural:

The weight surprises him, and opening the cupboard door he finds
Bob in hiding. The situation is explained to Bob, and he offers his
assistance. The pair put up a plucky fight . . . a party of the London
Scottish . . . are quickly on the scene. The enemy is soon over-
powered and led away.[89]

This dream-like transmutation of cupboard into man is matched by similar
metamorphoses in other spy dramas, such as the 1914 stage play *The Man
Who Stayed at Home*. As one reviewer noted:

Everybody at Mrs. Sanderson's guest-house on the East Coast
wondered why Christopher Brent . . . didn't answer Lord Kitchener's
call for recruits. He only laughed pleasantly when a girl staying at the
boarding-house ostentatiously presented him, in front of everybody,
with a white feather.

Brent is indeed a dangerous image for Britain in 1914, being at once a
member of respectable society and 'a coward . . . a waster and a shirker'
whom everyone must shun. The climax of the play thus centres on a
dramatic transformation which is dream-like in its simplicity: the manager-
ess of the boarding-house is shown to be the widow of a German general,
her son Carl and Fritz the waiter are revealed as German spies, and Brent
becomes a hero:

As a matter of fact, Christopher Brent was in the Secret Service of
the British Government . . . He suspected that there was treacherous
work going on in the boarding-house, and was convinced of it when he
discovered a Marconi signalling apparatus cunningly concealed behind
the fireplace.[90]

The play naturally proved enormously popular. The theatre, wrote one
reviewer, 'is full of people eight times a week watching the work of
the villains and their final capture and destruction', while the plot itself
brought a flood of rumours of secret transmitters worked by cunning

German spies.[91]

Dreamlike transformations could indeed resolve every human problem. *The Girl from Downing Street*, a film released in November 1918, introduces us to 'Peggy Marsden, the accomplished English female spy', who has stolen some vital German plans and been chased across Europe by Captain Muller, 'the chief of the German secret service staff'. Peggy attempts to deliver the plans to Lord Northwood, a government minister, but she is captured by Muller and his gang and tied up in a house outside London. Yet as *The Cinema* explained:

> She escapes, to go through many perilous adventures before finally reaching London, where she telephones to Lord Northwood, who orders the military to protect the courageous girl. The spies, however, headed by Muller, obtain an entrance to the Minister's house through a confederate butler, determined to make one last effort to recover the papers . . . Aided by sentries with fixed bayonets . . . Peggy safely reaches the Minister's room at last, only to be confronted by Muller, who takes them from her. And then she learns that he is not really Muller . . . but Cyril Godfrey [a British agent], and the play closes with Peggy and the man she looked upon as her enemy gazing into the fire and deciding to go through life together.[92]

As we can see from these examples, the secret world even has its own chronology. In Victorian pornography, as Steven Marcus notes, 'there is ideally no such thing as time', for its characters exist in 'a total, simultaneous present'.[93] The same is true of spy fiction, for in the hidden world the time is always now, the great plot is just about to mature, and the security of past and future both hinge upon the present.

An examination of early British spy fiction thus reveals an interesting paradox. The genre did not, as is often suggested, depend upon the construction and resolution of realistic dilemmas, but involved instead an imaginary parallel world of dream-like complexity. The spy, and anyone involved with him, had access to a world of great excitement – of flying, fighting and hiding. This world involved sudden and dramatic changes – explosions, transformations, disappearances and discoveries. It held bizarre juxtapositions of the strange and the familiar – treachery, androgeny, disguise and moral uncertainty. And, finally, it displayed its own logic – in distorted time, increased coincidence, and the overwhelming importance of trivial detail. It was indeed a world of heightened reality, which contemporaries found enormously enticing.

Yet the context of this hidden world was at odds with its content, for the overt message of spy fiction was throughout that this alternative existence had at all costs to be destroyed. The hidden world, as we have seen, contained very powerful and personal imagery, and yet it was presented as the clash of competing nations and impersonal forces. The hidden world lay parallel to reality, and yet it was presented as a deadly threat, which might at any moment break through and turn order into chaos. In short, the spy story depicts an attractive hidden world of great freedom, yet brands it as repulsive, dangerous, and constraining.

It is here that the function of the hidden world becomes plain, for its images are those of the subconscious, and the structure of spy fiction is that of the dream. As Freud explained in his *Interpretation of Dreams*, the process of dreaming operates at two levels. Dreams themselves are created at a deep emotional level, out of unconscious wishes, recollections and fantasies. Like spy fiction, dreaming is characterized by regression, in which satisfaction comes through magical wish-fulfilment, and by condensation, where diverse objects or individuals are combined to make a single image. The attempted resolution of subconscious fear forms the 'latent content' of the dream.

Yet the waking recollection of a dream is radically different, for the conscious mind suppresses the disturbing imagery of the dream, and creates instead a new set of images – the 'manifest content' – which lacks the power to shock. This 'dream censorship' conceals the true purpose of the dream, and in some cases, noted Freud, 'the wish-fulfilment was unrecognizable and often disguised by every possible mean'. Yet the dream's 'latent content' remains of paramount importance, for 'it is from these dream-thoughts and not from a dream's manifest content that we disentangle its meaning'.[94]

Spy fiction operates in the same way. It is a magical form of wish-fulfilment, played out through a series of bizarre images and irrational acts. These form its latent content, and herein lies its purpose and its appeal, but these images are too disturbing and revealing to be consciously faced. They are thus disowned, and consigned to a dangerous and unstable parallel world, within which all those elements that seem chaotic or against the natural order can be shown as the work of enemy agents. The emotional ambivalence of the spy story is fiercely denied, and a separate manifest content is created, retelling the story through patriotic and reassuring images.

Nevertheless, the principal function of the spy story is, like the dream, to give access to the subconscious mind, and this it achieves through a three-fold structure. The outer level is reality – the world of the reader himself. Within this is a second level of fictional reality, within which the hero of the story lives. This level holds the manifest content of the spy story, expressing and resolving the reader's conscious hopes and fears through foreign rivalry and destructive war. Yet contained within this second level is still a third – the hidden world of the spy. Here, in this fantasy within a fantasy, are acted out the fictional hero's hopes and fears, in a landscape drawn from the reader's subconscious. Only at this third level, twice removed from reality, can the latent content of the genre find open expression.[95] This, then, is where the army of fictional spies was born, and this is the world that they inhabit. In truth they owe almost nothing to reality, for, like the puppets in the hidden world of pornography, their sole purpose was to act out the subconscious fantasies of adolescents and of insecure middle-class men whose status had been undermined by a rapidly changing society.

NOTES

1. *Graphic*, 17 Oct. 1914, p.562, 'A Woman on Secret Service'.
2. Ibid.
3. C. Lowe, 'About German Spies', *Contemporary Review*, January 1910, p.43.
4. I.F. Clarke, *Voices Prophesying War 1763–1984* (London, 1966), p.125.
5. D. Stafford, *The Silent Game: The Real World of Imaginary Spies* (London, 1988), pp.3, 7, 13.
6. C.M. Andrew, *Secret Service: The Making of the British Intelligence Community* (London, 1985), p.34.
7. Clarke, *Voices*, pp.127, 161.
8. See for example D. Stafford, 'John Buchan's Tales of Espionage: A Popular Archive of British History', *Canadian Journal of History*, April 1983, pp.20–21
9. J.H. Brunvand, *The Vanishing Hitchhiker: American Urban Legends and their Meanings* (New York, 1981), pp.3–4,12.
10. L.J. Beeston, 'A Star Fell', in A.K. Russell (ed.), *Science Fiction by the Rivals of H.G. Wells* (Secaucus, NJ, 1979); E.S. Turner, *Boys Will Be Boys* (Harmondsworth, 3rd edn. 1976), p.195.
11. *Bioscope*, 3 October 1912, p.61, 'The Pick of the Programmes'.
12. D. McCormick, *Who's Who in Spy Fiction* (London, 1979), p.11.
13. Stafford, *Silent Game*, p.4.
14. 'Ole Luk-Oie' [E. Swinton] *The Green Curve and Other Stories* (London, 1916), p.238. 'An Eddy of War' first appeared in *Blackwood's Magazine* in April 1907.
15. *The Globe*, 7 May 1907, p.5,col.2, 'German espionage'.
16. Imperial War Museum, London: Kell Papers SVK/2, Lt.Col.J.E. Edmonds, 'Intelligence Systems/Germany', 9 Feb. 1909 [written in 1908], pp.8–9.
17. C. Holmes, 'Germans in Britain 1870–1914', *Beiträge Zur Wirtschaftsgeschichte, Band 6: Wirtschaftskräfte und wirtschaftswege III* (Stuttgart, 1978), p.582.
18. N. Hiley, 'The Failure of British Counter-Espionage Against Germany, 1907–1914', *Historical Journal*, Vol.28, No.4 (1985), pp.843–4.
19. W. Le Queux, *Spies of the Kaiser* (London, 1909), Ch.III: Hiley, 'Failure of British Counter-Espionage', p.861.
20. John Horace Dancy, Papers; Memoirs, Vol.13, pp.2006–7. I am grateful to Professor John Dancy for allowing me to quote from his father's papers.
21. *Daily Mail*, 10 April 1962, p.4, 'The Faceless Ones Spill a Secret'.
22. E. Gleichen, *A Guardsman's Memories* (London, 1932), p.344.
23. M. Drummond, *The Riddle* (London, 1985), pp.153–4.
24. H.C. Bywater and H.C. Ferraby, *Strange Intelligence: Memoirs of Naval Secret Service* (London, 1931), p.157:
25. PRO, WO 33/579, 'Special Military Resources of the German Empire', Feb. 1912, p.43.
26. Ministry of Defence, Naval Historical Library; F. Birch and W. Clarke, 'A Contribution to the History of German Naval Warfare 1914–1918' [typescript], Vol.I Part I, pp.44–5.
27. E. Swinton (ed.) *Twenty Years After: Supplementary Volume* (London, 1938), p.535.

28. V. Williams, *The World of Action* (London, 1938), p.334.
29. C. Mackenzie, *Greek Memories* (London, 1939), p.324.
30. M. Graham-White, *At the Wheel Ashore and Afloat* (London, 1935), pp.264–7.
31. F. Toye, *For What We Have Received* (London, 1950), p.129.
32. J.G. Millais, *Wanderings and Memories* (London, 1919), pp.232–3.
33. N. Everitt, *British Secret Service during the Great War* (London, 1920), pp.53, 72.
34. 'F. Douglas' [F. de Valda], 'The Greatest Secret Service Story,' *Sunday Chronicle*, 21 April 1929, p.7 col.1.
35. Mackenzie, *Greek Memories*, p.308; P. Brown, *Round the Corner* (London, 1934), p.233; P. Brown, *Almost in Camera* (London, 1944), pp.9–11.
36. E.P. Oppenheim, *The Pool of Memory* (London, 1941), p.38.
37. N. Hiley, 'Counter-Espionage and Security in Great Britain during the First World War', *English Historical Review*, July 1986, pp.646–7: Kell Papers [Frost]; Lecture headed 'Scottish Chief Constables, Edinboro' 26/2/25'. I am grateful to Robin S. Frost for allowing me access to this document.
38. M.W. Cannan, *Grey Ghosts and Voices* (Kineton, 1976), p.131.
39. Churchill College Cambridge, Archives Centre; Bull Papers 4/2, V. Brandon to L. Bull, 21 Sept. 1910.
40. *The Modern Eveline* (Paris, 1904: reprinted as *Eveline*, London, 1983), pp.52–3.
41. W. Le Queux *The Great Plot* (London, 1907), p.169.
42. E. Phillips Oppenheim, *The Secret* (London, 1907), pp.230, 246–8.
43. A. Conan Doyle, *Sherlock Holmes: The Complete Short Stories* (London, 1928), pp.125–6 ['The Man With the Twisted Lip', 1892].
44. *Eveline*, p.155.
45. Le Queux, *Great Plot*, p.169.
46. Oppenheim, *Secret*, p.239.
47. Conan Doyle, *Sherlock Holmes*, p.127.
48. V. Berridge and G. Edwards, *Opium and the People: Opiate Use in Nineteenth-Century England* (London, 1981), pp.197, 205.
49. T.M. Parssinen, *Secret Passions, Secret Remedies: Narcotic drugs in British society 1820–1930* (Manchester, 1983), p.67.
50. G. Holderness, 'Anarchism and fiction', in H. Gustav Klaus (ed.), *The Rise of Socialist Fiction 1880–1914* (Brighton, 1987), p.129.
51. S. Marcus, *The Other Victorians: A Study of Sexuality and Pornography in Mid-nineteenth-Century England* (London, 1966), p.268.
52. *'Frank' and I* (London, 1902: reprinted London, 1983), pp.137–8.
53. W. Le Queux, *The German Spy: A Present-day Story* (London, 1914), pp.17–18.
54. *The Imperialist*, 26 Jan. 1918, p.3, 'As I See It – The First 47,000'; *The Vigilante*, 16 Feb. 1918, p.2.
55. *Pleasure-Bound Afloat* (London, 1908: reprinted London, 1985), p.100; *Pleasure-Bound Ashore* (London, 1909: reprinted London, 1985), pp.96–8. The author of these novels, and of their companion *Maudie: Revelations of Life in London* (London, 1909), was possibly the aptly named George Bacchus: P.J. Kearney, *A History of Erotic Literature* (London, 1982), p.153.
56. H.J. Dyos and M. Wolff, 'The Way We Live Now', in H.J. Dyos and M. Wolff (eds.), *The Victorian City: Images and Realities; Vol.2* (London, 1973), pp.896–7.
57. *Eveline*, pp.120–3.
58. Kearney, *Erotic Literature*, p.151.
59. D. Thomas, *A Long Time Burning* (London, 1969), p.277.
60. J.A. Ferguson, *Stealthy Terror* (London, 1919), pp.242–3.
61. K. Sloan, *The Loud Silents: Origins of the Social Problem Film* (Urbana, 1988), p.85. Sloan refers specifically to American productions, but these dominated British cinemas even before 1914.
62. J. Buchan, *The Power-House* (London, 1916), pp.64–5.
63. J. Symons, *Bloody Murder: From the Detective Story to the Crime Novel; A History* (Harmondsworth, rev. ed. 1985), pp.21–2.
64. D. Stafford, 'Spies and Gentlemen: The Birth of the British Spy Novel, 1893–1914',

Victorian Studies, Summer 1981, pp.503–4.

65. PRO: HO45/10484/103444/file 4a, Maj.A. Law to C.E. Troup, 1 Sept. 1914.
66. B. Thomson, *Queer People* (London, 1922), pp.14–15.
67. H.C. Hoy, *'40 OB'* (London, 1935), p.92.
68. PRO: AIR1/551/16/15/28, p.118, 'Home Defence Intelligence Summary; 4th–10th June 1915'.
69. PRO: HO45/10484/103444/file 4a, Law to Troup, 1 Sept. 1914: AIR1/551/16/15/28, p.136, 'Intelligence Summary; 11th–17th June 1915'.
70. A. Pulling (ed.), *Manual of Emergency Legislation* (London, 1914), pp.516–20, Home Office statement issued 9 Oct. 1914.
71. N. Flower (ed.), *The History of the Great War: Volume I* (London, 1914), p.101.
72. Clarke, *Voices*, p.125.
73. PRO, AIR 1/551/16/15/28, p.17, report by Captain R.M. Crosse.
74. J. Buchan, *The Thirty-Nine Steps* (London, 1915), p.227.
75. R. Baden-Powell, *Aids to Scouting for N.C.O.s and Men* (London, revised ed. 1914), pp.140–1.
76. PRO, CAB 16/8, 'Report and Proceedings of a Sub-Committee . . . Appointed to Consider the Question of Foreign Espionage in the United Kingdom', 24 July 1909, pp.14–16, 43.
77. Scottish Record Office, Edinburgh; HH 31/1, 'Suspected Persons at Dalwhinnie', 18 Aug. 1914.
78. PRO AIR 1/550/16/15/27, pp.86–91, reports by Col.Cleeve, 15 Oct. 1914, and Col. Busche, 19 Oct. 1914.
79. C. Allen, 'The Deadly Plague: The Adventures of Pontifex Shrewd in the War', *Lot-O'-Fun*, 19 Sept. 1914, p.3.
80. B. Thomson, *Queer People* (London, 1922), p.40.
81. F. Gardner, *More Reminiscences of an Old Bohemian* (London, 1926), p.282.
82. S. Horler, *Excitement: An Impudent Autobiography* (London, 1933), p.118.
83. Thomas, *Long Time Burning*, p.277.
84. J. Munson (ed.), *Echoes of the Great War: The Diary of the Reverend Andrew Clark 1914–1919* (Oxford, 1985), p.124.
85. D. Stafford, 'John Buchan's Tales of Espionage: A Popular Archive of British History', *Canadian Journal of History*, April 1983, p.15.
86. P. Knightley, 'The Spy Through the Rosy Glass of Fiction', *The Independent*, 27 Nov. 1988, p.29.
87. Stafford, 'Buchan's Tales', p.15.
88. T. Jeal, 'Baden-Powell's Lost Boys', *The Independent*, 21 Oct. 1989, p.31: Baden-Powell, *Aids to Scouting*, p.143.
89. *Kinematograph Weekly*, 5 November 1914, p.62, 'By the Kaiser's Orders'.
90. *Newnes' Illustrated*, 5 June 1915, pp.62–3, 'The Man Who Stayed at Home'.
91. J. Waters, 'Popular Spy Plays', *Daily Mail*, 8 Feb. 1915; D. O'Callaghan, 'The Enemy in Our Midst', *Nineteenth Century*, Oct. 1919, p.700.
92. *The Cinema*, 7 November 1918, p.56: 'The Girl From Downing Street'.
93. Marcus, *Other Victorians*, pp.270, 279.
94. S. Freud (trans J. Strachey), *Pelican Freud Library Volume 4: The Interpretation of Dreams* (Harmondsworth, 1976), pp.381, 702.
95. It is interesting to note that most fictional forms which employ the imagery of the subconscious, where people can fly or change their shape and size, use this three-fold structure of reality, fictional reality, and fictional fantasy. In numerous examples, from *Alice in Wonderland* and *Peter Pan* to *Superman* and *Batman*, a level of fictional reality is carefully inserted between the readers and the central characters, to distance them from such disturbing images.

English Spy Thrillers in the Age of Appeasement

ERIC HOMBERGER

One morning in the late 1930s a smartly-dressed woman arrived at the office of *The Week*, a subversive left-wing newsletter edited by Claud Cockburn. She explained that she had more money than she knew what to do with, just loved *The Week*, and wanted to work in the office for nothing. Her striking good looks led her to be wittily described as a Gift from God by the proprietor. She was taken on at once. Cockburn's wife Patricia pointed out that the woman was obviously a spy.

> 'Likely enough. What of it?'
> 'But you can't have a spy working right here in the office.'
> 'We don't mind. So long as she works unpaid. Like that, the Special Branch or the Foreign Office Intelligence or whoever it is, will be actually helping to pay for the production . . .'
> 'But she'll report on you all.'
> 'First of all, there is nothing to report. The telephone and mail are tapped already. And no serious person would come to this office who could not afford to have his or her name noted down in a little book. And then of course, if she is a genuine spy, she could be fed false reports about matters arising . . .'[1]

Four decades of spy thrillers and a decade of the talkies accustomed people to see spies behind the blandest, most everyday façade. Spy-consciousness permeated popular mentality in the 1930s. When Miss Froy disappeared during a train journey in Ethel Lina White's *The Wheel Spins* (1936), the only explanation which seems to make sense is offered by one of the other characters: '"Miss Froy is a spy who's got some information which she's sneaking out of the country. So she's got to be bumped off. And what better way than a rail journey?"'[2] In the block of flats where the novelist and journalist Leonard Mosley and his wife lived in 1938, one of their neighbours, Mr and Mrs Stevens, seemed 'ridiculously ordinary' – until Mosley heard them one day switch suddenly from Russian into French when they suspected they were being overheard. Mosley's wife Isa nosed around in the building, asking questions, and came back with neighbours' gossip about the Stevens' drinking and violent arguments; she also reported her suspicion that a man across the street in a dark suit and a green trilby was actually watching the Stevens. Mosley was amused and somewhat skeptical at his wife's prowess as a counter-espionage agent:

> 'It's amazement, darling, at finding that you have delusions, too, just like all the other silly women. I'd never have thought it! You, who profess to sneer at spy novels! You, who sneer at feminine fantasies! You, of all people, turning two harmless neighbours into international spies – and Communist spies, by God, of all things! – accusing harmless little runts who happen to be waiting around to pick up a girl of being Secret Service men! Oh, God!'[3]

Mosley noticed the watcher in the trilby himself, and heard the Stevens' loud arguments. But when he saw Mr Stevens slap his wife, Mosley tried to intervene and was told to mind his own business. The couple were not seen again. Three weeks later Mosley read reports in the press about the trial of three employees at the Woolwich Arsenal who were charged with stealing plans for naval guns. They had been directed by a Mr and Mrs Stevens who lived in a flat on the Edgware Road. In other words, life in the 1930s showed an alarming capacity to imitate art.

When adaptations were made in the 1930s of Edwardian thrillers for the movies, they were brought into line with current fears about spying. Edgar Wallace's *The Four Just Men* (1905) was filmed in 1939 by Michael Balcon. (Its Enid Blytonish American title was *The Secret Four*.) Balcon had produced Hitchcock's versions of John Buchan's *The Thirty-Nine Steps* in 1935, and Conrad's *The Secret Agent* as *Sabotage* a year later: he was clearly the master of spy movies in the 1930s. Wallace's book, one of the great bestsellers of the day, set four wealthy men as avengers in a world in which great wrongs went unpunished: 'we kill and we will kill because we are each sufferers through acts of injustice, for which the law gives us no remedy'.[4] The three survivors from the original four were not British; though their base of operations was in Spain they functioned worldwide. The Four have decided that a law proposed by the British Foreign Secretary, Sir Philip Ramon, which would enforce the deportation from England of Manuel Garcia, exiled leader of Carlist Spain, was unjust. They have decreed Sir Philip's death. (Although it remained unexplained in the novel, the Carlists, Borbón pretenders to the Spanish throne throughout the nineteenth century, were utter reactionaries who had the support of the clerical party in Spain. The last Carlist pretender, Don Carlos, Duke of Madrid, spent some of his last years of exile in England before his death in 1909.) The Four Just Men have executed embezzlers, crooks, white-slavers and the operator of a sweatshop. In every case they gave their victim a warning, and if that went unheeded the execution took place as promised. Police across the world have painfully built up a dossier on their activities, but know nothing about their identities. The plot of Wallace's novel mainly depended upon the traditional devices of impersonation and locked-room mysteries. Buried beneath the cumbersome narrative mechanism was a suggestion that the Four, and their enemy, were equally dedicated to the pursuit of their vision of the right. Before his mysterious death Sir Philip explained that he, too, had total faith in what he proposed to do: "'I have been a just man according to my lights . . . Whatever happens I am satisfied that I am doing the right thing'".[5] Sir Philip was not an evil man, not a crook, but his stiff adherence to his intention brought about his death. Wallace populated the middle ground of the novel with politicians, policemen, journalists and petty thieves, men who appreciate principles but saw no reason to be martyred for them. The Four Just Men and their victim were locked in a duel which outsiders could not readily understand; the logic of their mutual inflexibility was extreme. For such men the ends always justified the means. The interest of the novel 'as literature' lies in the way the simple morality of the struggle of good against evil was made less clear. Perhaps Wallace, and not Childers' *The Riddle of the Sands* (1903), with its patriotic structure of good and bad, is the ancestor of the contemporary spy thriller as practiced by le Carré in which the morality of the antagonists in the Cold War has become hopelessly muddied and compromised.

When Balcon adapted Wallace, the ethical revenge motive was replaced by an attempt to foil an international conspiracy by an unnamed Germanic state (the opening scene takes place in a military prison in 'Regensburg') to destroy the British Empire by blocking the Suez Canal and thus prevent the movement of troops to the East. Balcon's film allows less introspective puzzling over the ethics of private revenge than Wallace's novel – in which ethical debate is thin on the ground anyway. The film makes two conventional assumptions of the spy thriller: that the most innocuous social occasion could mask a nest of traitors and espionage, and that the most innocent-seeming person could turn out either to be a spy or a Secret Service agent. The Four in the film retain only one named character from the Wallace novel, Poiccard, who is no longer a chemist 'who found joy in unhealthy precipitates', but now is the proprietor of an elegant fashion showroom in London.[6] The other Just Men in the film are an actor, a musical dramatist and a consumptive. The clear intention is to signal a break from the Bulldog Drummond style of tough, Hollywood heroes. The Four are, rather, in the vein of gentlemen-patriots like Leslie Howard, not given to excessive force or side-of-the-mouth dialogue.[7] There is a very Balconesque scene in Poiccard's fashion establishment, akin to a similar moment in *The Thirty-Nine Steps*, when spies, spy-hunters, inquisitive reporters and innocent customers go about their business, some understanding the devious counter-espionage operation being mounted to steal a message hidden in the purse of a customer, but most remaining in ignorance of what was going on. In the 1930s even rich customers and the affected salesmen of elegant clothing establishment could be part of the game between spy and spy-catcher. Almost any social occasions was laden with possibilities of espionage. (Graham Greene was the master of this device, as the use of the Entrenationo Language Centre as a cover for the meeting of D. and his contact, K., in *The Confidential Agent* [1939] suggests.)

The obsequious manager of the showroom, Poiccard, is shown to have a secret fierceness. His confederates have freed a colleague, the fourth man, from Regensburg prison by impersonating a high military officer and brought him back to England with information that there was an official in the Foreign Office whose wife, described as a 'temperamental' woman with a taste for the good life, was selling military secrets. These were being passed on to Sir Hamar Ryman, a pacifist and strong opponent of rearmament, to discredit the government. Of course there were moles in the Foreign Office and elsewhere, passing on information to dissident MPs, notably Churchill, who makes a brief appearance at the end of the film when it was reissued after the outbreak of war in 1939. Balcon's plot neatly reverses the politics of rearmament: the leaks were going to *advocates* of rearmanent, not traitorous opponents. The filmic Four were motivated solely by patriotic reasons (the desire to defend the Empire), and nothing survives of the equivalence which appears in the novel between the Four and Sir Philip. The film seeks to connect the old familiars of espionage – international conspiracy, murder, treason, impersonation, secret messages which go astray – with an urgent contemporary political issue. Wallace's novel had no such reference. In however confused a way, Balcon's film sought at least *some* reference to a world in which there were looming threats to national security.

The film substituted personal and ethical motives for the public and patriotic motives of Wallace's novel. The espionage thriller has from *The Riddle of the Sands* depended upon the interfusing of personal motive (revenge) with political ideals (patriotism). But in 'real' life people undertake dangerous missions out of many diverse motives, some of them, certainly, public and political.[8] The tendency to shift the emphasis of late 1930s espionage thrillers to the *personal* and away from the *political* is one of the most surprising features of these books. I will later suggest that there was 'something of a blind spot', as T.R. Fyvel remarked about Orwell, towards Nazi Germany, and that English espionage thrillers reinforced the national will to appease and not confront Nazism.

The complicated interchange between public and private motivation is evident in three books of this period of widely varying interest. The least notable was A.O. Pollard's *The Secret Pact*, an 'Anschluss' spy thriller which appeared somewhat belatedly in 1940. Within the larger plot, an attempt by a British Secret Service agent Leigh Garnett to foil a German plan to incorporate the Balkan state of Estavania by a coup by pro-German forces, there was a story of private revenge. Sidonie von Schegelmann's husband, the German ambassador to Estavania, died in a Gestapo prison after Hitler came to power. She organized a Murder Gang with the sole purpose of destroying Hitler. But in the end Sidonie was betrayed and killed by one of her men.[9] A similar theme of private revenge against Hitler appears in Geoffrey Household's *Rogue Male*, which was written in early 1939 and published in September.[10] The hero's solo mission to assassinate Hitler was undertaken out of grief at the death of his Jewish fiancée at the hands of Gestapo torturers. There were many good reasons to wish Hitler dead, but Sir Robert explicitly denied that patriotism or politics were of the slightest concern to him.

Greene used the theme of private revenge in *A Gun for Sale* (1936), but it was in *The Confidential Agent*, an 'Entertainment' written hurriedly in the immediate aftermath of the Munich 'conversations' in 1938, where he transformed the question from the narrow bounds in which it appeared in Pollard and Household into a more complex interrogation of the ethic of commitment. The motivation of Raven, the assassin with the hare-lip in *A Gun for Sale*, was profoundly overdetermined, as was Pollard's obsessive Sidonie von Schegelmann and Household's sportsman; such protagonists were not vehicles through which the ethics of revenge could seriously be considered. But the gentle D. in *The Confidential Agent*, victim of false imprisonment, a widower, a servant of a cause which he cannot fully accept, and someone who was distrusted by his own side, repeatedly asks himself where his loyalties belong. Sent to Britain to buy coal for the embattled Republic, the other side – and he suspects his own side as well – are determined to prevent the successful conclusion of his mission. They try to kill D., and to buy him off. L., the aristocratic agent of the (Spanish) rebels, tells D. that he will never be trusted by the Loyalists because he was a bourgeois. D. has more than adequate reasons to betray his own side (they executed his wife, by mistake), but he retained an inner core of ethical judgement which he refused to abandon. 'Unless people received their deserts, the world to him was chaos, he was faced by despair.'[11] In an important scene with Rose Cullen, daughter of the coal magnate Lord Benditch, D. is directly asked about his motives.

> 'Are you,' she said with a kind of angry contempt, 'what they call a patriot?'
> 'Oh no, I don't think so. It's they, you know, who are always talking about something called our country.'
> 'Then why don't you take their money?'
> He said, 'You've got to choose some line of action and live by it. Otherwise nothing matters at all. You probably end with a gas-oven.

I've chosen certain people who've had the lean portion for some centuries now.'
'But your people are betrayed all the time.'
'It doesn't matter. You might say it's the only job left for anyone – sticking to a job'.[12]

All three novels unsurprisingly suggest that the enemy was ruthless and capable of violence, but the *personal* motive (in Pollard and Household) curiously domesticates the threat of Nazism, and makes the hero's decision to oppose Hitler comprehensible only within the hoary traditions of the private and obsessive revenge, quest and adventure.[13] Both books are rather more conventional thrillers than Greene's, for D. alone makes his commitment with a full grasp of the ambiguousness of the act of commitment itself. Greene does not directly confront the complexity of the Nazi political and military onslaught; it remains a threat, a distant menace, which manifested itself in brutality and gangsterism. (The very terms, metaphorically transposed from criminal behavior to the action of states, suggests the problem: there was no terminology in England in the 1930s for what the Gestapo were doing to opponents of Nazism, and thus it tended to be described in the largely American terminology of 'gangsters' or as Public School bully-boy behavior.) When D. appeals to miners in a depressed Midlands colliery town to show solidarity with the beleaguered loyalists in his native land, Greene pitilessly writes:

'I wanted to tell him [George Bates, the local union leader] where the coal's going – to the rebels in my country.'
'Oh,' she said wearily, 'you're one of that lot, are you?'
'Yes.'
'What's it to do with Bates?'
'I want the men to refuse to work the pits.'
She looked at him with amazement. 'Refuse? Us?'
'Yes.'
'You're off your nut,' she said. 'What's it got to do with us where the coal goes?'
He turned away: It was hopeless . . .[14]

Commitment as Greene saw it emerged out of sympathy, almost out of an act of imagination, which those of narrow horizons were seldom able to make. It was a personal choice for D., and yet one which was also made impersonally out of a recognition of ethical necessity. England in *The Confidential Agent* is still remote from such choices. It remained a country which was ethically numb, or asleep. Orwell wondered whether it would take the the roar of bombs to jerk his fellow-countrymen out of 'the deep, deep sleep of England'.[15]

Ralph Harper has argued that thrillers 'are not concerned with the real or external world at all. Rather, they are written for the sake of and written about the interior life of man'.[16] On the contrary: if we leave Greene to one side, psychological insight, ethical concern, 'inner life' are the *weakest* aspects of the thriller. The complex machinery of plot and counter-plot, disguise and uncovery, are rooted in adventure tales and melodrama, not psychological insight. The 'revenge' motive in Household and Pollard is strictly conventional. It is only the exceptional practitioner like le Carré, and then not consistently or with great depth, who has sought to explore the deeper psychology and ethics of espionage. The relationship between such artefacts of popular culture and 'the real or external world', to use Harper's terminology, will express itself in versions of contemporary events which are sometimes surprising. Many writers of spy thrillers in the second half of the decade tried to link the forms and procedures of the thriller to contemporary political events. It would be surprising if they had not done so. (The spy thriller began as a way of drawing attention to the growing threat of German naval power in the Edwardian era.) But they do not necessarily retain the shape or spectrum of contemporary perceptions of those events. Indeed, the puzzling, protean, sometimes paradoxical relationship of the thriller to contemporary life, and the way ancient values of morality and revenge survive in our popular culture, give it continued relevance.

Mass-Observation's study of popular opinion about the negotiations in 1938 over the Czechoslovakia crisis points to the discrepancy between the enthusiasm for Chamberlain's 'conversations' with Hitler expressed in the popular press, and the feeling by working-class people that the 'whole tradition of England's pledges for honesty, fair play and resistance to threats' had been let down.[17] But in E. Phillips Oppenheim's 'Munich' novel, *The Spymaster* (1938), the crisis was resolved by a secret counter-espionage plan, masterminded by Admiral Cheshire of Naval Intelligence. Cheshire's plan did not involve naval mobilization, urged in 'real life' upon a reluctant Cabinet by Duff Cooper.[18] Nor did it contemplate the Prime Minister's Plan Z (a name straight out of Buchan and 'Sapper'), which would send Chamberlain flying to Germany in a last-minute plan to avert war.[19] The Admiral intended to plant truthful information about the extent of rearmament with the many foreign spies busily at work in Britain and to do so at the psychologically right moment during the 'conversations'. The idea was to get the truth to the enemy. "'They will be shown a plan of the blow we intend to strike if war comes, which will be paralysing to any hopes they might have had of success'", he explained.[20] The greatest danger to this scheme is Horace Florestan, whose activity as 'the keenest buyer of metals in the trade', shady connections with foreign interests, and terrible cruelty link him with the many arms-merchant villains in 1930s thrillers. After a last-minute race to catch Florestan at a secret aerodrome, of which England seemed to have a great excess in the thrillers of the 1930s, and a little timely gun-play, the crisis was resolved, peace assured, and a happy English people allowed to sleep soundly in their beds at night.

Perhaps most thrillers in the 1930s, and after, ended with such problematic reassurance. How did the thriller, which began as a clarion call against danger, become the unmistakable vehicle for lulling the public? It is abundantly clear that this was not only confined to right-wing thrillers. The 'politics' of *The Spymaster* is Chamberlainite, and it concludes with the success of appeasement. Even thrillers by authors at the opposite end of the political spectrum seemed to have contributed their mite to the politics of appeasement.

Consider *The Smiler with the Knife* by 'Nicholas Blake' (Cecil Day-Lewis), a thriller serialized in the *News Chronicle* in the summer of 1939 and published in October. The author – poet, fellow-traveller, countryman, philanderer – located the threat to England in traditionally the most unlikely setting of rural Devon.[21] The English Banner, rooted in the 'natural aristocracy' of the landowning class, was being used as a front organization by a secret inner conspiracy organized by the friends of Fascism. (It was like the Cagoulard conspiracy in France, organized by the best families, which sought to discredit the Popular Front government.) Sir John Strangeways, head of C Branch at Scotland Yard, asks his daughter-in-law Georgia to act as his agent within the EB. "'I'm asking you to do it for England'".[22] The aim of the conspiracy was to discredit democratic institutions, and to "'get rid of all these doddering old politicians and the greasy Jews and the agitators'".[23] Georgia's investigations lead her to Chilton Canteloe, a charismatic politician (who resembles Oswald Mosley *circa* 1931) who has devised a vast scheme to relieve poverty and unemployment by establishing co-operatives across Britain. She unmasks his role in the conspiracy, and after a series of Buchan-like adventures (she bribes one of a half-dozen Santa Clauses to let her wear his uniform to escape from a department store, and later joins a company of Englishwomen wearing little purple costumes who travel across the country doing aerobic dances) she escapes to inform Sir John of the identity of the inner conspirators.

As one might expect with Day-Lewis, the period detail is quite good. The English Banner was loosely modeled after Masonic Lodges, the British Legion and most importantly the Link, a movement which fostered Anglo-German fellowship in the 1930s. It was not explicitly designed to promote racist and Nazi ideology and thus retained an aura of respectability which was lost in the middle of the decade by the British Union of Fascists and other Nazi groups. Highly decentralized, the National Council of the Link had little control over individual branches. Members were often highly respected local citizens: aldermen, magistrates, headmasters, solicitors, local councillors, officers of the British Legion, clergymen, military officers, some of whom were stalwarts of the Labour Party and members of the Fabian Society. The West Country branches, where *The Smiler with the Knife* was set, were more 'county' than membership in the suburbs and the Midlands. Members of the Link probably did not see themselves as extremists. Rather, they wished to avoid the horrors of another war by sustaining links of friendship with the German people. There were inevitably Fascists among their number, but the public activities of the branches minimized their influence.[24] But what if such an innocuous body, mainly preoccupied with organizing talks, dances, social occasions and visits to Germany, were used as a front by an inner core of extremists?

The Smiler with the Knife is on the surface one of the beneficiaries of that change of paradigm which Ambler and Graham Greene effected earlier in the decade.[25] The politics of Buchan and 'Sapper' have been turned on their head: the baddies now are right-wingers, enemies of democracy. But the form of the thriller, and its reassuring message, remains the same: the novel ends with the arrest of the EB leaders, and with Georgia's return home to her lovely Devon garden. Although Oppenheim and Day-Lewis were on opposing political sides in the 1930s, *The Spymaster* and *The Smiler with the Knife* do not constitute opposing political alternatives within the spy novel. Rather, they share the same structure of feeling, the same reassuring defeat of 'the enemy'; and the same loyalty to a pastoral version of England, a myth of Englishness.

No 'serious' English novel of the 1930s registered the true nature of Hitlerian aggression. This was a widespread failure, from which popular culture was not exempt. Even where opposition to Fascism was the meat and drink of everyday politics, in the Labour Party and elsewhere on the left, the grasp in Britain of the nature of the threat was weak and bedevilled by pragmatism and insularity.[26] Ambler, the most political of the 1930s' espionage thriller writers, was obsessed by the dangers of international capitalism, and said nothing directly about Nazi Germany.[27] When he returned to Britain in late 1938, Tosco Fyvel was intrigued to find that his friend George Orwell was deeply pessimistic about Europe. He feared Britain would succumb to Fascism:

> . . . in the two years before the war, it is perfectly evident that it was his own Spanish experience which shaped his thinking and not the build-up of Hitler's Germany of which he knew little, about which, indeed, I think he had something of a blind spot.[28]

In Orwell's novel of this period, *Coming Up for Air* (1939), George Bowling attends a Left Book Club lecture on 'The Menace of Fascism'. *The Menace of Fascism* was a book published by John Strachey in 1933. Though they both had been at Eton, they had not met, and their only contact had been over Orwell's *The Road to Wigan Pier* about which Strachey, as a selector of the Left Book Club, made a complaint to the publisher Victor Gollancz.[29] Whatever he felt about Strachey, his picture of the speaker at the meeting was characteristically caustic. While the speaker ranted on ('. . . Democracy . . . Fascism . . . Democracy . . . Fascism . . . Democracy . . .'), Bowling closed his eyes and tried to enter the skull of the speaker:

> I saw the vision that he was seeing. . . . It's a picture of himself smashing people's faces in with a spanner. . . . Hitler's after us! Quick! Let's all grab a spanner and get together, and perhaps if we smash in enough faces they won't smash ours. Gang up, choose your Leader. Hitler's black and Stalin's white. But it might just as well be the other way about, because in the little chap's mind both Hitler and Stalin are the same. Both mean spanners and smashed faces.[30]

Totalitarianism, and not the specific threat of Hitler, was Orwell's subject.

Household, alone of the writers discussed here, seems to have known central Europe well. With a Jewish wife, Nazism was a direct and personal threat: 'My feeling for Nazi Germany had the savagery of a personal vendetta'.[31] But we will search far and wide, at the moment when the threat of war dominated the concerns of politicians and filled newspapers with screaming headlines, to find English spy novels which take these concerns as more than a useful pretext or background. It is probably best to avoid genetic or structural explanations. Espionage thrillers do not necessarily have to offer reassurance, as the recently reissued Constantine FitzGibbon's *When the Kissing Had to Stop* (1960) makes clear. His powerful warning against the election of a Labour Party committed to unilateral disarmament was specific and highly political, and is now, in the age of *glasnost* and Gorbachev, offered as 'The Classic Novel of the Cold War'.[32] It was not the *form* of the thriller which was incapable of capturing the threat of Nazism. It was the age itself to which we must look for conjunctural explanations of the failure of the espionage thriller in the age of appeasement.

NOTES

1. Patricia Cockburn, *The Years of 'The Week'* (Harmondsworth, 1971), pp.224–5. Maxwell Knight specialized in this kind of penetration operation for section B(5)b of MI5. See Anthony Masters, *The Man Who Was M: The Life of Maxwell Knight* (Oxford, 1984). Joan Miller, recruited at the age of 21 by MI5, one of three agents from B(5)b in the Right Club in 1939, describes her experiences in *One Girl's War: Exploits in MI5's Most Secret Station* (Dingle, Co. Kerry, 1986).
2. Ethel Lina White, *The Wheel Spins* (1936; reissued London, 1962 as *The Lady Vanishes*), p.144.

3. Leonard Mosley, *Down Stream* (London, 1939), pp.105–6. The Woolwich Arsenal case was widely regarded as one of the most professional of Maxwell Knight's achievements as a spy-runner. See Masters, *The Man Who Was M*.
4. Edgar Wallace, *The Four Just Men* (London, 1905), p.58.
5. Ibid., p.168.
6. Ibid., p.149.
7. Noted by Charles Barr in his *Ealing Studios* (New York, 1980), p.182.
8. See the discussion below of Greene's *The Confidential Agent*. Hemingway's *For Whom the Bell Tolls* (1940) is particularly interesting when seen in this context.
9. Captain Alfred Olwen Pollard, a V.C. from the first World War, was a prolific author of spy stories in the late 1930s. His autobiography, *Fire-Eater* (London, 1932), deals with his years before he became a novelist; *The Secret Pact* (London, 1940).
10. See Household's *Against the Wind* (London, 1958), pp.209–11; and *Rogue Male* (London, 1939; Harmondsworth, 1974), p.151, on motive.
11. Graham Greene, *The Confidential Agent* (London, 1939; Harmondsworth, 1978), p.117.
12. Ibid., p.60.
13. The typology of these literary forms is described in John G. Cawelti, *Adventure, Mystery, and Romance: Formula Stories as Art and Popular Culture* (Chicago and London, 1976).
14. Greene, *Confidential Agent*, p.199. There were considerably more miners than poets in the British Battalion of the International Brigades in Spain.
15. George Orwell, *The Complete Works of George Orwell*, ed. Peter Davison, Vol.6, *Homage to Catalonia* (London, 1986), pp.187.
16. Ralph Harper, *The World of the Thriller* (Cleveland, 1969), p.79.
17. Charles Madge and Tom Harrison, *Britain by Mass-Observation* (Harmondsworth, 1939), p.106.
18. Wesley K. Wark, *The Ultimate Enemy: British Intelligence and Nazi Germany 1933–1939* (Oxford, 1985), p.146.
19. John Charmley, *Chamberlain and the Lost Peace* (London, 1989), p.95.
20. E. Phillips Oppenheim, *The Spymaster* (1938; London, 1950), p.136. Oppenheim's naïveté is of course everywhere on display. Why would the enemy believe such reports? Would they not seem to be classic examples of disinformation? Among many examples, Stalin similarly was unwilling to believe the detailed reports he received about German preparations to invade Russia in 1941.
21. Sean Day-Lewis in *C. Day-Lewis: An English Literary Life* (London, 1980), pp.125–6, suggests that some of the principal locales and characters were autobiographical.
22. Nicholas Blake, *The Smiler with the Knife* (London, 1939; reissued with a new Introduction by Patricia Craig and Mary Cadogan, London, 1985), p.56.
23. Ibid., p.95.
24. Richard Griffiths, *Fellow Travellers of the Right: British Enthusiasts for Nazi Germany 1933–39* (London, 1980), pp.307–17.
25. As suggested by Graham Greene in *Ways of Escape* (London, 1980), p.72.
26. Sabine Wichert, 'The Enigma of Fascism: The British Left on National Socialism', in John Bossy and Peter Jupp (eds.), *Essays Presented to Michael Roberts* (Belfast, 1976), pp.146–58; Brigitte Granzow, *A Mirror of Nazism: British Opinion and the Rise of Hitler, 1929–33* (London, 1964).
27. See David Stafford, *The Silent Game: The Real World of Imaginary Spies* (London, 1988), pp.134–6.

28. T.R. Fyvel, *George Orwell: A Personal Memoir* (London, 1983), pp.86–7; there were only six references to Hitler in Bernard Crick's 1980 biography of Orwell.

29. Bernard Crick, *George Orwell: A Life* (Boston, 1980), p.204.

30. George Orwell, *The Complete Works of George Orwell*, ed. Peter Davison, Vol.7, *Coming Up for Air* (London, 1986), pp.153, 156–7. Arthur Koestler, who made a four-week lecture tour in England for the Left Book Club in 1938, saw nothing of the bloodthirstiness recorded by Orwell: 'Their meetings, compared with those on the Continent, were like tea parties in the vicarage; they put decency before dialectics and, even more bewilderingly, they tended to indulge in humour and eccentricity – both of which were dangerous diversions from the class struggle.' Koestler, *The Invisible Writing* (London, 1954), p.382. In this context, I think Koestler's was the more reliable account of the Left Book Club ethos.

31. Household, *Against the Wind*, p.94.

32. Reissued with a Foreword by Julian Amery (London, 1989).

Ireland in Spy Fiction

KEITH JEFFERY and EUNAN O'HALPIN

This essay examines the treatment of Ireland and Irish themes in twentieth-century spy fiction. The term is taken to include general thrillers involving espionage, terrorism or subversion. The works under consideration deal with a variety of themes arising from the complexities of the Irish question, which range from that of German intrigue in the two world wars to contemporary terrorism involving the IRA and other republican groups. Sometimes the Irish elements are incidental, as in the Sherlock Holmes story *His Last Bow* (1917); sometimes they are central, as in Gerald Seymour's *Harry's Game* (1975).[1] The treatment of Ireland and of Irish issues in such fiction raises questions about the intentions of authors and the impact of stories which cannot be addressed in detail in a brief essay such as this. What is provided here is a necessarily impressionistic survey of the treatment of Irish affairs in spy and related fiction since the turn of the century.

Ever since the 1880s Britain has been subject to sporadic bombing campaigns by Irish separatists. Britain came close to civil war on the issue of Ulster during the Irish home rule crisis of 1912–14, which absorbed the energies of its leading politicians at the expense of attending to European affairs. During the crisis both the Ulster Volunteer Force (UVF), pledged to resist home rule, and the Irish Volunteers, formed to defend it, bought large quantities of weapons from arms dealers in Germany, Britain's imperial rival. During the First World War Germany encouraged and assisted the Irish rebellion of Easter 1916, and links were maintained with some Irish separatists for the rest of the war. Irish rebels were brought back to Ireland by German submarine in 1916 and 1918, and it was widely believed in Britain that U-boats were being refuelled and replenished in remote areas along Ireland's western coast.

Between 1919 and 1921 Irish separatists fought a violent campaign against the British authorities in Ireland which ended with the grant of qualified independence to Southern Ireland, at the expense of partition from the six counties of north-east Ulster, which became known as Northern Ireland and remained within the United Kingdom. In the late 1930s the IRA established links with the German *Abwehr* and, in January 1939, launched an indiscriminate bombing campaign in England. When the Second World War broke out southern Ireland remained neutral and maintained diplomatic links with the Axis countries. For this it was

publicly excoriated as a spineless and treacherous neighbour and a haven
for Britain's enemies. The potent First World War myth of Irish succour
for German submarines was revived, and the enemy diplomatic missions in
Dublin were portrayed in Britain and America as nests of Axis spies.

There was a lull in separatist violence after 1945, although the IRA
waged a sporadic campaign of bombings and shootings along the border in
1956–62. In 1969, however, the Northern Ireland troubles erupted, and
soon resulted in considerable republican terrorism in Great Britain itself,
including the spectacular bombing of the Grand Hotel. Brighton, in 1984
in which the Prime Minister, Mrs Thatcher, came close to losing her life.

If spy fiction serves partly to reinforce popular beliefs and myths, and
to propagandize, it might be expected that Irish material would repeatedly
have been woven into British books of the genre. In fact, what is curious is
that despite the enduring nature of the Irish problem, and the close political
and cultural links which the country has with both Britain and the United
States, Ireland is characterized in spy fiction chiefly by the small amount of
attention that it has received, with the partial exception of developments
in Northern Ireland over the last 20 years. Works with Northern Ireland
backgrounds now form a distinct stream within the thriller genre.[2] In
addition, IRA members have increasingly been accorded walk-on parts
in books dealing with non-Irish themes, such as contemporary European
or Middle Eastern terrorism and even ordinary crime. Irish terrorists
now occasionally also feature in stories set in earlier eras, such as Julian
Symons's *The Detling Secret* (1982), set in 1890s England.[3] Finally, recent
years have brought the publication of a few books concerning the spill-over
of the Northern troubles into Southern Ireland, an obvious but previously
unexplored theme.

Spy fiction first found a mass audience in Edwardian Britain through
exploiting fear of Germany. Ironically in view of the later conversion to
Irish separatism which was to cost him his life, the first man to popularize
the format was Erskine Childers, who adopted it in *The Riddle of the Sands*
(1903). His intentions were patriotic: to show the public that Germany
was Britain's most likely enemy and to illustrate the country's blissful
unpreparedness for war. Childers was followed by less able but more
prolific authors warning of the German menace, the best known being
William Le Queux.

Christopher Andrew and David French have shown how 'spy fever' had
a marked influence both on popular perceptions of the German threat and
on government planning for war. The fever, however, was a strictly British
affair, and its themes were espionage and invasion assisted by Germans
already resident in Britain. The possibility that Germany might seek to
damage Britain by encouraging sedition in Ireland was not canvassed,
despite historical precedents and despite the Irish home rule crisis which

erupted just before the First World War. Yet, as events showed, the German arms dealers who supplied both Ulster and nationalist Ireland between 1912 and 1914 did far more damage to Britain's interests than the harmless assortment of waiters, barbers, musicians and cooks believed to be the Kaiser's secret vanguard.[4]

One Irish writer, George A. Birmingham, took up the theme of German interference. Birmingham was the pen-name of James Owen Hannay, a Belfast-born Anglican clergyman and liberal home ruler. His novel *The Red Hand* (1912) describes the elaborate armed preparations which Ulster unionists make to resist the imposition of home rule on the north-east of Ireland. Hannay initially intended the novel to conclude with the Germans offering direct assistance to the Ulstermen, and provoking such a revulsion of feeling that unionists and nationalists combined in the face of the common enemy. Worried about the political implications of the plot, Hannay's publishers sent the manuscript to 'a statesman of the Foreign Office', who requested that it not be published 'in view of the delicacy of the international situation at this time'.[5] Reluctantly the author removed any reference to German involvement from the conclusion, an ironic procedure since he had, in fact, correctly predicted the immediate reaction of unionists and nationalists to the outbreak of war in 1914.

The only other notable attempt by a contemporary fiction writer to argue a pre-war link between Irish politics – in this case militant separatism – and Germany came in Arthur Conan Doyle's Sherlock Holmes adventure *His Last Bow*. Conan Doyle was part-Irish, and was in favour of home rule. He was also an independent-minded man, willing to speak up for unpopular causes. Although hostile to physical force separatism, he was one of the few people in Britain to stand by Sir Roger Casement, the former consular official who sought German aid for a rebellion in Ireland and who was tried for treason in 1916. Conan Doyle was the main contributor to Casement's defence fund, and when officials tried to persuade him to withdraw his support by showing him documents proving that Casement was a homosexual, he sent them packing.[6] While *His Last Bow* was evidently written for patriotic purposes, therefore, it was plainly not intended to add to anti-Irish feeling.

The story, set on 2 August 1914, concerns Von Bork, a German master spy who since 1910 has played the 'hard-drinking, hard-riding country squire', considered 'quite a decent fellow for a German' by his English friends. In conversation, Von Bork expresses doubts whether Britain would come to the aid of her continental friends 'especially when we have stirred her up such a devil's brew of Irish civil war, window-breaking Furies [suffragettes], and God knows what to keep her thoughts at home'. Von Bork then meets his lieutenant Altamont, an elderly 'real bitter Irish-American' with 'a small goatee beard which gave him a general resemblance to the caricatures of Uncle Sam', who is 'a wonderful worker'. In fact Altamont is Sherlock Holmes, who had spent two years penetrating Von Bork's ring. He tells his friend Watson that 'I started my pilgrimage at Chicago, graduated in an Irish secret society at Buffalo, gave serious trouble to the constabulary at Skibbereen' in county Cork and 'so eventually caught the eye of a subordinate agent of Von Bork, who recommended me as a likely man'. But the only function his Irish-American background and his consequent hatred of Britain serves in the story is, disappointingly, to provide an explanation of his recruitment as a German agent in the first place. He does most of his work spying in navy towns around the coast. Von Bork's safe has rows of pigeon-holes with titles such 'as "Fords", "Harbour-defences", "Aeroplanes", "Ireland", "Egypt", "Portsmouth forts", "The Channel", "Rosyth", and a score of others. Each compartment was bristling with papers and plans', most of it disinformation supplied by Altamont.[7]

Overall, the Irish dimension in the story does not amount to much, and it does not ring true. The suggestion that the home rule crisis was German-inspired is an interesting one, since it was unionist Ulster rather than the nationalist south which first armed itself to resist the British government, but it is merely an aside and is not developed. Altamont's Irish-American background is plausible enough – the arrangements for German aid for the 1916 rising were agreed between German diplomats and Irish *émigrés* in the United States, and became known to Britain very quickly through Room 40's codebreaking – but the idea that an Irish-American agitator would have been a useful spy in England, least of all to suborn men of the Royal Navy, is not. Germany's principal object in cultivating Irish-American groups during the First World War was to encourage unrest in Ireland (an aim in which it was brilliantly successful), not to recruit men to spy in Britain.[8] Besides all this, it must be said that Von Bork himself is a most unconvincing master spy, even by the modest standards of tradecraft of real German agents in Britain. Not only does he receive Altamont openly at home, explain the operation of the combination lock on his safe and tell him all his business, but he pays him by cheque.[9]

A second British author to touch on Irish themes in contemporary patriotic spy fiction was John Buchan. A strong imperialist and a Conservative MP from 1911, in 1917–18 he was involved in covert propaganda work as Director General of Information. His Richard Hannay novels, published during and shortly after the war, carry a distinct political message. Despite the cosmic scale of German intrigue uncovered by his hero throughout the empire, ranging from espionage and industrial subversion in Britain to holy war in the east, German-aided sedition in Ireland did not attract Buchan's interest as a writer. It is only in *The Three Hostages* (1924), the fourth Hannay adventure, set in 1921, that

Ireland comes into the story at all. Although this is not strictly speaking a piece of spy fiction, the underlying premise of the book is that Britain is threatened by a vast conspiracy feeding off and manipulating the post-war chaos in international affairs. Hannay finds himself up against a powerful criminal combine whose tentacles, in the best traditions of such fictional organizations, stretch all over the world. The Irish angle is provided by Buchan's villain, the graceful, sallow-skinned, charismatic Dominick Medina, whom even the dour Ulsterman Inspector Macgillivray of Scotland Yard is moved to declare 'the handsomest being alive'. Although he is Spanish by descent, his 'people live in Ireland, or did live, till life there became impossible'. Hannay later encounters Medina's mother, a blind lady possessed of mystic powers who converses with her son in Irish. It is hard to say quite what message Buchan intended to convey to the public about Ireland, by then independent, unless it was that its denizens were an untrustworthy and fractious lot of 'sullen hobbledehoys' capable of causing trouble the world over.[10]

The dearth of Irish themes is British spy fiction of the 1910s and 1920s may simply reflect the fact that no one, author or reader, was much interested in Ireland, despite or perhaps because of actual events in that country. In British eyes Ireland was dangerous but not glamorous, and the Irish problem intractable but not exciting. In Ireland, despite the country's strong literary traditions, Irish writers evidently felt much the same. Erskine Childers, the pioneer of the patriotic spy story, had become a convert to Irish separatism and was a key Irish propagandist after the First World War, but no one in Ireland followed his lead. There was no outpouring of patriotic stories of espionage and skulduggery, whether for propaganda or for escapist purposes. The spy or agent or gunrunner, if he appears at all in the Irish writing of the times, is usually only an author's device in some broader literary endeavour. The most celebrated story of the Irish troubles, Liam O'Flaherty's *The Informer* (1925), in which a petty criminal betrays a rebel friend to the police for a small reward during the civil war, is primarily a study in individual treachery and guilt.[11]

The Second World War provides the next significant examples of Irish themes in spy fiction. Despite strong pressure Ireland remained neutral because of partition.[12] This decision presented Britain with a number of serious problems. Ireland had an open land border with Northern Ireland, and since independence there had been free movement of people between the two jurisdictions. Ireland was also of some strategic importance in naval terms, particularly after the German defeat of France left Britain isolated and dependent for survival on transatlantic shipping. It was feared that Germany might invade Ireland to encircle Britain and cut its Atlantic supply routes. Britain also expected that Germany would use Ireland as a base for espionage, and would encourage the republican movement to step up violence in Northern Ireland and Great Britain. The maintenance of a German legation in Dublin was particularly worrying, and a good deal of effort went into monitoring its activities and communications. In fact, the legation confined itself almost entirely to straightforward political reporting, the German minister taking the view that to engage in covert work would only antagonize the Irish authorities and might jeopardize Irish neutrality. Germany's alliance with the IRA, which was the responsibility of the *Abwehr* and which did not involve the Dublin legation, never bore much fruit. Although a number of agents were sent to Ireland between 1940 and 1943, they were all captured by the Irish security forces before they could fulfil their missions.[13] From the outset, and despite its declared position of pious neutrality, the Irish government secretly co-operated very closely with British security agencies, the links being maintained through the army's G2 intelligence directorate and MI5.[14]

German intrigue in wartime Ireland has been a theme of a number of books. An early example is Peter Cheyney's *Dark Duet* (1942). Cheyney, a journalist of Irish descent and a one-time Fascist, was already the author of successful and rather lurid thrillers.[15] *Dark Duet* describes the violent adventures of two counter intelligence officers tracking German spies who, it emerges, mostly belong to a network controlled by agents based near Dublin. 'We're nearest, and we do most of the work', explains one German, though infiltration into Britain has become very difficult because 'the damned English get more cautious every day, and the Irish are a sick headache'. The Irish episode involves the killing by his comrades of a German spy thought to be wavering in his commitment to the war. *Dark Duet* is noteworthy because it reinforces the contemporary myth that Ireland was a safe haven for German spies, but it does so only in passing and without malice. Apart from the fact that it rains all the time, and that the roads are pot-holed, there is nothing particularly Irish about the setting and there are no Irish characters involved. While the book does presume that German agents could operate with impunity in Ireland, it also suggests that England is full of spies. The two British heroes are ruthless killers, distinguishable from the assortment of Nazis they slaughter only by their nationality. The book describes with relish how they use 'Process 5' (assassination) on one suspect, as 'there is nothing official on the woman . . . You can't *prove* anything'.[16] Overall, German spying from Ireland is treated simply as a fact of wartime life, and the book makes no attempt to denounce Irish neutrality or to suggest collusion between the Irish government and Germany.

Brian Garfield's novel *The Paladin* (1980) adopts a different and more censorious approach in portraying wartime Ireland. The book describes the adventures of 'Christopher Creighton', a 16-year-old schoolboy recruited to spy for Winston Churchill in the summer of 1940. His first mission is

to travel to the north-western Irish border county of Donegal to check
for signs of German submarine activity. When he reaches the coast he
discovers makeshift but functioning submarine pens, where U-boats are
refuelled and replenished. These installations are guarded by a combination
of German personnel and Irish soldiers. The hero eventually makes his
way to Londonderry in Northern Ireland. Once Churchill receives this
information, he uses it secretly to coerce the Irish government into ending
their assistance to Germany.

Garfield styles his book 'a novel based on fact', and cites his hero
Creighton as the source for his stories. As the Irish section of the book
demonstrates, Creighton was evidently educated in the Dr Josephine Butler
school of historical research.[17] His Irish adventure takes place in what both
he and Churchill term 'the Republic', a remarkable piece of prescience since
southern Ireland adopted that style only in 1948. More importantly, both
the surviving records and the recollections of British and Irish intelligence
officers confirm that the possibility of German submarines being succoured
or supplied with intelligence along the west coast of Ireland was thoroughly
investigated in 1939 and 1940, as it had been during the First World War.[18]
No evidence of such activities was found then or after the war, although
U-boats were used to land agents on a number of occasions. The additional
suggestion that the Irish government allowed Germany to establish a U-boat
base a few miles across the border from the key port of Londonderry is
doubly absurd. Irish foreign policy was geared towards keeping the country
out of the war, an attitude which Germany applauded. Providing the British
with an incontrovertible *casus belli* in 1940 would have been insane. By the
time that *The Paladin* was written a good deal had been published on Irish
neutrality; neither 'Christopher Creighton' nor his amanuensis lets this get
in the way of their tale.

The theme of German intrigue in Ireland is taken up to much better
effect in another novel published in 1980, *Emerald Decision*, by David
Grant. This book links events in 1940 with the present troubles, through
the interesting though far-fetched device of the existence of a guilty secret
in the war record of the British minister responsible for Northern Ireland.
In order discreetly to wreck crucial Northern Ireland peace negotiations,
the IRA attempt to have the minister exposed by the hero MacBride,
an American thriller writer investigating Germany's wartime designs on
Ireland. They manipulate his enquires to ensure that he discovers the
appropriate evidence. Continuity between 1940 and 1980 is also maintained
through the machinations of the Hun: in 1940 the Nazis, in 1980 the East
German secret service which arms and largely directs the IRA. At the heart
of the book is the build-up to and aftermath of a small-scale German landing
in county Cork on Ireland's southern coast, the prelude to a full invasion.
The plot centres on a British agent who discovers a network of German

spies, including a treacherous Royal Navy officer who is the Admiralty's intelligence man in the area, making preparations for the invasion with the help of the IRA. Although the author has a feel for the Cork coastline, his portrayal of conditions in wartime Ireland is fanciful. Despite a good deal of shooting and killing in town and country, and the eventual arrival of German paratroopers, the pervasive Irish wartime security system, embracing the police, army, local defence force and coastal observer units, does not feature at all. A German officer, bemused by the lack of opposition, asks one of the protagonists: 'Where is the Irish army?' Despite wartime rationing, everyone seems to have a car and, stranger still, petrol to put in it. There are also some curiosities at the British end of events: Winston Churchill, fresh from his appearance in *The Paladin*, remains under the illusion that Ireland is a 'Republic'. The British foil the invasion attempt by re-laying mines in a channel previously swept by the Germans, and thus they destroy the submarines carrying the main invasion force. Churchill also takes one of those tough but expedient decisions routinely accorded him in fiction when he allows a British convoy to be wiped out in the same minefield. As well as concealing the fact that the navy has discovered the German-cleared channel, this secures the death of a pessimistic adviser of Roosevelt's on a mission to observe Britain's impending defeat. *Emerald Decision* is, its plot notwithstanding, surprisingly unpolemical about Irish neutrality: indeed, when describing the Irish Prime Minister de Valera as 'crafty, and not without courage', Churchill's 'eyes misted for a moment'.[19]

   A relatively common thriller technique is to weave a story around some actual historical event. In Anthony Burton's *The Coventry Option* (New York 1976), an IRA man in England in alliance with the *Abwehr* sets up a radio transmitter to guide the Luftwaffe to bomb Coventry in November 1940. Other novels claim historical veracity for the events they narrate. Like *The Paladin*, Belfast-born Jack Higgins's *The Eagle has Landed* (1975, revised edition 1982) claims to be based on fact. It deals with a German attempt to abduct Winston Churchill in 1943. Its Irish element is provided by the IRA killer and littérateur Liam Devlin,[20] rescued by the *Abwehr* from a Spanish jail in 1940 after capture during the Spanish Civil War, who is brought to Berlin to help with operations into Ireland. Devlin whiles away his time giving tutorials in English at the University of Berlin, while the *Abwehr*'s attempts to spy in Ireland collapse ignominiously. As a character Devlin is a curious combination of plausibility and absurdity. In his background he resembles a composite of three Irishmen, Sean Russell, Frank Ryan and Francis Stuart, all of whom advised the Germans on Irish affairs while in Berlin in 1940. One was an uncomplicated gunman, the second a left-wing republican who had fought in the Spanish Civil War, and the third a writer, lecturer and occasional broadcaster in English on German radio.[21] Devlin is eventually brought into the kidnap plan, and is dropped by parachute into Ireland. He crosses the border into Northern Ireland, and makes his way to Norfolk, where the kidnapping is to take place, in the guise of an Irishman invalided out of the British Army. Devlin is a rather strange choice to send to East Anglia, since he is already known to and wanted by both the British and the Irish police. Unlike almost everyone involved in the plan, however, he escapes death. He resurfaces in an epilogue, when Jack Higgins discovers he is 'a prime architect of the Provisional IRA movement' and interviews him in Belfast in the early 1970s.[22] This rather unconvincing resurrection seems to be designed as much to tie up some loose romantic ends of the plot as to emphasize the continuity of republican violence against Britain.

Two novels published in the 1940s illustrate the IRA playing no more than a marginal role. *Lieutenant Commander* (1944), one of George A. Birmingham's last books, deals with the smuggling of an English airman, who also happens to be a jockey, from Ballymoy on the coast of Connacht, where his plane has crashed, to Newmarket racecourse in England, just in time to win the 2,000 Guineas on a horse part-owned by Commander John Vandaleur VC, a retired Anglo-Irish naval officer living in Ballymoy. The local IRA man, Murphy, recognizable by his 'Sinn Fein quiff' (a distinctive hairstyle apparently sported by republicans) is an impediment to this until, moved by the substantial gains to be made by betting on the horse, he co-operates with the local police and Vandaleur to get the jockey out of neutral Ireland. The closest the book gets to treating serious secret information is Birmingham's comment on two bookmaker's touts: 'like the intelligence officers of nations at war, they knew that even the smallest piece of gossip might have its value'. For Birmingham, who mostly wrote light social comedy of the Somerville-and-Ross variety, the relationships between militant republicans, the Irish police and British loyalists, even during the Second World War, were apparently easy-going enough for him to envisage these divergent groups combining in a sporting venture. The serious business of politics is firmly excluded from the narrative. As Vandaleur unoriginally remarks, 'politics are the curse of this country'.[23]

F.L. Green's *Odd Man Out* (1945) is a tense psychological study of a gunman, Johnny Murtah, on the run in Belfast after a bungled wages-snatch. Murtah is chief of an unnamed 'Revolutionary Organization', clearly modelled on the IRA. He and his colleagues are 'menacing, desperate men', but they are also heroes, possessing 'the immeasurable heat of courage, resource, patience and unyielding resolve'.[24] Murtah's nerve, however, has been affected by imprisonment and months of hiding in a cramped inner-city house; he shoots a man dead during the robbery and is himself wounded. Although policemen appear only rarely in the narrative, Murtah's response to their relentless pursuit gives the story much of its power. Murtah, too, is a fugitive from his own past and represents one of the classic genre types: the loner who has lived by violence ultimately facing nemesis. This type recurs repeatedly in novels set in the current Irish troubles.

Between the end of the Second World War and the renewed outbreak of civil disorder in 1969 only a very few 'Irish' thrillers were published. James Bond passed the island by, although in Ian Fleming's *From Russia, with Love* (1957) the chief executioner of SMERSH is a man called Donovan Grant, the illegitimate son of a German professional weight-lifter and a Southern Irish waitress, who had briefly met in Belfast. Grant, a psychopath, is brought up in 'Aughmacloy' on the Irish border, and becomes a strongarm man for both republican subversives and local smugglers. He later joins the British Army, but defects to the Russians after being posted to Berlin. Here, perhaps, Fleming was inspired by information which he could have acquired while personal assistant to the Director of Naval Intelligence, Admiral J. H. Godfrey, in 1939–42. Bearing in mind the Admiralty's special worries about German activity in Ireland, Fleming must have known that in April 1940 a German agent, Ernest Weber-Drohl, appeared in the Dublin District Court charged with entering Ireland illegally. Weber-Drohl was actually a former professional wrestler and weight-lifter who had worked in Ireland before the First World War as 'Atlas the Strong'. He succeeded in persuading the court that he had merely returned to Ireland in search of two illegitimate sons fathered during his earlier visit, and escaped with a fine of £3.

In 1960, using the pseudonym Harry Patterson, Jack Higgins published *Cry of the Hunter*, which deals with the theme of the disenchanted terrorist and is set historically in the 1956–62 IRA campaign. Martin Fallon, a retired IRA commander turned thriller-writer, is persuaded to return to Northern Ireland to spring his successor, Patrick Rogan, from police custody. Fallon succeeds, but quickly discovers that Rogan is little more than a common killer ('You're just about the lowest rat I've ever come across'). Fallon eventually kills Rogan and himself dies from gunshot wounds just as he reaches sanctuary once more across the border in the Irish Republic. This book is significant in that it is the first of a kind of novel which has become very common since 1969 and which addresses the violence of Irish terrorism with bleak realism and also attempts to examine the morally and spiritually corrosive effect of this violence. Fallon's contempt for Rogan's promiscuous killing is regarded simply as a sign of weakness by the younger man. Rogan is fighting a 'total' war, in which there can be no scruples: 'That's what I'm here for. To kill people. That's what the Organization needs.' But there is also a social and educational gulf between the two: Fallon is university-educated, Rogan is not. 'The Organization', reflects Fallon, 'has to take what it can get these days . . . They aren't getting the educated idealists like they used to.' Here Patterson touches on the social and political context of Irish political violence, and indicates another common theme: that of tension between the generally middle-class, educated idealists and the proletarian gunmen and bombers. In the end Fallon comes to realize the futility of it all: 'I'm just a dead man walking . . . [and] have been since the day I joined the Organization'.[25]

A legacy of the the 1956–62 campaign occurs in *Vendetta in Connemara* (1968), by the romantic novelist Nora Kent. A developing love affair between a holiday-making British physiotherapist and tall, good-looking Clive Conway is given extra spice by the attempts of Niall O'Flaherty to kill Conway in revenge for the death of his younger brother during a border attack in 1959. Conway had been a member of the 'B-Specials' – the wholly-Protestant Northern Ireland part-time reserve police force, whose excesses during rioting in 1969 led to their disbandment. This force (erroneously described by the author as the 'Ulster Special Branch') was vilified by Northern republicans and scarcely ever receives credit for anything at all, save the exacerbation of tension in Northern Ireland. *Vendetta in Connemara* is unique in containing an admirable, sympathetic, romantic hero who is also a B-Special.

The incompetence of the police and intelligence agencies in the Republic is the underlying message of Andrew Garve's thin tale, *The House of Soldiers* (1962). The reader is asked to believe that the authorities have not the slightest inkling at all that a heavily-armed group of 200 fanatics is planning to use a historical pageant as cover for a coup d'état. The plot is only exposed by a mild-mannered archaeology professor. This is an impressive example of individual initiative (and, perhaps, a precursor for Indiana Jones), but wildly improbable, especially bearing in mind another staple of the genre: the ubiquity of the Irish informer. One other novel published during this period, *The Invisible Evil* (1963), by Robert Gaines, deals with Ulster Protestant activists who attempt to blow up the British House of Commons while the Prime Minister is speaking about a plan for the unification of Ireland.

Since renewed and persistent violence broke out in Northern Ireland in the summer of 1969[26] a comparatively large number of thrillers has been written about various aspects of the 'troubles'. In preparing this essay we have reviewed over 50 such novels, covering the security situation in Northern Ireland itself, as well as Irish and Irish-related terrorist activity elsewhere in Ireland, Great Britain, Europe and North America.[27]

A Little Bit British (1970) written by an Ulsterman, Martin Waddell, who had already made a name for himself as an author of comedy thrillers, was perhaps the very first of the 'troubles' novels. Completed in September 1969, it comprises the secret diary of a fervent Orangeman, Augustus Harland, for the violent first two weeks in August 1969. Although not strictly a thriller, the novel does contain an interesting example of 'covert action'. Harland discovers that his daughter's boyfriend, whom he had thought to be a respectable Englishman, had actually 'come over to Northern Ireland at the behest of certain Republican and Anarchist (Anti-Christ) organizations to foment civil disorder'.[28] The youth had set up an illegal radio transmitter, and had been broadcasting subversive sentiments from the outside W.C. at the rear of Harland's house in 'Boyne Villas'. The novel, too, wittily illustrates aspects of Protestant loyalist mentality.

The stream of spy fiction and thrillers proper began soon afterwards. Following Martin Waddell's prompt example, two other Ulster-born writers got novels out in 1972. Jack Higgins returned to an Irish theme with *The Savage Day* in which a corrupt British officer, Vaughan, is sprung from a Greek prison by the SIS on condition that he worked to prevent arms and gold from reaching the IRA. Shaun Herron, a Protestant born in Carrickfergus and educated in Belfast, but who subsequently emigrated to Canada, gave a Northern Irish setting to *Through the Dark and Hairy Wood* (1972), the third of his books about John Miro, a retired CIA agent trying to lead a quiet life. Miro finds both British Army intelligence and the IRA worried and perplexed by the attempts of a mysterious terrorist group to precipitate a complete destabilization of the province by, for example, abducting children and elderly Presbyterian ministers. What Herron has in common with Waddell is that, within the context of their novels, both writers show Protestant extremists as representing a serious force in the Northern Ireland situation. This is unusual, since for the most part, the Northern Ireland problem has been simplistically perceived as a violent struggle between the IRA (or some analogous republican group) and the British. This perception undermines the veracity of Irish spy novels as much as it has, at times, handicapped security policy in Northern Ireland.

Herron is one of a number of authors who have taken the opportunity to include an Irish angle in a continuing series of thrillers. The first of the Miro books[29] was published in 1969 and was set substantially in Canada. In the second[30] Miro has moved to a house in the west of Ireland, but in this novel the location has only scenic significance for the plot. Other series have cashed in on the troubles. The exploits of Joe Gall, 'freelance super spy . . . America's ace hit man, [who] accepts contracts from American intelligence to bounce around the world liquidating difficult problems before they become acute embarrassments to the United States government',[31] are dealt with in more than 20 books, including *Joe Gall: The Shankill Road Contract* (New York, 1973), by James A. Phillips, writing as Philip Atlee. Richard Camellion, 'Death Merchant', is another private-sector agent devoted to helping the CIA out of little local difficulties, such as in *Death Merchant: The Shamrock Smash* (New York, 1980) by Joseph Rosenberger. A similar kind of book is Steve White's *The Fighting Irish* (New York, 1982), the fourth in a series about a group of mercenaries calling themselves S-Com, or Strategic Commandos. S-Com are hired to 'root out the true terrorists' by an American company with a factory in Northern Ireland which has recently been bombed. With a mixture of cartoon violence, low comedy and the usual gratuitous sex, the novel depicts every contending group in Northern Ireland as being equally repellent. The security forces rule by torture and repression. A unit of British paratroops is particularly sinister: 'their function was secret and simple. Needle civilian terrorists into violent response and wipe them out'.[32] Ultimately S-Com, the Provisional IRA and loyalist paramilitaries actually combine to destroy the 'real terrorists'. They turn out to be a Communist commando, who helpfully identify themselves by wearing orange armbands emblazoned with a green hammer and sickle. The most exotic of these series novels is *Furie à Belfast* (Paris 1974), by Gérard de Villiers. It is also the only non-English language spy novel about the troubles we have discovered.[33] The detail is good, the locations are well researched, and even the *'argot irlandais'* is impressive. But the plot is preposterous. Prince Malko Linge, an central European aristocrat and experienced secret agent, has been engaged by the CIA to discover the fate of one of their men in Belfast. Malko succeeds and also uncovers a Soviet plan to exploit the IRA.

A significant category of novels is those written by journalists who have worked in Northern Ireland. In the words of one commentator, 'these documentary thrillers can be seen as the fruits of their authors' tours of duty as political tourists'.[34] As might be expected, the novels all tend to include good technical and corroborative detail. *The Bomb that could Lip-read* (1974) by Donald Seaman, a *Daily Express* journalist, is 'dedicated to the officers and men of "Felix"' (the British Army's bomb disposal branch) and contains much interesting information about constructing bombs and the security techniques for countering them. *Harry's Game* (1975), by Gerald Seymour, who was a TV reporter in Belfast from 1969 to 1976, is perhaps the best of these journalist novels and is quite convincing on police and intelligence methods and the frequently strained relations between the Royal Ulster Constabulary (RUC) Special Branch and the military. Seymour's subsequent novel, *Field of Blood* (1985) is also impressively realistic and concerns the difficulties the security forces have in securing and sustaining a major republican informant. The novel reflects the real problems posed by the 'supergrass' or 'converted terrorist' (the official term) system which operated in Northern Ireland in the early 1980s.[35]

Inside knowledge certainly seems to have informed *The Patriot Game* (1973), by John de St. Jorre and Brian Shakespeare, two London journalists who had formerly served in the British Diplomatic Service. The intelligence aspects of this novel are especially good and the authors have left little clues for the informed reader to indicate their own specialist knowledge. The RUC Special Branch, as was the case in reality, are joined by British officers with colonial experience in Palestine and Kenya. SIS and MI5 are strongly competitive, with SIS upsetting their MI5 colleagues by muscling in on the Irish scene. The plot of the book concerns a disillusioned IRA man, James Grogan, himself a former soldier in the British Special Air Service (SAS) regiment, who leaves Northern Ireland on a lone mission in Great Britain. Grogan considers planting a bomb at the 'Government Communications Centre' near Bath, an establishment which 'had grown out of the famous code-breaking team that had cracked the German Secret Service's cyphers during the Second World War'.[36] The allusion is clearly to the Government Communications Headquarters (GCHQ), the principal British Sigint agency, which is located at Cheltenham, not far from Bath. The reference to its wartime achievement is noteworthy, coming as it did in the year before Group Captain Winterbotham's celebrated exposé, *The Ultra Secret*, was published. Grogan eventually decides to bomb the headquarters of the SIS, which six years earlier had been removed from Westminster to 'Millenium House' in London EC 3. The real headquarters of the SIS did move out of Westminster in the 1960s, but to Century House in SE 1.

Harry Finn, the central character of *In Connection with Kilshaw* (1974), by a South African journalist Peter Driscoll, has a realistic Army intelligence background. Having begun in the Intelligence Corps, he had moved to the Field Security Branch and the Special Investigation Branch, and worked in Malaya and Cyprus. His controller Partington, however, who is something senior in British Intelligence, has a less credible background. During the war he was in a British Intelligence Unit in Dublin, apparently assisting the Irish authorities to deal with IRA internees in Mountjoy Prison. The plot crucially turns on some contacts with republicans Partington had maintained from that time.

There is a sub-group of journalist novels which concern themselves with the impact of the troubles and the security forces on the Catholic-nationalist community. In Jimmy Breslin's ironic *World Without End, Amen* (New York, 1973) a New York policeman, suspended from duty for beating up a black suspect, comes to Ulster to visit his family. While in the Belfast ghetto he himself becomes the victim of official violence. In *The Prisoner's Wife* (New York, 1981), Jack Holland describes some of the techniques used by the security forces in (as the dust-jacket announces) the 'deadly game played by the police and the guerrillas struggling for supremacy in the blood-stained streets of Belfast'. In order to demoralize the Provisionals' supporters, the police, for example, quietly spread the word that Nora, wife of a prominent imprisoned Provo, is having an affair with a visiting journalist. Desmond Hamill's *Bitter Orange* (1979) is an everyday story of Catholic West Belfast folk. The father of the Malone family has died of a heart attack following his attempts to prevent rioters from burning down a neighbouring house. One son, Vincent, is involved with the IRA, but is 'kneecapped' unjustly as a suspected 'tout' (informer). After a city-centre bomb leaves Vincent's sister and girlfriend terribly injured (the sister loses three limbs), he begins a personal bombing campaign against Protestant targets. His twin brother does not sympathize with the IRA and debates matters with Vincent. The Malones' family life breaks down under the manifold strains. In security terms, the book contains much detail about the running of a terrorist bombing campaign, the attendant technical problems and its wider psychological and social impact.[37]

A final type of the journalist novel comprises those written by British-based authors, and which deal with events in Great Britain itself. Chapman Pincher, the well-known writer on intelligence and security affairs, fic-tionalized many of his journalistic concerns in *The Eye of the Tornado* (1976), which recounts a very nearly successful Soviet attempt to subvert the country using various front organizations, including the IRA who threaten to set off a captured nuclear device. Sir Mark Quinn, Director-General of SIS, solemnly warns that 'the links between the IRA and Russia go right back to 1927'. Britain, in any case, had suffered from 'many years of Socialist softness and indecision' and was ripe for a Communist coup. MI5's counter-subversion capabilities 'had been progressively weakened by cuts and changes imposed by successive Labour governments'. After the coup has successfully been reversed Quinn reflects that 'the only thing that can arouse this nation out of its lethargy is a really convulsive shock'.[38] Sentiments like this, held within the British intelligence community, are thought to have prompted discussion of direct action against Labour governments in the 1960s and 1970s.[39] The other novel in this category, *Operation 10* (1982), by the former BBC Political Editor, Hardiman Scott, has no strong political message, but describes the kidnapping of Mrs Thatcher by the Provisional IRA. Other novels which concentrate exclusively on IRA bombing teams in Britain are G. W. Target, *The Patriots* (1974) and Paul Theroux, *The Family Arsenal* (1976).

A few novels about the troubles have been written by politicians. Although intelligence is not central for any of them, they can be revealing regarding the politician's perception of security matters and security agencies. Douglas Hurd, the senior British Conservative (who has written several thrillers with Andrew Osmond) published *Vote to Kill* in 1975. Events in Northern Ireland have precipitated a political crisis in London and there are widespread demands to bring the British Army 'home'. The Prime Minister asserts that 'no military solution is possible. No political solution can be imposed from here',[40] and the army must stay to hold the peace until the Protestants and Catholics agree some solution among themselves. A largely reactive security policy such as this which, *faute de mieux*, has more often than not existed in Northern Ireland, is anathema to most thriller-writers. It is, literally, not very thrilling. Tales of violent action and derring-do, however, can powerfully influence the popular image of the conflict. Two Northern Ireland politicians, one Protestant and one Catholic, have ventured into fiction. In *The Last Ditch* (Belfast, 1981), Roy Bradford, a former Cabinet Minister in the Northern Ireland unionist government who served in military intelligence during the Second World War, has set his thriller in the context of deep disagreements between London and local Ulster politicians over security policy. Not only does the book convincingly, and presumably accurately, depict the security policy-making process in action, but it also provides a vivid picture of Protestant hopes, fears and capabilities. More recently, Danny Morrison, Director of Publicity for Sinn Fein, the legal political wing of the Provisional IRA, has written *West Belfast* (Cork, 1989), which looks at the impact of the troubles in the early 1970s on a Catholic family in that part of the city. In the book Morrison has sought to explain why ordinary people have resorted to the armed struggle when 'everything mitigated [*sic*] against violence: the family structure, the church, morality, the awesome power of the British army'.[41] The book provides a perspective on Belfast republicanism and the motivations behind the IRA.

Novels by members of the security forces are even rarer than those by politicians. *A Breed of Heroes* (1981) is by Alan Judd (a pseudonym), who served in Northern Ireland on the military side. It is a comic novel which covers the four-month tour of one British battalion to Northern Ireland. Here we have grassroots security and intelligence work, together with convincing detail about military tactics in inner-city Belfast. The cynical analysis of one company commander, moreover, rings true for the army's view of the situation: 'Northern Ireland is perfectly simple really . . . All you have to do is to thump 'em when they step out of line, and the rest of the time leave 'em alone'.[42]

Apart from Judd's book, there have been some well-informed novels concentrating on the army and police. Sarah Michaels' *Summary Justice* (1988) is very authentic about the RUC, especially the Special Branch and its relations with the rest of the force. Barney Somerville, an RUC inspector with a lot of army covert operations experience, turns vigilante after his wife and children die in a bomb attack meant for him. He kills a substantial number of IRA men and any police or soldiers who get in his way. With the help of the Northern Ireland head of MI5, he uncovers a conspiracy between republican and loyalist terrorists, a senior Special Branch officer and millionaire businessmen to protect racketeering and arms dealing operations. The book implies that the crucial actors in the security effort come from the intelligence community. Cecil Rose, the MI5 controller, had been responsible for new covert hard-line tactics, including a 'shoot-to-kill' policy, and he has the direct authority of the Prime Minister in London to take charge of affairs in Northern Ireland.

Another 'police' novel, G.F. Newman's, *The Testing Ground* (1987), also touches on the interaction of the RUC and intelligence agencies. In effect this is a fictionalized account of the 'Stalker affair', in which a senior British policemen, John Stalker, was brought in to investigate the circumstances surrounding the killing of six people by the security forces in late 1982.[43] Like Stalker, Newman's character, John Bentham, is taken off the investigation before it is quite complete. But he discovers close links between the RUC Special Branch, the SAS, MI5 and SIS, corrupt policemen covering up for each other on the grounds of their common membership of the Masonic Order, and a homosexual vice ring centred on the 'King's House Community Home for Boys'. Among the judges and senior civil servants involved with the boys' home was Sir Michael Newfield, Security Co-ordinator in the province. In the end Bentham compromises and uses the information he has gathered to protect his police career, rather than ending it gloriously as a 'whistle-blower'. But in any case the real power lies with the security establishment and the strong common interest the RUC and intelligence agencies have in not washing their dirty Irish linen in public. Newman's underlying thesis is clearly critical of the establishment cover-up, and the reader is no doubt meant to draw instructive parallels with the real-life Stalker affair. The names of his characters indicate this: for example, John Bentham/John Stalker and Sir Michael Newfield/Sir Maurice Oldfield (Security Co-ordinator 1979–80).[44] Presumably Newman's publishers' lawyers read the typescript closely before publication.

A number of novels has been published taking a Republic of Ireland perspective and with important characters coming from the Southern security forces. The lurking presence of the IRA and the Northern violence in Bartholomew Gill's 'McGarr' detective stories, illustrates the extent to which the Northern Ireland unrest has spilled over into the South. Peter McGarr is head of the Murder Squad in Dublin and Gill's stories are superior murder mysteries. On occasion McGarr has to deal with terrorism directly. In *McGarr at the Dublin Horse Show* (New York 1979), the policeman is faced with a terrorist attack during the Dublin Horse Show. His problem in *McGarr and the Method of Descartes* (New York 1984) is to stop a planned assassination of the Protestant politician Ian Paisley, which is intended to foment civil war in the North, provoke the withdrawal of the British and finally break the power of the Northern Protestants. There is some reflection about the nature of police and intelligence work in Ambrose Clancy's *Blind Pilot* (New York, 1980). Raymond Murray, the Trinity College, Dublin, and Oxford-educated 'wonder boy' of the Irish Special Branch, thinks that his deputy, Costello, is too 'soft and romantic', qualities which he believes are 'incompatible with police work'.[45] But Costello's intuitive approach succeeds very well indeed when he takes charge after Murray is killed. A similar standpoint (though hardly one to follow slavishly) is revealed by Cecil Rose, the MI5 man in *Summary Justice*, when he advises: 'Don't clutter your mind with facts like our Special Branch colleagues . . . We have to think ahead. It's no use relying on Intelligence source reports'.[46]

John Brady has written two admirable novels set in southern Ireland. In *A Stone of the Heart* (1988), Sergeant Matt Minogue of the Dublin Murder Squad is asked to investigate the death of a student at Trinity College, Dublin. He discovers that an English lecturer in psychology and a retired Irish Army captain with an administrative post at the College are closet republicans, involved in a scheme to smuggle arms through Dublin into the North. A number of police get killed by some IRA volunteers down for the arms operation and by a mysterious 'Yank', the link man from the foreign (American?) end of the smuggling operation. The nameless 'Yank' eventually dies in a bloody shoot-out while the Trinity psychologist and an innocent girl drive north. Minogue follows by helicopter, to find that the Special Branch have arranged to let the car go through into Northern Ireland so that the Northern security forces can get the credit for intercepting it. The occupants get shot up by the British Army and RUC when the psychologist tries to drive through a checkpoint. Minogue is restrained by the Special Branch, who tell him that as an ordinary detective he just doesn't understand how things work along the border. Brady's *Unholy Ground* (1989), is among the very best of the Irish spy novels. A retired British agent is murdered in Dublin, and Minogue finds himself involved in a lethal intelligence game which is likely to cause an international incident and wreck the imminent Anglo-Irish Border Security Conference. As in Brady's first novel, one of the book's qualities is that it treats the Irish police as intelligent and capable players in the drama, rather than 'stage Irish' comic relief.

Apart from the early troubles novels of Waddell and Herron (and, to a certain extent, Sarah Michael's *Summary Justice* and Roy Bradford's *The Last Ditch*), the Protestants of the North have received fairly short shrift in the literature. Andrew Lane's *The Ulsterman* (1979) follows the same general model as *Summary Justice*. The hero, Detective Christian Boggs, is an embittered Protestant RUC officer who decides that counter-terrorism is the only answer since 'the permissive laws were all geared in favour of the criminal'.[47] In *Operation Emerald* (1985), Dominic McCartan represents the Protestant paramilitary group 'Emerald' as posing as serious a threat to political progress as the IRA. The group is led by a senior unionist politician, a Presbyterian clergyman, a merchant banker and a retired British Army general. It has ample finance and arms, some of which have been acquired jointly with the IRA in order to secure discount for bulk purchase. The plot is more than usually incredible, and falls within the 'omnipotence of intelligence' category of thriller. The 'Commander of British Intelligence in Northern Ireland' has, with American co-operation, fomented a fiendishly clever covert operation by which all the 'crack troops' of the IRA and the Protestant paramilitaries concentrate on the Emerald headquarters for a final showdown. Those terrorists who are not killed in the ensuing battle are finished off with nerve gas administered by two CIA men. Thus, satisfactorily, 'the principal forces of sectarian violence in Ulster had . . . been removed in a single calculated act of modern warfare'.[48]

There is nothing so simplistic in Maurice Leitch's excellent *Silver's City* (1981), in which 'Silver' Steele, leader of a Protestant paramilitary group, but suspected of disloyalty, is sprung from police custody in hospital and later hunted by his own side. The novel graphically reveals some of the pressures under which terrorist organizations operate. There is also a moment when one of Silver's colleagues, in charge of the operation to free him, ponders that it is as important to have information about your own side as about the enemy. He had included a girl in his team, and

> had anticipated how valuable she would prove if and when some chit of a nurse decided on throwing a fit of hysterics. Curious how much more afraid they always were of their own kind in such a situation. Knowledge like that, and the use of it, reflected Galloway, was the real 'intelligence', not the other sort, the messing about with street-maps and timetables, that Bonner and his boy scouts set such store by.[49]

Blind Pilot and Ian St James's *The Balfour Conspiracy* (1981) both exemplify the internationalization (as it were) of the Irish thriller. In *The Balfour Conspiracy* Irish expertise is exploited by Palestinians, Libyans and an unexpected Taiwanese fanatic. *Blind Pilot* has a sexy German Baader-Meinhof terrorist teaming up with a romantic Irish-American and a strongly socialist Provo. Palestinians are popular partners for Irish gunman. In Gerald Seymour's *The Glory Boys* (1976), introspective Ciaran McCoy, a Provo from Crossmaglen in south Armagh, goes to London to help a Palestinian group kill a visiting Israeli atomic scientist. Walter Nelson in his novel *The Minstrel Code* (1979) covers most of the likely possibilities with a group of IRA gunmen, two German anarchists and a Japanese Red Army psychopath, financed and run by the fanatically anti-Israeli Professor Ahmed ibn Abdullah who is based in Syria. The Irish gunman (or woman), experienced and hardened by the years of warfare in Northern Ireland, has now become an almost indispensable partner – indeed a cliché – in any international terrorist operation.

The Minstrel Code, in which the group hold Queen Elizabeth hostage in Buckingham Palace, illustrates a common device in the genre: the spectacular terrorist exploit. This usually involves the kidnapping or attempted assassination of some prominent figure. Queen Elizabeth is also threatened in *The Sovereign Solution* (New York, 1979), by Michael N. MacNamara, and in *Hennessy* (1975)[50], by Max Franklin, where the eponymous hero threatens to blow up the State Opening of Parliament. There is an elaborate Irish National Liberation Army (INLA) – a particularly violent republican splinter-group – plan to assassinate the Queen at Epsom on Derby Day in Peter Lauder's *Noble Lord* (1986). The project is backed up with over $15 million of Arab money, used to buy a racehorse. But the plan is foiled after an Antiguan police sergeant turns up in England with vital information at the last moment. The Pope is the target in Jon Cleary's *Peter's Pence* (1974) and Jack Higgins's *Confessional* (1985), while in *Blood Scenario* (New York 1980), by Peter Spain, IRA terrorists plot to take over the United States by kidnapping the President. A real IRA assassination, that of Lord Mountbatten in 1979, is written into *Juniper* (1987), by James Murphy. In this case MI5 are behind the IRA killers. They decide to remove Mountbatten because he is publicly beginning to doubt the value of nuclear weapons, and so endangering British national security. Buildings are not immune from attack. As noted above, the headquarters of SIS is a target in *The Patriot Game*, and in Nelson DeMille's *Cathedral* (New York, 1981) the IRA seize St. Patrick's Cathedral in New York. Listing spectacular targets like this might make the plots ridiculous, yet the IRA's bombing of the Grand Hotel, Brighton, in 1984 was real enough. Underpinning the whole idea of the spectacular, however, is the notion that such an attack, if successful, will have a dramatic and definitive impact on the political situation. The target in *The Bomb that Could Lip-read* is a top-level ministerial conference. One of the terrorists asserts that by killing the Secretary of State for Northern Ireland and other senior officials they can 'strike a blow that would change the whole course of Irish history'.[51] No doubt a belief such as this is necessary for dramatic tension, and the Provisional IRA seem to believe it too, but the real-life 'spectaculars' of the Mountbatten killing and the Brighton bomb produced no extraordinary shift in policy.

A persistent theme in spy fiction generally, and certainly in the Irish literature, is that of the loner, the 'odd man out'. Harry Brown in *Harry's Game* is a classic case on the security forces' side. In the novel, not only is he very much his own man, but when working undercover in Belfast, he deliberately moves out of touch of his controllers. Terence Strong's *Whisper Who Dares* (1982) has a rather more polished character. SAS Lieutenant Charles Harrington-Corbett, an upper-crust British officer with Ulster relatives, works alone in dangerous south Armagh and strikes up an improbable romance with a girl from a strongly republican family. This character is obviously based on Captain Robert Nairac, a public-school and Oxford-educated Guards officer who worked undercover in south Armagh. In May 1977 Nairac was taken from a south Armagh pub and murdered by the IRA.[52] Harrington-Corbett meets a similar end, although first he is forced to witness the kneecapping (by electric drill) of his girlfriend. One of the most interesting 'odd men out' is Arthur Apple in M. S. Power's accomplished *The Killing of Yesterday's Children* (1985). Apple is a former minor British diplomat who has been found a job managing a seedy betting shop in his native Belfast. Here he is used by both the IRA (for laundering funds) and the security forces (for snippets of information). The Dublin-born author balances realism and fantasy in this novel in a way which echoes the desperate, lethal games played by intelligence officers and terrorists alike. In *Jig* (1987), by Campbell Armstrong (a pseudonym for Campbell Black), two loners fight it out: 'Jig', an IRA assassin, who never harms 'innocent' bystanders, and Frank Pagan of British intelligence. Pagan comes to respect the IRA killer who has, he believes, introduced 'dignity' to the Irish struggle.[53]

Other 'loners', such as the maverick RUC officers Christian Boggs or Barney Somerville, are concerned less with dignity than effectiveness. These men, and other covert operations specialists who take the law into their own hands, dangerously reinforce the notion that the only way to take effective action against the terrorists is to operate outside the law, with a species of counter-terror. For these men, as for the terrorists, the end justifies the means. The intelligence chief in *Operation Emerald* concludes a briefing for a 'shoot-to-kill' operation against republican and loyalist gunmen with apparently sincere assurances about 'our fundamental belief in freedom and democracy'.[54] Some types of people, however, do not qualify for the usual democratic rights. This has long been the case in Northern Ireland. In *A Bomb and a Girl* (1944), by Hugh Shearman, Stanislas McOstrich, a disaffected student at Queen's University, Belfast, blows up an unpopular professor. The police are convinced of the student's guilt, but cannot prove it. When another professor suggests arresting McOstrich, the RUC Sergeant McGusty is horrified: 'You can do no such thing. This is a free country. You can only do that sort of thing with Sinn Fein rebels and communists'.[55]

Fiction of the kind discussed in this study both influences and reflects popular perceptions of security and intelligence matters. Most of the books are simple adventure stories which characterize soldiers, police, intelligence agents and terrorists merely as players in a violent Irish pantomime. On the whole the novels embody a generalized assumption concerning the corrosive effect of violence on its practitioners. Such moral judgements as are made about the nature or direction of the violence (which is invariably graphic) tend to favour the security forces. Republican and loyalist violence is frequently portrayed as misguided, mindless and counter-productive, which ignores the fact that in Ireland this century politically-motivated violence, or the threat of it, has undoubtedly paid political dividends on a number of occasions: for republicans in 1916–21 and in the early 1970s when the British government was brought to the negotiating table with the IRA; and for loyalists in 1912–14 and 1974, when they brought down the Northern Ireland power-sharing executive. One critic has argued that since Irish thrillers have, for the most part, given the IRA a 'bad press', they thus 'may have played a part in the British campaign to restore order, if not justice, to Ulster. In bold strokes of black and white, they have painted the jolly ploughboy, the Irish Rebel, the romantic gunman, as a terrorist, futile, brutal, at best misguided, at worst a callous killer. Surely,' he concludes, 'the British could ask for no more'.[56] But this is a little unreasonable. The fact that the IRA comes out badly in most of the books reflects wider political realities. However sincere and apparently justified the IRA may be, their political wing, Sinn Fein, has manifestly failed to secure much popular support outside a few localized areas in Northern Ireland.[57] Since the British, Irish and American governments (among others) are firmly committed to the destruction of all Irish terrorist groups, it is scarcely likely that the majority of Irish thrillers would, in general terms, do anything other than favour the security forces rather than the IRA.

Few of the novels under consideration attempt to explain in any depth the commitment to 'physical force' methods in Ireland. The usual explanation for IRA activism is that the individual's mother/wife/sister has been beaten up/raped/shot by the British Army, the RUC or loyalist thugs. Some authors begin to touch on the social and political circumstances, as well as the personal, which might lead to violence, but most simply fall back on the convenient popular literary convention of the innately violent, 'fighting' Irish. It is, says Anne Murray in *Cry of the Hunter*, 'something that's inherent in the Gael. A sort of agonized eternal struggle inside that moves him to self-destruction'.[58] The Prime Minister in *Vote to Kill* remarks on 'the Irish fever, the worst variety known to man. It destroys all gentleness, truth, sensible calculation'.[59]

What sort of 'real' intelligence, then, does Irish spy fiction describe? Most of it – run of the mill stuff, indeed – peddles the common thriller currency of mysterious spymasters running fiendish covert operations and hardened, brutal agents fighting it out with mirror-image terrorists attempting to pull off some spectacular coup which will finally 'liberate' Ireland. It is a simplistic approach which feeds the dangerous illusion that there might be a purely 'military' solution to the Northern Ireland – or any – problem. But the best of it – Seymour, Brady, Newman, Power – possesses no such certainty. The terrorist challenge is complex, as is the response. The security force personnel in these novels are realistic, neither superhuman nor incompetent. While they are frequently violent, they do not exist in the moral or legal vacuum of 'pulp' spy fiction. In this, no doubt, the best Irish spy fiction is no different from the best of the literature generally, whatever the precise subject matter.

NOTES

1. The original date of publication is given at the first mention of a book in the text. Unless otherwise indicated, place of publication is London and quotations are taken from the first edition.
2. The volume of Irish-related thrillers should not, however, be overstated. Myron J. Smith Jr., *Cloak and Dagger Fiction: an Annotated Guide to Spy Thrillers* (Santa Barbara and Oxford, 2nd edn, 1982) lists 3,435 books published between 1940 and early 1981. Of these barely 40 are 'Irish'.
3. Published in paperback as *The Detling Murders* (Harmondsworth, 1984).
4. Christopher Andrew, *Secret Service: The Making of the British Intelligence Community* (1985), pp.34–85; David French, 'Spy Fever in Britain, 1900–1915', *The Historical Journal*, Vol.21, No.2, (1978), pp.355–70.
5. R.D.B. French, 'Introduction', pp.xv–xvi, in George A. Birmingham, *The Red Hand of Ulster* (Shannon, 1972 edn).
6. Owen Dudley Edwards, *The Quest for Sherlock Holmes: a Biographical Study of Arthur Conan Doyle* (Edinburgh, 1983), pp.16, 135.
7. Arthur Conan Doyle, 'His Last Bow: an Epilogue of Sherlock Holmes', in *His Last Bow* (1962 edn), pp.191, 201–2.
8. Eunan O'Halpin, *The Decline of the Union: British Government in Ireland, 1892–1920* (Dublin, 1987), pp.109–13.
9. Conan Doyle, 'His Last Bow', pp.198–9.
10. John Buchan, *The Three Hostages* (Harmondsworth, 1953 pbk edn), pp.48–50, 43, 103–9. Irish characters turn up in a couple of other novels by celebrated thriller writers. In *Moon of Madness* (1927), the creator of Fu Manchu, Sax Rohmer (Arthur S. Wade), recounted the story of 'an Irish secret service agent and an American girl [who] track an international spy across Europe and into a death-fight in Madeira'. (Plot synopsis from Smith, *Cloak and Dagger Fiction*.) In Raymond Chandler's *The Big Sleep* (New York, 1939) one of General Sternwood's daughters has married ex-IRA officer Rusty Regan, 'a big curly-headed Irishman from Clonmel, with sad eyes and a smile as wide as Wilshire Boulevard' (1971 pbk edn, p.8).
11. *The Informer* was made into a celebrated film (directed by John Ford, 1935) in which Victor McLaglan, in the title role, won an Academy Award.
12. J.J. Lee, *Ireland 1912–1985: Politics and Society* (Cambridge, 1990), pp.221–70, gives a stimulating account of all aspects of Irish neutrality.
13. One novel mentions German activity in Ireland in the summer of 1939. In *The Private Wound* (1968) by Nicholas Blake (Cecil Day-Lewis), a romance and murder story set in the west of Ireland, one character who belongs to an extremist group of the IRA is involved in making contacts with Nazi agents. The Irish police, however, efficiently expose his activities and arrest him.
14. Eunan O'Halpin, 'Intelligence and Security in Ireland, 1922–45', *Intelligence and National Security*, Vol.5, No.1 (1990), pp.50–83.
15. Julian Symons, *Bloody Murder: From the Detective Story to the Crime Novel: A History* (London, 1972), p.126.
16. Peter Cheyney, *Dark Duet* (Harmondsworth, 1949 pbk edn), pp.136, 134, 131–54.
17. Dr Josephine Butler wrote *Churchill's Secret Agent: Code Name 'Jay-Bee'* (1983), which she maintained was an account of her work as a wartime spy under the direct command of the Prime Minister. Her claims have been greeted with scepticism by intelligence veterans and by historians.
18. O'Halpin, *Decline of the Union*, p.109.
19. David Grant, *Emerald Decision* (1981 pbk edn), pp.259, 301, 319.
20. Devlin was played unconvincingly by the Canadian actor Donald Sutherland in the 1977

film of the book.

21. J.P. Duggan, *Neutral Ireland and the Third Reich* (Dublin, 1985), pp.148–50, 209. Sean Russell died of appendicitis on board a U-boat which was bringing him back to Ireland to organize an IRA uprising timed to coincide with the invasion of Britain. Ryan, who had embarked with him, returned to Germany and died there in 1944. His association with Nazi Germany did not prevent his becoming one of the patron saints of the Irish revolutionary left. Stuart's wartime activities proved no bar to his progress afterwards. He is now one of Ireland's most celebrated writers of serious fiction.

22. Jack Higgins, *The Eagle has Landed* (1983 pbk rev.edn), p.374. Higgins has used Devlin in other novels. In *Touch the Devil* (1982), having retired in 1975 from the Provisional IRA, Devlin has become a professor of English at Trinity College, Dublin, but he still provides help for British intelligence in running to earth Frank Barry, an Ulster-born freelance terrorist. Devlin also appears in *Confessional* (1985). When in 1982 an IRA contact asks Captain Harry Fox of DI5 ('that branch of the British Secret Intelligence Service which concerns itself with counter-espionage') if the rumours about Devlin's wartime exploits were true, Fox dismissively says that it 'sounds straight out of a paperback novel to me' (1986 pbk edn, pp.40, 63).

23. George A. Birmingham, *Lieutenant Commander*, pp.78, 41.

24. F.L. Green, *Odd Man Out* (Harmondsworth, 1948), pp.38, 29. James Mason starred as Johnny Murtah in the distinguished film version of the story (directed by Carol Reed, 1947).

25. Harry Patterson, *Cry of the Hunter* (1979 pbk edn), pp.72, 81, 139, 147. One scholar has remarked on how common in 'troubles' novels is the opposition between conscience (a middle-class virtue) and ruthlessness (the vice of the low-class political fanatic). Joseph McMinn, 'Contemporary Novels on the "Troubles"', in *Etudes Irlandaises*, No.5 (Dec. 1980), p.119.

26. The background and course of the Northern Ireland conflict can be followed in Paul Arthur and Keith Jeffery, *Northern Ireland since 1968* (Oxford, 1988), among many other works.

27. Thrillers only represent approximately one half of the total volume of novels written about the troubles.

28. Martin Waddell, *A Little Bit British*, p.147.

29. Shaun Herron, *Miro* (New York, 1969).

30. Shaun Herron, *The Hound and the Fox and the Harper* (New York, 1970).

31. Smith, *Cloak and Dagger Fiction*, p.285.

32. Steve White, *The Fighting Irish*, p.29.

33. There is an English translation: *Malko: the Belfast Connection* (New York, 1976).

34. McMinn, 'Contemporary Novels on the "troubles"', p.114.

35. Some of the problems of police-military relations are discussed in Keith Jeffery, 'Intelligence and Counter-insurgency Operations: Some Reflections on the British experience', *Intelligence and National Security* Vol.2, No.1 (1987), pp.118–49. For the supergrass system, see Stephen Greer, 'The Supergrass: a coda', in *Fortnight* (Belfast), No.249 (March 1987), pp.7–8.

36. John de St. Jorre and Brian Shakespeare, *The Patriot Game*, p.195.

37. Hamill has also written *Pig in the Middle: The Army in Northern Ireland 1969–1984* (1985).

38. Chapman Pincher, *The Eye of the Tornado*, pp.28, 124, 113, 264–5.

39. See David Leigh, *The Wilson Plot* (1988).

40. Douglas Hurd, *Vote to Kill*, p.161. Hurd has subsequently held office as Secretary of State for Northern Ireland, Home Secretary and Foreign Secretary. Any future thriller he might write ought, therefore, to be unusually well-informed on security and intelligence matters.

41. Danny Morrison, quoted by Mark Lieberman in *Fortnight*, No.280 (Jan. 1990), p.23.

42. Alan Judd, *A Breed of Heroes*, p.9. Judd has gone on to write spy thrillers set in South Africa and Latin America.

43. For the 'Stalker affair' see Peter Taylor, *Stalker: the Search for the Truth* (1987) and John Stalker, *Stalker* (1988)

44. There is also what appears to be a joke. In *The Testing Ground* a 'Timothy Faligot' is Minister of State for Northern Ireland. Roger Faligot, a radical French journalist, is the author of *Britain's Military Strategy in Ireland: the Kitson Experiment* (1983), a book sympathetic towards the IRA and very highly critical of security policy in the province. Faligot is not a common British surname.
45. Ambrose Clancy, *Blind Pilot*, p.20.
46. Sarah Michael, *Summary Justice*, p.230.
47. Andrew Lane, *The Ulsterman*, p.13.
48. Dominic McCartan, *Operation Emerald*, pp.197–8.
49. Maurice Leitch, *Silver's City*, p.21.
50. Published in the United States as *The Fifth of November*.
51. Donald Seaman, *The Bomb that Could Lip-Read*, p.161.
52. See Hamill, *Pig in the Middle*, pp.213–6.
53. Campbell Armstrong, *Jig*, p.312.
54. *Operation Emerald*, p.168.
55. Hugh Shearman, *A Bomb and a Girl*, p.139.
56. J. Bowyer Bell, 'The Troubles as Trash', in *Hibernia* (Dublin), 20 Jan. 1978, p.22.
57. In the May 1989 local council elections in Northern Ireland, Sinn Fein won 11.3 per cent of the vote (as opposed to 21.2 per cent for the constitutional nationalist Social Democratic and Labour Party) and in the European Parliament election the following month gained only 9.2 per cent (SDLP 25.5 per cent). In the Republic of Ireland general election in June 1989, Sinn Fein won only 1.2 per cent of the vote.
58. Patterson, *Cry of the Hunter*, p.142.
59. Hurd, *Vote to Kill*, p.215.

Our Man in Havana, Their Man in Madrid: Literary Invention in Espionage Fact and Fiction

DENIS SMYTH

One striking aspect of the relation between fiction and reality evident in some of Graham Greene's novels is their prescient, perhaps even their prophetic quality. Thus, in *The Quiet American*, published in 1955, Greene accurately anticipated the American intention to intervene on a massive scale in Vietnam to prevent the Vietminh from consolidating their rule over a united country. The author attributed his own clairvoyance on this issue to the personal experience of Vietnam that he had gained during lengthy visits there in the early 1950s, while researching a series of magazine articles.[1] However, Greene was by no means the only Western observer to visit Vietnam during the dying days of French colonial authority there, and there were doubtless many potential models for the eponymous character of the novel. Yet, few, if any, of these 'quiet' Americans, for all their exposure to Vietnam and its people, proved capable of comprehending the local political scene with as much perspicacity as Greene displayed in a short passage in his novel:

> This was a land of rebellious barons. It was like Europe in the Middle Ages. But what were the Americans doing here? Columbus had not yet discovered their country.[2]

Obsessed as they were with the preoccupations of the contemporary Cold War between the capitalist and Communist blocs, Washington's policy-makers ignored this critical distinction between historical and chronological time. Consequently they embarked upon the hopelessly anachronistic mission of arresting not so much the progress of Communism as the march of time itself.

In *Our Man in Havana* (1958), Greene exhibited such a power of anticipating actuality in his fiction as apparently to transcend informed inference and attain veritable second sight. For, within four years of the publication of this novel, life appeared to imitate art. Thus, the Cuban missile crisis of 1962 conferred retrospective credibility on Greene's tall tale of the British Secret Service being taken in by fabricated reports of clandestine rocket installations in the Oriente province of the Caribbean island. Yet, Greene has denied any particular foresight on his part in this instance, ascribing the convergence of literary invention and international incident to pure chance: 'My story of concealed missiles in Cuba was a sheer fluke'.[3] Indeed, the geographical coincidence that Greene and Kruschev should both decide to locate their respective missile bases in Cuba was fortuitous. For it was just after the close of the Second World War that the author had first conceived of the basic plot for this work in which be sought 'to make fun of the Secret Service' – a disrespect he believed it 'amply merited' – as an outline for a film entitled 'Nobody is to Blame' whose action would take place 'in some Baltic capital similar to Tallinn'.[4] However, whether because the Brazilian film director, Alberto Cavalcanti, did not really like Greene's movie sketch or whether because, as the former maintained, he was informed by the British film censor that 'no certificate could be issued to a film that made fun of the Secret Service', the project was shelved.[5]

Still, the basic idea of the film outline – that of a paper merchant/mill whose reports, which have been fabricated for personal profit, are believed by a gullible London centre for so long that, even when subsequently discredited, he cannot be disowned – lingered on in Greene's mind undergoing 'the wise criticism of the pre-conscious',[6] to resurface as the kernel of a new novel in the 1950s. By then, Greene had also decided on a change of scene for his story, from pre-war Estonia to pre-revolutionary Cuba. Havana replaced Tallinn for the following reasons:

> Suddenly it struck me that here in this extraordinary city, where every vice was permissible and every trade possible, lay the true background for my comedy. I realized I had been planning the wrong situation and placing it in the wrong period. The shadows in 1938 of the war to come had been too dark for comedy; the reader could feel no sympathy for a man who was cheating his country in Hitler's day for the sake of an extravagant wife. But in fantastic Havana, among the absurdities of the Cold War (for who can accept the survival of Western capitalism as a great cause?) there was a situation allowably comic, all the more if I changed the wife into a daughter.[7]

Doubtless, the inherent humour of this new milieu eluded anybody reading *Our Man in Havana* during the Cuban missile crisis when the 'absurdities of the Cold War' threatened the world with nuclear Armageddon. Yet, Greene's very shift of his *locus in quo* from the Baltic to the Caribbean further proves that he did not divine the shape of things to come there. After all, why abandon one setting, geographical and chronological, because its dubious historical associations might subvert its comic impact, for another context where one suspected the moral enormity of a global nuclear war might be precipitated? In any event, Greene's decision to end his search for a site that would not prove to be 'too black a background for a light-hearted comedy' in Havana turned out to be an unfortunate one, on account of subsequent, internal, as well as external, developments. For, the Castro regime, despite allowing Carol Reed and Graham Greene to make the film version of *Our Man in Havana* on location in Cuba, inevitably had misgivings about a story that seemed to trivialize the Batista dictatorship and, by implication, the revolution that had overthrown it.[8]

However, if the relation between fact and fiction in the choice of location of this novel was more problematical than providential, its theme certainly derived from the reality of personal experience. For Greene has admitted that the subject-matter of *Our Man in Havana*, that of a paper merchant, was suggested to him by his own wartime experience within the British intelligence community. The novelist was recruited by the SIS to serve in West Africa during the years 1942–43, where he vainly attempted to dispatch agents into the neighbouring Vichy French colonies from his base in Freetown, Sierra Leone. He was then recalled to London for the period 1943–44, to work under Kim Philby in the Iberian sub-division of SIS's counter-intelligence department, Section V.[9] His new posting carried with it responsibility for monitoring the activities of *Abwehr* agents in Portugal. Their antics were more cause for amusement than concern:

> Those Abwehr officers who had not been suborned already by our own service spent much of their time sending home completely erroneous reports based on information received from imaginary agents. It was a paying game, especially when expenses and bonuses were added to the cypher's salary and a safe one. The fortunes of the German Government were now in decline, and it is wonderful how the conception of honour, alters in the atmosphere of defeat.[10]

Sustained surveillance of these practitioners of this entrepreneurial espionage made Greene reflect on how easy it would have been to dupe his own gullible superiors from his field station in Sierra Leone, susceptible as they were for psychological and professional reasons to fraud and fabrication. Indeed, Greene recalls one occasion when his London spymasters, even though he cautioned them against lending any credence to a report from an illiterate and barely numerate informant alleging the presence of an army tank in a building (which the novelist himself believed contained old boots) on an airfield in Vichy-controlled French Guinea, officially pronounced the item to be 'most valuable'.[11] Thus, wartime involvement in counter-espionage at home and abroad conjoined to suggest the theme of the book:

So it was that experiences in my little shack in Freetown recalled in a more comfortable room off St. James's gave me the idea of what twelve years later in 1958 became *Our Man in Havana*.[12]

Of course, the particular subject-matter of this spy novel must have had an additional appeal for the author. For, in focusing not upon the activities of spies in general but the actions of paper merchants in particular, Greene had singled out for literary attention precisely that branch of espionage which so resembled his own art. In choosing to explore these different varieties of the practice of 'imaginative writing' (Greene's own term), the novelist had conjured up a golden opportunity to examine the complex interaction between the literary and the real worlds, between the internally invented and the externally experienced. Indeed, one of the most suggestive passages in the entire novel is the exchange which occurs between Greene's paper merchant, Wormold, and his German friend, Dr Hasselbacher, when they are forced by circumstance to address that very congruence between the creative writer and the counterfeit agent:

> [Wormold:] '. . . I invented Raul' [one of his supposed sub-agents].
> [Hasselbacher:] 'Then you invented him too well, Mr. Wormold. There's a whole file on him now.'
> [Wormold:] 'He was no more real than a character in a novel.'
> [Hasselbacher:] 'Are they always invented? I don't know how a novelist works, Mr. Wormold. I have never known one before you.'[13]

Naturally, the literary critics have their own devices for measuring the extent of Greene's success in exploring the resemblances and replications between these respective modes of literary invention in *Our Man in Havana*. However, the novel does also provide historians with scholarly opportunities. For, in its treatment of an often neglected sub-species of spy, the paper merchant, it affords analytical insights and conceptual perspectives of considerable potential utility in the study of this aspect of secret intelligence.

Moreover, perhaps the most appropriate case with which to prove the virtues of Greene's novel as a manual for the study of the paper-merchant phenomenon is that of the Spaniard, Angel Alcázar de Velasco. This is so for two reasons. For a start, Alcázar de Velasco was one of the most spectacularly spurious spies unearthed by the Iberian sub-division of SIS's counter-intelligence section, to which Greene returned to work after his West African sojourn. It is true that the Spaniard's espionage activities had been revealed as largely fraudulent by the investigations of the British security and secret services before Greene's return to London, but it is likely that they remained a part of the counter-intelligencers' departmental folklore for long afterwards – long enough, indeed, for Kim Philby to recount his own version of the episode in the autobiography he wrote in Moscow, after his defection to the Soviet Union.[14] However, even if the Alcázar de Velasco affair did not provide any direct inspiration for Greene's novelistic treatment of the spy as fabricator, there are sufficient parallels and coincidences between these literary and historical examples of the paper merchant to justify a comparison and contrast between them. The motives, *modus operandi* and management of these two agents – the one created by fiction, the other a creator of fiction – will be analysed in turn to elucidate the nature and significance of this joint literary-historical phenomenon.

On first examination, the motives prompting Wormold and Alcázar de Velasco respectively to embark upon their ostensible careers seem of quite a different order. It is Wormold's predicament as a neither forceful nor successful vendor of vacuum cleaners, with a need to cater for the extravagant tastes of his teenage daughter, Milly, on whom he dotes, that renders him a ready candidate for recruitment by MI5's Caribbean control, Hawthorne. On the other hand, Alcázar del Velasco impressed those who encountered him, whether friend or foe, as a much more natural desperado than his fictional counterpart: to his British opponents he appeared as a 'colourful . . . adventurer', while to his Japanese associates he seemed 'a cavalier – one who will do anything on earth for his friends and those he likes; of strong character but rather quixotic and hot-headed'.[15] But Alcázar de Velasco was not only more of a born buccaneer than Wormold, he was also seemingly driven by an ideological commitment to Spanish Fascism and German Nazism absent in Greene's politically agnostic anti-hero. Indeed, so intense was Alcázar de Velasco's devotion to the purity of Falangist (Spanish Fascist) principles that he joined other 'old-shirt' militants in resisting General Franco's enforced unification of the main political factions within the Nationalist civil-wartime camp, in 1937. His opposition to Franco's absorption of the radical Falange into the ideologically amorphous Falange Española Tradicionalista y de las Juntas de Ofensiva Nacional-Sindicalista landed him in a Francoist prison. However, one of the Caudillo's most senior advisers, Ramón Serrano Suñer, who would also serve as Spain's Foreign Minister between October 1940 and September 1942, managed to persuade Franco to release Alcázar de Velasco within a couple of years, in recognition of the part he had played in foiling an escape by Republican prisoners from the Fort of San Cristóbal in Pamplona where he had been incarcerated along with them.[16] Upon his release from prison, Alcázar de Velasco became both a protégé of and propagandist for Serrano Suñer, who, as President of the Junta Política of the F.E.T. de las J.O.N.S., was trying to establish his ideological credentials as the legitimate successor of the Falange's dead leader, José Antonio Primo de Rivera.[17] All the better to aid his powerful patron in this task, Alcázar de Velasco was appointed as Secretary of the Institute of Political Studies. The Institute had been established in September 1939 to function both as an official think-tank to fashion a more juridically sound justification for the Franco regime than the imperatives of military dictatorship, and as a school for the education/indoctrination of senior party officials.[18]

Actually, Alcázar de Velasco claims, in his rambling and often unreliable memoir of his adventures in espionage, that even before – indeed, as early as 1935 – he had been elevated to a position of influence within the Francoist state, his ideological sympathy with the Third Reich had attracted the attention of the *Abwehr*. However, although he allegedly received some training as an agent in that year, it was only in 1940 that he was activated by the Germans to engage upon an important espionage mission, the gathering of secret intelligence inside wartime Britain.[19] Again, unlike Wormold who, with neither natural inclination for nor previous experience of clandestine activity, had no option but to play the part of a paper merchant throughout his career as a spy, Alcázar de Velasco did set about his covert commission with apparently authentic application. Thus, the Spaniard managed to secure the sponsorship of the British Council and the British Embassy in Madrid for a visit to wartime Britain by a representative-cum-reporter from the Institute of Political Studies, an individual called 'del Pozo'. In reality his name was Miguel Piernavieja, and he abused the privilege granted him by the British Ministry of Information of sending his articles back to Spain in its diplomatic bag, by copying in invisible ink on to their reverse pages secret messages reporting such matters as bomb damage inflicted by the Luftwaffe. However, even before Piernavieja's arrival in Britain, SIS's counter-intelligence department had warned British security authorities of his espionage mission for the *Abwehr*, a fact which he confirmed by establishing covert contact with one of the putative German spies already carefully controlled by MI5's 'double-cross' system. Indeed, MI5 proceeded to engineer the departure of Alcázar de Velasco's spy from Britain by having a senior double-cross agent caution the *Abwehr* that 'del Pozo's personal and political indiscretions threatened to blow his cover'.[20]

Undaunted, however, by this set-back Alcázar de Velasco himself actually stayed in Britain for two lengthy periods in 1941. There in the guise of press attaché at the Spanish Embassy in London he recruited and ran agents, many of whom again came under the control of the 'double-cross' system's Twenty Committee, which proceeded to use them to channel information and disinformation of its own choosing via the Spaniard's unwitting good offices, to the unsuspecting Germans. This advantageous state of affairs explains why the British counter-intelligence and security authorities were prepared, for a time, to tolerate Alcázar de Velasco's espionage activities inside Britain, despite SIS's receiving a report early on that the Falangist journalist was 'a high level and dangerous agent'.[21] Indeed, Alcázar de Velasco's control was none other than Specialist-Captain Karl-Erich Kühlenthal of the *Abwehr* station in Madrid, who according to David Kahn was 'in charge of recruiting and controlling' its 'most important spies abroad'.[22]

However, Britain's security supremos eventually took fright in early 1942 at the apparently serious threat posed to the national war-effort by Alcázar de Velasco's espionage operations, as revealed by decrypts of *Abwehr* Enigma traffic and Japanese 'Purple' communications. Impressed by the revelations of a seemingly extensive Spanish-run spy-ring at work in Britain contained in this Ultra and Magic material, senior officers in MI5 decided to ignore the concern of the W Board and the Twenty Committee (the authorities that managed the double-cross system) that the arrest of one of Alcázar de Velasco's sub-agents could conceivably compromise the security of the entire double-cross enterprise. Thus, one of the most active Spanish spies in Britain, Luis Calvo, the London correspondent for the Madrid daily newspaper, *A.B.C.*, was officially apprehended on 12 February 1942.[23] Ironically, it was precisely this security counter-action, provoked by the seeming size and substance of Alcázar de Velasco's espionage network in Britain, that eventually led the British to conclude that the Spaniard was running a largely bogus outfit.

For, although an intense interrogation of Calvo – including it seems a degree of physical intimidation – over a period of months did eventually persuade the Spaniard to confess to espionage at Alcázar de Velasco's behest and to identify a couple of the other personalities involved – Vice-Consul Lojiendo and assistant press attaché Brugada – the prisoner also steadfastly denied any knowledge of a more extensive ring being run by his Falangist spymaster in Britain.[24] At some stage in the proceedings, according to Kim Philby, SIS's counter-intelligence department, Section V, resolved to ascertain the truth about the activities of this 'particularly nasty Falangist' by indulging in a piece of skulduggery of its own.[25] Thus, Section V's man in Madrid, Kenneth Benton, bribed Alcázar de Velasco's secretary with a sum of £2,000 to be allowed to open his employer's safe and to photograph its contents.[26] The principal item turned up by this action was a document that, on first inspection, appeared to justify British apprehensions:

> The diary stated explicitly that he [Alcázar de Velasco] had recruited a network of agents on behalf of the German Abwehr; names, addresses and assignments were given in detail.[27]

However, after a considerable expenditure of time and energy by Britain's counter-intelligence and security agents, it was concluded 'that the diary, though undoubtedly the work of Alcázar del Velasco himself, was fraudulent from beginning to end'. Moreover, Philby was not in any doubt as to why the Spaniard had perpetrated such a thorough-going fraud against the *Abwehr*; he was convinced that the diary 'had been concocted solely for the purpose of extracting money from the Germans'.[28]

That is to say, Kim Philby, who as a double-agent in his own right conscientiously maintained the purity of his ideological commitment to Soviet Communism as the primary inspiration of his own intelligence double-dealing, was not inclined to ascribe any nobler motive to Alcázar de Velasco's espionage activities than an obvious desire to line his own pockets. Thus, according to one insider's expert appraisal, whatever may have prompted Alcázar de Velasco to work for German intelligence in the Second World War in the first place, he soon succumbed to the opportunity for personal enrichment which a career in espionage offered. In practice then, if not in principle, this real-life Spanish paper merchant turns out not to be too different in fundamental motivation from Greene's fictional character, the impecunious Wormold. Of course, as Graham Greene's fellow-writer and wartime intelligence operative, Malcolm Muggeridge, has commented, money is an omnipresent element in clandestine and covert operations:

> In Intelligence operations, money is an essential ingredient; even where other motives arise – as patriotism or ideological affiliations – money, however little, or its equivalent must be dropped in, like a touch of bitter in a mint julep, to validate the deal. Only when money has passed is the mystical union fully established; it's money that makes Intelligence go round.[29]

Naturally, it is all too easy for such an all-pervasive influence to become an all-consuming passion.

Certainly, the sums that Alcázar de Velasco managed to mulct from the Japanese Minister in Madrid, Yakichiro Suma, to support a putative extension of the Spaniard's espionage network ostensibly operating inside Britain to the United States – the enemy power of greatest interest to Japan – were not insubstantial. Suma, an individual whom Serrano Suñer has characterized as an 'innocent', seems to have been a natural victim for con-men of all types (much of his cherished art collection consisted of forgeries). Again, according to Serrano Suñer's testimony, Alcázar de Velasco proceeded to make an absolute fool of the Japanese envoy (*'le tomaba el pelo como ningún peluquero del mundo'*).[30] The scale of the financial depredations which the Spaniard managed to practise against both the Japanese and the Germans in exchange for his doubtful intelligence services is suggested in a communication that Suma sent from Madrid to Tokyo, by the Purple diplomatic cipher, on 21 August 1942:

. . . as you know, the espionage net in England was founded by Germany regardless of expense, with the cooperation of the Spanish Government . . . Through the good offices of Foreign Minister Suñer we are using it free of charge. As a matter of principle, Germany is paying operating and salary expenses for the agency's work in England. All we do is send some of these spies special bonuses, so to speak, when they do fine work. However, when it comes to the United States we will have to pay it all. The expenses for getting started and operating expenses from then on will be our burden. These agencies [*sic*] . . . will be in the direst danger of their lives; and from the very nature of their work they will require very large amounts of money. So please see that this is taken care of.

When we first started out on this undertaking, you sent some money, 300,000 paper dollars [this figure was later reduced to $30,000 in a later Sigint evaluation report – D.S.] of which is still left. When we embark on the adventure in the United States, we may need much money instantly, so please send 400,000 yen [$100,000 at that time] to the Yokohama Specie Bank in Berlin to be placed on our account there (if possible in Swiss francs – otherwise in German marks).[31]

The Japanese Foreign Ministry duly complied with Suma's request for additional funding for what the envoy had come to designate as the 'TO' intelligence network. However, Alcázar de Velasco was soon back for more, arguing with an impudent ingenuity that it was the niggardliness of the Japanese themselves that was responsible for the poor output of the 'TO' agents inside the USA. They were allegedly complaining that 'because of lack of funds their activities did not come up to expectation'. Suma immediately obtained another 500,000 yen from Tokyo to finance the espionage enterprise but once more, doubtless in response to Alcázar de Velasco's importuning, he asked, in early 1943, for as much again to be dispatched to him inside a few weeks.[32] However, although there is ample evidence to prove Alcázar de Velasco's great interest in securing generous financial returns for his secret services, it is true that the official historians of British security and counter-intelligence operations in the Second World War attribute the Spaniard's 'claim to be running a large network' to a yearning for reputation rather than remuneration, to 'vanity' rather than venality.[33] Yet, of course the prestige and profit motives could be mutually sustaining in such an endeavour. For the greater the fame Alcázar de Velasco enjoyed as a successful spymaster, the greater the fortune he was likely to earn in the process. Self-esteem and self-interest conjoined. Thus, this real-life paper merchant turns out after all not to be too fundamentally different in motivation from the more modestly mercenary figure of Wormold in *Our Man in Havana*.

If the espionage frauds of Wormold and Alcázar de Velasco were inspired by kindred ambitions, then the means that they employed to realize them are also similar. Wormold is able to expand his clandestine income rapidly once he elaborates a factitious circle of agents, for whom both regular payments and additional expenses are required, drawn mainly from the membership list of Havana's Country Club. However, while he is able to glean enough material from the local press to make up routine economic and political reports, Wormold comes to appreciate that he will really impress his new covert employers in MI6 only by furnishing them with 'something they would enjoy for their money, something to put on their files better than an economic report'. It is his insight that his control 'Hawthorne and his kind were credulous . . . (that) what they swallowed were nightmares, grotesque stories out of science fiction' that prompts Greene's paper merchant to spin his yarn of secret missile installations hidden on Cuba, whose rockets so resemble vacuum-cleaners – the only mechanical model available to Wormold for the drawings he makes to substantiate his sensational reports.[34]

However, it seems again on first encounter that in this area of *modus operandi* Alcázar de Velasco's case does differ from Wormold's. For, the literary inventions employed by the Spaniard to promote his profits and prestige with his real-life spymasters seem pedestrian in comparison with Wormold's extravagant imaginings. Thus, the Sigint evaluation section of the US Military Intelligence Service, the Special Branch, delivered the following damning verdict in late January 1943 upon the 'TO' network, having monitored its intelligence output from the USA for the previous six months on the basis of Purple decrypts:

> . . . some 80 reports have been received . . . This Branch has checked the accuracy of most of them. Usually they are either vague or quite inaccurate. Only occasionally has a report been partially correct and of some importance. The impression is obtained from the reports that they are bread and butter stuff . . . and that where facts are lacking the writers draw on their imaginations.[35]

Actually, Alcázar de Velasco's literary devices as a paper merchant appear to have been two in number: the specification of may individual 'low-grade' items of information on which it was next to impossible to check; and the making of such deliberately imprecise and general predictions concerning future moves by the enemy that almost any subsequent action by the Allies would seem to confirm these forecasts, however vaguely. Thus, one report ostensibly emanating from the Spanish spy-ring active inside Britain, and dispatched from London to Madrid on 24 August 1942 for relaying to the German and Japanese, contained the following seemingly concrete piece of information:

On August 13 a convoy of 36 ships left the port of Sligo, Ireland, for the Cape of Good Hope, loaded with tanks and anti-aircraft guns.[36] The several weeks' lapse that ensured before this message reached Berlin or Tokyo not only meant that this item was so dated as to be useless for all practical military purposes; it also meant that no physical verification of the report was feasible. All the paper merchant had to do to prosper with such a procedure was to avoid any obvious error or contradiction in concocting the contents of such reports. Of course, in this instance, Alcázar de Valesco had manifestly failed to do just that. He had committed an obvious 'howler' in reporting this notional convoy's departure from neutral Ireland (and from a small port at that without the facilities to handle such a concentration of shipping). In displaying such ignorance either of Ireland's neutrality or, perhaps more likely, of Sligo's position south of the border with Northern Ireland, Alcázar de Velasco was running the risk of compromising the credibility of the 'TO' network.

The second literary trick up this paper merchant's sleeve, that of the grand strategic speculation, which sought to cover all the enemy's options, usually contained no such pitfalls, as the following example from a 'TO' report relayed from Madrid to Tokyo on 26 October 1942 demonstrates;

> Among local diplomatic circles there is a rumour that ere long the Soviet [sic] will embark on a large scale offensive. Depending upon whether or not this succeeds, there is a possibility that an invasion of the continent will be carried out. If this drive fails before the United States and England can establish their second front, these two nations will turn to their other alternative, that is a very large scale drive in Africa.[37]

Such general speculation covered a myriad of contingencies, any one of which, if it occurred, should serve to confirm this prediction, after a fashion.

Yet, Alcázar de Velasco, like Wormold, seems to have appreciated that his spymasters, with their cultivated taste for dramatic revelations, would not be content forever with the diet of 'chicken-feed' and conjecture that he was providing. So, although Alcázar de Velasco was bound by more practical limits in his literary fabrications than Wormold, who operates in a fictional world underpinned by a willing suspension of disbelief, the Spaniard too tried to pander to his employers' appetite for more exotic items. Thus, on 9 April 1942, Suma informed Tokyo that he had 'obtained by a certain method an exact copy of a highly secret message from British Foreign Minister Eden to British Ambassador to Madrid, Hoare, containing the outline of the views and opinions on the war situation of the highest war council in the United States', the original of which had been allegedly carried across the Atlantic by Roosevelt's Special Adviser, Harry Hopkins, and the US Army Chief of Staff, General George C. Marshall. In this instance, Alcázar de Velasco was careful to attend to such details as the correct day of the Americans' arrival in London (probably learnt from press reports), but he offered no explanation as to why such a top-secret, high-level document would be communicated, verbatim, to Sir Samuel Hoare in Madrid, when none of the information it contained had any bearing on British policy towards Spain. Again, the actual contents of the message, which purported to be the American's assessment of likely future moves by the Japanese (including action against Burma and in India) and the Germans (including action against Egypt and in the Near East), were neither specific nor substantial. Moreover, the final paragraph of the supposed US report employed neither the tone nor the terminology normally encountered in such official documents:

> Above is all in all a major disaster for the British Empire, and its allies but these objectives can be gained, as for Japan, through hitting back Russian and Allied offensives in the North . . . and as for Germany, through the elimination of the forces of Turkey and the Middle East.[38]

Certainly, the bizarre references to Japan's 'hitting back' at 'Russian . . . offensives', when no state of war existed between the Soviets and the Japanese, and to Germany's elimination of 'the forces of Turkey', a neutral country, hardly reinforced the credibility of the document. However, the Americans who intercepted Suma's communication to Tokyo, containing the alleged report, took no chances and checked on its authenticity. The US Sigint evaluation agency, the Special Branch, reported on the investigation, thus:

> The Navy Department says the British Admiralty reported to the Navy Department on April 11th as follows: 'No such wire . . . was dispatched from London. It is considered that the Japanese Minister has been duped.'[39]

Yet again then, Wormold and Alcázar de Velasco turn out to have almost as much in common in the ways and means of their literary inventions as they do in the motives prompting them.

However, given the patent falsity of so much of these paper merchants' reports, it might seem that what the English vacuum-cleaner salesman and the Spanish fascist really shared most was a singularly gullible set of handlers – spymasters whose credulity made them soft targets for even such amateurish confidence tricksters as Wormold and Alcázar de Velasco. Again, Wormold – as befits a literary exemplar of this genre of espionage – is a more perfect specimen of the paper merchant: he hardly supplies any real

information to his control. Alcázar de Velasco, on the other hand, as has
been noted, did initially try to conduct some genuine espionage activities
inside Britain – and later, too, inside North America. However, it was
precisely because his real-life agents, like the few individuals – Spanish
journalists and diplomats – he recruited to spy inside the USA and Canada,
yielded such meagre pickings that he had to embroider so in his actual
reports to the *Abwehr* station and the Japanese embassy in Madrid.[40]

Of course, in the case of his network in Britain Alcázar de Velasco was
materially aided by the British themselves in the inflation of his modest
intelligence product. They seized upon the opportunity offered by the
Spaniard's espionage operation to further their own double-cross of the
German intelligence services by channelling misleading information to them
via Alcázar de Velasco's good offices. Indeed, in one of the very first uses of
the double-cross system for the active deception of the Germans, Alcázar
de Velasco's spy-ring based on the Spanish embassy in London was used in
later 1941 as the conduit for the delivery of false intelligence about Britain's
practices in the convoying of merchant ships and about the damage caused
by the Luftwaffe's bombing attacks on that country.[41] This ruse consisted of
an effort to mislead the Germans into redirecting their damaging bomber
raids away from the vulnerable urban and industrial centres of Britain
and towards the better defended aerodromes. It sought to persuade the
Germans to switch the main targets for their bomber attacks by providing
them with an allegedly stolen folder of official British documents, which
appeared to demonstrate considerable alarm at the damage already done to
the airstrips and aircraft of the Royal Air Force by the Luftwaffe's bomber
raids.[42] It was only after the defeat of Nazi Germany that the perpetrators
of this deception were able to judge its seemingly substantial success, as
recorded by Sir John Masterman in his official report on the operation of
the double-cross system in the Second World War:

> The folder, after other attempts had failed was successfully conveyed
> . . . through the Spanish embassy. The exact effect of the plan was
> impossible to gauge, but in 1945, when German Air Ministry files
> fell into British hands, it was discovered that the plan had apparently
> had very considerable success. The Germans accepted the documents
> at their face value and drew the conclusion which was desired, that
> attacks on aerodromes would be the most effective use of the
> Luftwaffe. The first conclusion which the German commentator
> makes reads in translation as follows: 'The British ground organisation
> concentrated in the southeast of England is the Achilles heel of the
> R.A.F. A planned attack on the ground organisation will hit the
> British air force at its most tender spot'.[43]

Undoubtedly, the much more professionally prepared false reports and forged documents which the British fed to the unwitting Alcázar de Velasco, for relaying to the Germans, helped to boost the apparent competence, and therefore the ultimate credibility, of his espionage enterprise. However, even without this helping hand from the British, there is every reason to believe that he could have prospered if left to his own limited devices. For, as British security and counter-intelligence operatives found when processing another case within the double-cross system, it turned out 'that an agent could not only survive while supplying the Germans with wildly inaccurate information but could thrive on doing so . . . '.[44] Nor was this disparagement of the *Abwehr*'s gullibility confined to its British opponents. Thus, the chief of the Luftwaffe's intelligence group monitoring the United States Army Air Force and the Royal Air Force came to view spies' reports 'almost humorously', while a head of German naval intelligence could maintain that 'the effectiveness of the spy is small'.[45] The Japanese intelligence services were, by all accounts, even less inclined, professionally and psychologically, to subject Alcázar de Velasco's intelligence product to the critical scrutiny it so obviously deserved.[46]

Yet, Alcázar de Velasco's employers in espionage like Wormold's own intelligence service superiors, Hawthorne and 'the Chief', also persisted in taking their paper merchant's fantasies seriously, not least because they had staked their own reputations on the continued credibility of their imaginative underlings. Indeed, in *Our Man in Havana*, Hawthorne sees through Wormold's notional illustrations of the Cuban-based missiles, on first inspection. However, his Chief's own credulity and the fulsome congratulations that he presses upon his Caribbean control mean that any expression of scepticism would be professional suicide:

> [The Chief:]　'You know, Hawthorne, we owe a great deal of this to you. I was told once that you were no judge of men, but I backed my private judgement. Well done, Hawthorne.'[47]

The same vested interest in maintaining the prestige and therefore the intra-governmental influence of the Secret Service – its power to command administrative resources and rewards – prevents Wormold's spymasters from either officially repudiating his literary inventions or disowning him professionally, once his fictions are revealed. Recognizing that any admission of the truth about 'our man in Havana' would 'ruin' the Secret Service's relations with the intelligence departments of the armed forces' ministries, the Chief proposes a way out of this embarrassing imbroglio: '. . . perhaps the simplest plan was to circulate one more report from [Wormold] – that the construction had proved a failure and had been dismantled'.[48] Moreover, to ensure Wormold's acquiescence in the cover-up, he is to be the recipient of benefits, both material and honorific, as the Chief informs him:

We thought the best thing for you under the circumstances would be to stay at home – on our training staff. Lecturing. How to run a station abroad. That kind of thing . . . Of course, as we always do when a man retires from a post abroad, we'll recommend you for a decoration. I think in your case – you were not there very long – we can hardly suggest anything higher than an O.B.E.[49]

Again, Alcázar de Velasco's career as a paper merchant resembles Wormold's in this regard. For the former's main secret-service employer, the *Abwehr* was operating in a much more cut-throat bureaucratic environment than the administrative milieu inhabited by MI6 in *Our Man in Havana*. So, engaged in an intense competition, less for supremacy than survival, with rival security and intelligence services of the Nazi party and state, the German military intelligence service could ill afford to discredit and disown one of its senior foreign agents, even supposing it were efficient enough to detect his deceit.[50]

Moreover, if the demise of the Third Reich, and its intelligence community along with it, in 1945 deprived the Spaniard of any possibility of imparting any of his professional experience to future generations of Nazi spies, Alcázar de Velasco did achieve a belated renown for his intelligence-gathering exploits. This development constitutes perhaps the most uncanny coincidence between the fictional story of Wormold and the actual case-history of Alcázar de Velasco. For, on 10 September 1978, *The Washington Post* printed a front-page story on the alleged espionage activities of the 'TO' network inside the United States during the Second World War. The report was prompted by the release of 30,000 pages of declassified documents from the records of the National Security Agency to the US National Archives in Washington, DC, including 'Magic' material. However, although the newspaper report cited a number of individual items from the 'Magic' intelligence summaries relating to the 'TO' organization, inexplicably it made no reference to the considerable evidence contained in these documents pointing to the spurious character of most of this supposed espionage effort. Instead, the author of *The Washington Post's* story, Thomas O'Toole, attributed the fact that the 'TO' network was left unmolested in the conduct of its espionage activities inside wartime America to the concern of US intelligence officers that any attempt to round up this spy-ring might alert the Japanese to the American cryptanalysis of the Purple cipher.[51] Naturally, Alcázar de Velasco confirmed this newspaper version of his wartime intelligence career, and the story was repeated in other Spanish and international papers and journals.[52] The result was that the 'TO' network was rapidly and retrospectively endowed with a substance and significance it never had in real life. Thus, despite commenting on the control exercised by MI5 on all the notional *Abwehr* agents active inside wartime Britain, Ronald Lewin in his book, *The American Magic: Codes, Ciphers and the Defeat of Japan*, does not allude at all to the serious doubts entertained by America's military intelligence about the authenticity of the espionage ring being run there by Alcázar de Velasco (whom he does not identify by name) during the Second World War. Indeed, he treats the espionage efforts of the Spaniards ostensibly at work inside the USA, after the attack on Pearl Harbor, as entirely a matter of fact.[53]

The new lease of life conferred on Alcázar de Velasco's wartime creations by this surprising turn of events might well have caused him to muse in similar fashion to Wormold, when the latter is confronted by the alarming tendency of his imaginatively invented agents to elaborate their own increasingly palpable personalities: 'Sometimes he was scared at the way these people grew in the dark without his knowledge'.[54] Ironically, Wormold's downfall as a paper merchant comes when his imaginings are taken so seriously by a rival secret service as virtually to turn his agents into real people who escape the confines of his authorial control into a more autonomous existence. So, in this coincidence – that in both the fictional story of the paper merchant, Wormold, and the actual history of the paper merchant, Alcázar de Velasco, the distinction between fiction and reality becomes blurred, that their literary inventions come to assume an independent existence – there is further mutual illumination. Indeed, in this way, as in the others specified above, *Our Man in Havana* affords a number of valuable insights into the real-life career of the Spanish 'literary' agent, Angel Alcázar de Velasco. Certainly, the novel's heuristic worth in this instance supports the judgement of that sometime OSS operative and academic literary critic, Norman Holmes Pearson, on its practical utility for the aspirant agent: 'Manuals on either espionage or counterespionage are after all rare. Graham Greene's *Our Man in Havana . . .* is perhaps as good as most'.[55]

NOTES

1. Marie-Françoise Allain, *The Other Man: Conversations with Graham Greene* (London, 1983; Harmondsworth, 1984) p.100.
2. *The Quiet American* (London, 1955), p.33.
3. Quoted in Allain, *The Other Man*, p.100.
4. Graham Greene, *Ways of Escape* (Toronto, 1980), pp.204–5, and 214; idem, *The Tenth Man* (New York, 1985), Introduction, pp.19–20; Allain, *The Other Man*, pp.58–9.
5. Greene, *Ways of Escape*, p.206; Graham Greene, *Our Man in Havana* (*The Collected Edition*, London, 1970), Introduction, p.viii.
6. Greene, *Ways of Escape*, p.264
7. Ibid, pp.206–7.
8. Ibid., p.214; Greene, *Our Man in Havana*, Collected Edition, Introduction, p.xviii; Allain, *The Other Man*, p.59.
9. Kim Philby, *My Silent War* (London, 1968; Frogmore, St Albans, 1969), p.81; Greene, *Ways of Escape*, pp.204–5.

10. Greene, *Ways of Escape*, p.205.
11. Ibid., p.205.
12. Ibid., pp.205–6.
13. *Our Man in Havana: An Entertainment* (London, 1958), p.175.
14. Philby, *My Silent War*, pp.57–8. See also, Phillip Knightley, *Philby: The Life and Views of the K.G.B. Masterspy* (London, 1988), pp.103–4.
15. J.C. Masterman, *The Double-Cross System in the War of 1939 to 1945* (New Haven and London, 1972), p.99; RG 457 (Records of the National Security Agency, National Archives, Washington, DC, (Records of 'Magic' Summaries, 1943, SRS 847) 24 January 1943, annex entitled, 'Summary of Information received by this Branch concerning the Organization and Operation of the "TO" Intelligence Net in the United States', p.2.
    See also the record of a meeting that T.F. Burns, the press attaché of the British Embassy in Madrid, had with Alcázar de Velasco in February 1942, in which the Spaniard made the following impression: 'Violent, blustering, foul-mouthed and eloquent, he is an extraordinary mixture of astuteness and sheer brute fanaticism of the Nazi type'. (Public Record Office, Kew, FO 371/31229, C2004/186/41)
16. See, e.g., Heleno Saña, *El Franquismo sin Mitos: Conversaciones con Serrano Suñer* (Barcelona, 1982) p.230, and Sheelagh M. Ellwood, *Spanish Fascism in the Franco Era: Falange Española de las Jons, 1936–76* (Basingstoke and London, 1987), pp.41–7.
17. Saña, *El Franquismo sin Mitos*, p.230; Herbert Rutledge, Southworth, *Antifalange: Estudio crítico de 'Falange en la Guerra de España: la Unificación y Hedilla ' de Maximano García Venero* (Paris, 1967), pp.14 and 55.
18. Stanley G. Payne, *The Franco Regime, 1936–1975* (Madison, Wisconsin, 1987), pp.240–41, Ellwood, *Spanish Fascism*, p.68; Viscount Templewood, *Ambassador on Special Mission* (London, 1946), p.76.
19. Angel Alcázar de Velasco, *Memorias de un Agente Secreto* (Barcelona, 1979), pp.19 and 35. The year for Alcázar de Velasco's activation as an agent by the *Abwehr* is specified in the text on p.35 – incorrectly – as 1930, when it should obviously be 1940.
20. This account of 'del Pozo's' mission is drawn from the following sources: F.H. Hinsley *et al. British Intelligence in the Second World War* (5 vols., London, 1979–90) Vol IV (1990), with C.A.G. Simkins, *Security and Counter-Intelligence*, pp.94–5; Masterman, *Double-Cross System*, pp.57–8 and 92; Alcázar de Velasco, *Memorias de un Agente Secreto*, pp.42–4; Confidential report of 'Headquarters United States Forces European Theater Military Intelligence Service Center, APO 757, Subject: Referat II KO Spanien', of 12 January 1946, Annex IV, in John Mendelsohn (ed.), *Covert Warfare: Intelligence, Counterintelligence and Military Deception During the World War II Era* (18 vols. New York, 1989), Vol.13, with an introduction by David Kahn, *The Final Solution of the Abwehr*.
    The official history of *British Intelligence in the Second World War* does not give 'del Pozo's' real name and Alcázar de Velasco only identifies him in his memoir by Christian name and initials, 'Miguel P.-V.', but his full name, Piernavieja, is mentioned in the post-war report of US Military Intelligence (cited above) at the following place: Annex IV; Operation of II KO Spanien in Other Countries', Subject: Referat II KO Spanien, para. 6, *Wales*, p.20.
21. Hinsley and Simkins, *British Intelligence in the Second World War*, Vol.IV, pp.104–5 and 107; Masterman, *Double-Cross System*, pp.83–4, 92–3 and 99.
22. Mendelsohn (ed.), *Covert Operations*, Vol.13, Confidential report of 'Headquarters U.S. Forces European Theater Military Intelligence Service Center, APO 757, Subject: Referat II KO Spanien', of 12 January 1946, Annex IV, para. 6, p.20; David Kahn, *Hitler's Spies: German Military Intelligence in World War II* (London, 1978), p.356.
23. Hinsley and Simkins, *British Intelligence*, IV, pp.107–9.
24. Ibid., pp.109–10, Philby, *My Silent War*, p.58.
25. Philby, *My Silent War*, p.57.
26. Nigel West, *M.I.6: British Secret Intelligence Service Operations, 1909–45* (London, 1983), p.184. Philby, writing from memory alone, does not specify the precise date of the operation but he does suggest that it preceded the arrest of Calvo and indeed that it yielded the evidence however dubious, for the latter's arrest. However, Hinsley and

Simkins, on the basis of access of official MI5 records, state that it was Magic and Enigma decrypts that incriminated Calvo. (Philby, *My Silent War*, p.58; Hinsley and Simkins, *British Intelligence*, IV, p.108.)

Phillip Knightley asserts, on the basis of conversations with Philby in Moscow in January 1988, that Calvo's espionage activity 'had nothing to do with de Velasco' but this contention, too, is contradicted by the official historians of British security and counter-intelligence in the Second World War (Knightley, *Philby*, p.104; Hinsley and Simkins, *British Intelligence*, IV, p.109).

27. Philby, *My Silent War*, p.57.
28. Ibid., pp.57–8.
     In a discussion with the author Michael Bloch in the autumn of 1983, Alcázar de Velasco claimed that he had received advance warning of the British intent to steal his espionage records and had replaced them with the fabricated diaries that the SIS discovered, all the better to mislead and misinform its agents. This latter assertion is not corroborated by the incontrovertible evidence of Alcázar de Velasco's espionage inventions and fabrications contained in Allied decrypts of enemy communications and especially the Magic material cited below. (Michael Bloch, *Operation Willi: The Nazi Plot to Kidnap the Duke of Windsor* (Toronto, 1984), p.155.)
29. Malcolm Muggeridge, *Chronicles of Wasted Time* (2 vols. London, 1972–73), Vol.II, *The Infernal Grove*, p.154.
30. Saña, *El Franquismo sin Mitos*, p.244.
31. RG 457, 'Magic' Summary, 28 August 1942, annexed Memorandum, Subject: 'TO' Intelligence Reports, pp.9–10; SRS 847, 'Magic' Summary, 24 January 1943, annex, p.16.
32. RG 457, SRS 847, 'Magic' Summary, 24 January 1943, annex, pp.15–18; SRS 697 'Magic' Summary, 28 August 1942, annex p.1.
33. Hinsley and Simkin, *British Intelligence*, IV, p.110.
34. Greene, *Our Man in Havana*, pp.70–72 and 89.
35. RG 457, SRS 847, 'Magic' Summary, 24 January 1943, annex, pp.11–12.
36. RG 457, SRS 706, 'Magic' Summary, 6 September 1942.
37. RG 457, SRS 769, 'Magic' Summary, 7 November 1942.
38. RG 457, SRS 573, 'Magic' Summary, 16 April 1942.
39. Ibid.
40. RG 457, SRS 847, 'Magic' Summary, 24 January 1943, annex, pp.5–9; Antonio Marquina Barrio; 'TO', Espias de Verbena, *Historia 16*, No.32 (December, 1978), p.14; 'Spanish diplomat admits spying in US and London', *The Times* (London), 21 September 1978, RG 457, SRS 901, 'Magic' Summary, 11 March 1943.
41. Hinsley and Simkins, *British Intelligence*, IV, p.127.
42. Masterman, *The Double-Cross System*, p.83.
43. Ibid., p.84
44. Hinsley and Simkins, *British Intelligence*, IV, p.127.
     The case in question was that of Juan Pujol, code-named 'Garbo', who graduated from misinforming the Germans, on his own initiative, to becoming the double-cross system's star agent in the promotion of Operation 'Fortitude', the deception scheme intended to aid and abet the Allied invasion of Normandy in June 1944. (See, eg., Juan Pujol, with Nigel West, *Garbo* (London, 1985), *passim*.)
45. Kahn, introd., *Final Solution of the Abwehr*, pp.XIII–XIV.
46. See, e.g., J.W.M. Chapman, 'Japanese Intelligence, 1918–1945: A Suitable Case for Treatment' in Christopher Andrew and Jeremy Noakes (eds.), *Intelligence and International Relations, 1900–1945* (Exeter, 1987), pp.145–90. However, the following sharp reply from Foreign Minister, Shigemitsu, in July 1943, to yet another request from Suma in Madrid for additional funds – to support the dispatch of three Spanish journalists to Latin America on an espionage mission for Japan – indicates, perhaps, a growing awareness on the part of Japanese intelligence officials that they were not getting value for their money:

I have just read your telegram. You must think that we are made of money. As a matter of fact, we haven't any money at all to throw away. I too would like to carry out some such plan as you mention, but, if we were to do it in the way you suggest, then you would find yourself greatly hampered by a lack of funds in much of your other work.

(RG 457, SRS 1031, 'Magic' Summary, 20 July 1943).

47. Greene, *Our Man in Havana*, pp.96–100.
48. Ibid., pp.268–9.
49. Ibid., pp.267, 268–70.
50. See, e.g., Michael Geyer, 'National Socialist Germany: The Politics of Information', in Ernest R. May (ed.), *Knowing One's Enemies: Intelligence Assessment before the Two World Wars* (Princeton, 1984), pp.310–46.
   Interestingly, Walter Schellenberg, as chief of the *Reichsicherheitshauptamt*, the SS's Foreign Intelligence Service (the eventual victor over the *Abwehr* in the power struggles within the Third Reich's intelligence community), was presented, probably in late 1941, with a scathing report by one of his assistants, on the insecurity and inefficiency of that department's organization in Spain. However, Schellenberg, too, decided, in the end, to let sleeping dogs lie (idem, *The Schellenberg Memoirs* (London, 1956), pp.259–60).
51. *The Washington Post*'s headline for Sunday, 10 September 1978 read thus: 'Spanish Diplomats Spied on U.S. for Japan in W.W. II'.
52. See, e.g., *The Times*, 21 September 1978, *El País* (Madrid), 20 September 1978 and *Cambio 16* (Madrid), 24 September and 1 October 1978.
53. Ronald Lewin, *The American Magic: Codes, Ciphers and the Defeat of Japan* (New York, 1982), pp.239–40.
54. Greene, *Our Man in Havana*, p.127.
55. Norman Holmes Pearson, 'Foreword', in Masterman, *The Double-Cross System*, p.IX.

The Development of the Espionage Film

ALAN R. BOOTH

It is not surprising that the development of the espionage film in the twentieth century should roughly parallel that of the spy novel. Some of the similarities are obvious. Both genres were turn-of-the-century phenomena,[1] originating in the pre-war mania of the 1890s (the novels), and events of the First World War itself (the films). Each featured certain common plot elements: adventure, suspense, politics and romance; and both incorporated similar themes: good vs. evil, loyalty, betrayal, patriotism, xenophobia and war. Both were 'reflections of the times and societies which produced them'.

Of course 'the times' were fearful. The industrialized nations of Europe, having invented a new generation of lethal weaponry (tanks and machine guns, submarines and aircraft), were careening towards the First World War.[2] For turn-of-the-century Britain (the wellspring of the modern spy novel), the danger of France to its continental dominance gave way to the specter of a Germany risen to power by virtue of its aggressions against Austria and France, the successes of which lay in no small part in Prussian intelligence and espionage. It was no coincidence that the new generation of early twentieth-century British spy novels revolved around plots of continental invasion threats, and of stolen secret plans and documents.[3]

SPIES INVADE THE SILENT SCREEN

The development of the espionage film did not quite follow the pattern of the books. In the first place, the society which first produced it was Californian, not British. So it was the American view of 'the times' – the First World War and the US's avoidance of it until its belated entry in 1917 – that the earliest espionage films reflected. Some themes, as in the novels, revolved around the theft of war plans and technology; but others were new, particularly as they reflected a burgeoning fear and fascination with the German submarine, the one new weapon with ocean-spanning potential and threatening implications to America's shores. The 1915 German U-boat sinking of the *Lusitania* with heavy loss of American life contributed to that fear, and to the anti-German bias of many of the early American spy features.

Those were reflected in one of the earliest Hollywood films, *Our Secret Wires* (1915), which depicted an American secret service operator discovering German agents sending messages to an enemy U-boat stationed off the Oregon coast. In fact by 1916 Hollywood was producing an increasing number of films making Germans the villains of their plots, as a way of urging American intervention. *The Hero of Submarine D-2* (1916) depicted an attempt by German operatives to destroy a US naval base, while in *As In a Looking Glass* (1916) the heroine was a double agent who halted German attempts to spirit away the defense plans for New York harbor. Still another, *The Secret of the Submarine* (1916), involved foreign attempts to steal an invention enabling a submarine to remain underwater indefinitely.[4]

The year 1917, bringing America's entry into the war, unleashed an avalanche of spy dramas reflecting heightened concerns of war's immediacy. Plots continued to reflect filmgoers' preoccupations with the U-boat, and played on war-inspired patriotism and xenophobic fears of treachery and conspiracy. Romance – and the vulnerability of women – were the constant stuff of plots. In *The Little American* (1917), Mary Pickford ('America's Sweetheart'), a war relief worker in Belgium, was taken prisoner by the Germans and held as a spy. Ethel Barrymore in *The Greatest Power* (1917) turned in her lover after discovering him to be a German agent. German spies staged (in Rubenstein's words) a 'virtual invasion of the silent screen', establishing secret submarine bases and signalling U-boats off the New England coast, suborning German-born aliens to work for the Fatherland, sabotaging war factories, and stealing plans for secret weapons. D.W. Griffith's 1918 feature *The Great Love* combined the dual themes of national and personal betrayal, portraying a Canadian soldier whose English girlfriend married another man while he was away at the front, only to discover that the counterfeit lover was into the bargain a German agent.[5]

With the armistice and the popular shift away from war toward the frenzied pleasures of the 1920s, public taste in the United States tired of espionage as cinematic lore. Anti-war revulsion for the most part cooled the market even for the wartime staple of the romantic drama within the spy vehicle. Few memorable Hollywood spy films were produced during the 1920s, and those that were dealt with espionage motifs safely removed from the recent conflict: the American Civil War; the French Foreign Legion vs. Arab nationalism; foreign threats to American security; or thefts of exotic new technologies ('electronic death rays') or priceless gems.

One manifestation of this reaction was the introduction of the screen comedy based on spying, a genre which (with its cousin the espionage film parody) would be responsible for half a dozen of the best espionage films over the next 60 years. The most notable of the early spy comedies was Buster Keaton's legendary portrayal of a Confederate spy in *The General* (1928).[6]

Europe, by contrast, came down with a touch of renewed spy fever during the 1920s, undoubtedly a spin-off from the Russian Revolution of 1917 and the post-war economic catastrophes befalling many countries (notably Germany). It produced one epic melodrama (nearly three hours in the original) by the German producer/director Fritz Lang: *Spione* [*Spies*] (1928).[7] Lang's master villain, Haghi, was both the head of a multinational banking house and an international spy network concealed within it – all modelled, Lang later maintained, on incidents surrounding a Soviet trade delegation-cum-spy ring in London during the 1920s.[8]

Romance and sexual entrapment drove the plot ("*"Spies"* projects like "*Perils of Pauline*"', wrote one reviewer). One of Haghi's beautiful seductresses compromised and drove to suicide the Japanese diplomat/spy Dr Masimoto; another, Haghi's arch female spy, Sonia, fell in love with her designated quarry, saved his life, and turned on her spymaster, entrapping him in his own web of romantic betrayal.[9]

Spione was the first true espionage feature, as opposed to adventures, romances or comedies on the spy motif. Haghi, the arch villain and archetypal spy of an era, was a professional agent and a master of disguise. His profession, like that of the prostitutes he employed, was morally tainted. His soul (hence the soul of the spy) was evil and corrupt; his method was treachery. His female agents were also dedicated professionals (along with nearly everyone else in the film), who vamped their victims for secret information. No longer merely reacting to their romantic predicaments, *Spione's* women chose actions which determined not only their own fates, but those of networks and states as well. So Sonia, Haghi's trusted agent, opted for heart over loyalty and brought the enemy down on him.

If *Spione* gave a different dimension of importance to the female agent, two films of the same era (*Dishonored* [1931], and *Mata Hari* [1932]) brought the complexities of her character to a new level. Casting was in part responsible, for the heroines were played by the two most popular romantic actresses of the time: Marlene Dietrich (Agent X-27), and Greta Garbo (Mata Hari). These two stars took the supporting characters of *Spione's* women (treacherous *femmes fatales*) and fashioned them into the multifaceted and compelling starring roles they became.

Other borrowings from Lang included the clown disguise, the seduction/ suicide of the espionage victim (*Dishonored*), and the central idea of the female agent as the calculating and crafty professional. But 'X-27' and Mata Hari, as played by these legendary actresses, became women of many faces: flirtatious yet utterly ruthless, both vulnerable and courageous, and always – however calculating and deadly – feminine romantics to the core, fatal qualities which placed each before the firing squad at the ends of both films. Dietrich's 'X-27' fell in love with her quarry, Russian Agent 'H-14', and in allowing him to escape sealed her own fate. Garbo's Mata Hari pleaded guilty at her trial rather than let her betrayed Russian aviator lover (Ramon

Navarro), learn the awful reality of her past, and died with a bravery that was pure melodrama.

THE BRINK OF WAR: THE SPY AS AMATEUR GENTLEMAN HERO

Dishonored and *Mata Hari* reintroduced American audiences to the spy film by looking back to the First World War. It was the European film-makers, notably the British, who viewed the current world around them and reflected it cinematically. It was not so much the Depression which heightened anxieties of European film producers and audiences as the violent polarization of world politics as evidenced by the accession to power of new governments in Soviet Russia, Fascist Italy and Nazi Germany, each with an open commitment to aggression and subversion. Lang's *Spione* were, after all, Bolsheviks operating against the post-war West. But they were also despicable characters (with the exception of Sonia), just as Dietrich and Garbo were treacherous vamps before finally choosing romance over state.

The 1930s generation of pre-war films produced by the Europeans marked a turning away from earlier themes of the spy as morally tainted professional. Indeed, it struck many that these new continental regimes were so odious and threatening that they *warranted* being spied upon.[10] In any event, these films (reminiscent of the early British espionage novel) restored the spy to amateur standing and reasserted his essential goodness, making him the thwarter of totalitarian regimes and their subversive schemings. Agent heroes were, like their literary antecedents, upper-class gentlemen who accidentally discovered foreign plots against the state or found themselves thrust against their will into a world of intrigue and incipient violence, taking up the defense of democratic 'good' against authoritarian 'evil'. Aside from their heroism, like Edwardian gentlemen they were cosmopolitan, honorable, humane – and terribly witty. Women likewise were relegated to their previous incarnations as auxiliaries or foils to the heroes, reacting to events and (except for the occasional *bon mot*) contributing little in the way of intellect or insight.

One of the most notable and enduring of these British films was *The Scarlet Pimpernel* (1935). It was set in the French Revolution, but its message was clearly allegorical to the times: political tyranny of either extreme was the enemy of civilized mankind. The hero, the simpering and foppish Sir Percy Blakeney (Leslie Howard), secretly set out to rescue French aristocrats from certain death at the hands of the radicals. The irony of his position (since he was the last person to be suspected of such derring-do) was heightened by the attitude of his French-born wife (Merle Oberon) who, passionately devoted to the Revolution's ideals, estranged herself from her husband's effete attitudes, only to discover his true role after leading him into a nearly fatal trap sprung by the French ambassador, Chauvelin (Raymond Massey).

Lest the allegory be lost on wartime audiences (notably in still-neutral America), Mr Howard – himself to be shot down and killed in 1943 while furthering the British war propaganda effort – produced an updated version, *Pimpernel Smith* (1941). This time, Professor Horatio Smith (Howard), an absent-minded Cambridge archaeologist supposedly looking for a lost Aryan civilization in pre-war Germany, snatched intended Nazi victims from under the large nose of the oleaginous but deadly Gestapo General von Graum (Francis L. Sullivan). Using a device borrowed from *Spione*, Howard accomplished his bravura feats (as he had in *The Scarlet Pimpernel*) partly by the masterly use of disguise.

But 'disguise' comes in many forms. While Lang's clowns and Howard's false faces and scarecrows dissembled to perfection, it was left to another director to take the device to new levels of subtlety and innovation. The greatest innovator of disguise in all its forms during this (or any) period was the master director of espionage films, Alfred Hitchcock. To Hitchcock 'disguise' was deception: wigs and rubber noses gave way to false names and seemingly innocent professions to mask the real work of espionage. As Rubenstein put it:

> Hitchcock's villains did not wear traditional signs, neither distinct foreign accents nor melodramatic cloaks. Pronounced or subtle, their mannerisms indicated the faint clues to their position in the English director's morality tales. And it is a morality tale that his films often resembled, with a naive character introduced to a world of intrigue and terror. Most of his protagonists were more or less forced by circumstances to become spies, and it was assumed by all that the film's end that they would never undertake such work again.[11]

No film director has ever produced more first-quality spy films, many of which have become classics; none has consistently filmed better quality screenplays or introduced more plot devices to draw the viewer into his films and to heighten and sustain audience tension.[12] In a series of films from the 1930s to the 1950s (*The 39 Steps* [1935]; *The Secret Agent* [1936]; *The Lady Vanishes* [1938]; *Foreign Correspondent* [1940]; *Notorious* [1946]; *North by Northwest* [1959]), Hitchcock established himself as the crowning genius of sophisticated humor and suspense, and the nonpareil of creativity in all aspects of film-making, from casting, staging and editing to nearly every imaginable audio and visual technique.

'My hero,' Hitchcock once said, 'is the average man to whom bizarre things happen, and not vice versa.' The independent nature of the amateur hero makes him a character with whom the audience can easily identify. At first glance the Hitchcock hero is an uncomplicated, even one-dimensional character – certainly less complicated than the villain. In this manner the director makes his protagonist easily understandable and at the same time evokes a keen sense of empathy with him. Admiration for the hero is heightened by the understated, off-hand, sophisticated humor with which he goes about entrapping the spies and saving England. Humorless by contrast, the Hitchcockian villain is invariably introduced behind a facade of utter charm and respectability – quickly demonstrated to be fearfully enigmatic.[13]

One of the finest examples of Hitchcock's artistry was one of his earliest, *The 39 Steps* (1935). The quintessentially suave and handsome hero, Richard Hannay (Robert Donat), was a Canadian visiting Britain.[14] In a favorite Hitchcock device, the audience was immediately thrust into sympathy with Hannay who found himself isolated on every side, chased by the London police for a murder he did not commit, and both pursuer of and fugitive from the secret agents of the '39 steps,' whose information he had to intercept if Britain were to be saved. 'The audience will wonder,' the director later said, '"Why doesn't he go to the police?" Well, the police are after him, so he can't go to them can he?'[15]

The villain was the enigmatic Professor Jordan (Godfrey Tearle), the man with the missing fingertip Hannay had been warned about. Here Hitchcock revealed one of his many plot twists: for against all spy film tradition it was the eminently respectable Briton, Professor Jordan, who sought to betray the motherland, while Hannay, the foreigner, determined to save it.

Nothing (except Hannay's intentions) was as it seemed. The unwitting hero first mistakenly placed his trust in Jordan, and then in a Scottish police official who betrayed him to the spies, each time barely escaping. The heroine, Pamela (Madeline Carroll),[16] first attempted to turn him in to the police, and later betrayed him to the spies disguised as the police. Indeed, her inability to grasp the nuances of what was transpiring brought them both repeatedly to the brink of ruin, escaping from one dangerous situation into another, each refuge becoming a greater danger. During the crucial chase segment, Hannay both literally and figuratively dragged Pamela along after him, handcuffed as they were together. Hitchcock deftly moved from the gripping tension of that chase to the light comedy of sexual tension, as the antagonistic yet attracted couple were forced to spend the night cuffed to each other at an inn.[17]

But Hitchcock's 'equivocal' portrayal of Pamela was an example of why some modern feminists take issue with his women in this and other early films.[18] The world of *The 39 Steps* was a man's world. Gone, at least for the moment, were the days of the female prime protagonist. Pamela, no 'Agent X-27' or Mata Hari, was auxiliary, reactive and slow to catch on. Every woman in the film was used in one way or another, and one (the farmer's wife) was brutally slapped, her scream fading into the laughter of Hannay and a policeman in the following scene.

Hitchcock's dominant metaphor driving the film's plot through sequential deceptions and misunderstandings was the theater. The film's opening sequence was in a London music hall and its final scene was at the Palladium. Hannay, to extricate himself from sticky situations, played many roles: a politician; a milkman; Pamela's lover; a Salvation Army marcher. Some of those fictions achieved a measure of truth, notably when Hannay, who pretended to be Pamela's lover while escaping on a train, became so at the film's end.[19]

The 39 Steps was representative of several mid-1930s spy films which were mildly anticipatory of war. Set in between-the-wars Britain, it reflected Britain's spirit of hope that peace could be preserved if everyone kept their heads, and kept their powder dry. So, for instance, *The 39 Steps* never named the offending foreign power attempting to make off with British defense secrets.

But as war clouds gradually approached, Hitchcock became one of several late-1930s filmmakers who registered their growing apprehensions with the spread of Fascist adventurism on the continent through more explicitly allegorical films. One, *The Secret Agent* (1936), based on Somerset Maugham's *Ashenden* (1928), involved two British intelligence agents (Madeline Carroll and John Gielgud) dispatched to Switzerland to assassinate a mysterious and troublesome German spy. It was distinctly anti-espionage and pacifist in tone: Gielgud killed the wrong man, and both he and Carroll, lovers at the end, vowed never to spy again.

Noticeably less anti-war was the other period Hitchcock allegory, *The Lady Vanishes* (1938), his last important and most acclaimed British film before he moved to the United States.[20]

The Lady Vanishes was in many ways vintage Hitchcock. Well-paced and sprung with mounting tension, it conveyed the bewilderment and growing apprehensions of ordinary Britons caught up in extraordinary circumstances – all in exotic settings featuring beautiful mountains and speeding trains. Thrown together among a group of British travelers stranded in a small 'third-rate [European] country',[21] a holidaying man (Michael Redgrave) and woman (Margaret Lockwood) discover that an elderly lady among them (Dame May Whitty) is a British agent in possession of damaging state secrets and in the process of being kidnapped by the German secret service. Their efforts to save her, involving drugged drinks, false-bottomed trunks, melodic ciphers, and a notably un-Hitchcockian gunfight at the border, are ultimately successful.

In fact Hitchcock's *The Lady Vanishes* proved so spectacularly successful as a plot formula that it spawned what was arguably one of the early examples of the critically successful sequel, a classic on its own. The British film *Night Train to Munich* (1940) was not directed by Hitchcock, who by then had migrated to the United States, but its other borrowings were copious. Both films were produced, scripted and scored by the same men. Furthermore, *Night Train to Munich* reprised the gripping climactic scenes of *The Lady Vanishes*, the chase on the hurtling train, and the shoot-out – this time atop a cable car – both devices which were imitated many times.[22]

Filmed after the outbreak of the Second World War, *Night Train to Munich* marked the mobilization of the spy film to war duty. Its plot (like *The 39 Steps*) involved British foiling of the theft of defense technology – but this time clearly at the hands of the Gestapo. Into the bargain the film laid on some licks against Hitler's legitimacy and for Britain's secret service, to a filmgoing public for whom in 1940 'even a cinematic victory was welcome'.[23]

ESPIONAGE GOES TO WAR

As the Second World War was a major turning point in the history of espionage, so was it a milestone in the development of the spy film. That was so partly because the years since the First World War had witnessed an awareness among governments of the cinema's potential as a propaganda vehicle. No state made better use of that knowledge than Nazi Germany, and its films (especially those of Leni Riefenstahl) glorifying its Aryan heritage became the standard of effectiveness for others (notably Frank Capra's *Why We Fight* [1942]) to be measured against.

Consequently with rare exception the quality of the espionage film fell victim to the exigencies of war. Subtlety and ambiguity gave way to the necessity of indoctrination. Typecast characters, predictable plots and ham-handed depictions of the enemy made for wartime spy films that were for the most part 'painfully mediocre'. Even Hitchcock fell victim to accusations of propagandizing his enemy characters.[24]

Three films produced early in the war were memorable exceptions. One, *Confessions of a Nazi Spy* (1939), was noteworthy not so much for its plot – a too-melodramatic tale of an FBI 'G-man's' (Edward G. Robinson) successful entrapment of a nest of Nazi spies in the US – as it was for its method. Its pioneering *cinema vérité* style, utilizing the voice-over (Reed Hadley) to dovetail newsreel footage with dramatized sequences, was to be copied with greater success in later semi-documentary Second World War spy films. The technique was made possible, and the film's popularity guaranteed, by the basing of the film on the 1938 Nazi spy trials which had shocked the American public into awareness of the dangers of a German fifth column in their midst. Still it was overdrawn, even for the tenor of the times: 'We can endure,' complained one review, 'just so much hissing, even when Der Fuehrer and the Gestapo are its victims.'[25]

Another memorable propaganda vehicle, *Watch on the Rhine* (1943), was adapted from a 1941 agitprop play by Lillian Hellman whose message was that Fascism was just as barbaric and threatening at home as abroad. Set largely in a Washington drawing room, it portrayed the efforts of an undercover anti-Nazi German engineer (Paul Lukas) and his American-born wife (Bette Davis) on a family visit to fight off the attempts of a Fascist Romanian count (George Coulouris) to blackmail them with the threat of exposure to the German embassy. Yet by modern standards *Watch on the Rhine* was little more than a filmed stage play, a drama of words relieved by a single dramatic action, Lukas's shooting of Coulouris.[26]

The third film – and of all the spy films of the early war the greatest and most enduring classic – was *Casablanca* (1942). It was in fact far more propaganda vehicle and incandescent romance than it was espionage cinema. Like *Night Train to Munich* and other spy romances, its plot turned on a love triangle, two men vying for a woman's love, set in the North African city which had become a definition of the crossroads of intrigue. 'Rick's Café Américain' was the stopping-off point for agents of all sides: Free France, Vichy France and Nazi Germany, along with assorted anti-fascist freedom-fighters, profiteers and refugees, and all the riff-raff which imagination linked them with.[27]

The café's owner was Rick Blaine (Humphrey Bogart), whose cynically cold exterior shielded a soul thirsting for world justice and romance. His passion was focused on Ilsa (Ingrid Bergman), with whom he had had an intense affair in Paris before the Germans closed in, and who now appeared at Rick's place with her husband, Free French underground leader Victor Laszlo (Paul Henreid). Rick had in his possession the tickets to the Lazlos' freedom, exit visas which would get them to Lisbon and thence America; the question was whether Rick and Ilsa would choose love (remaining with him) or duty (following Laszlo). Rick made the choice for her, dispatching her with her husband from the airport, then dispatching the Nazi agent in a classic eighteenth-century pistol duel. Finally, Bogart, the metaphorical American, went off with Police Captain Renault (Claude Rains) to Brazzaville, to fight and to spy another day, for world justice – and for money.

Casablanca's popularity as a romance somewhat masked its effectiveness as a stirring piece of anti-Fascist and pro-espionage propaganda. It was, to quote one reviewer, 'a sturdy if glossy study of how a sense of fair play and patriotism leads all manner of individuals into the world of spying and underground work'. On the other hand *Casablanca* perpetuated the spy film's traditional portrayal of the woman as passive. Bergman was indecisive, vacillating between her husband and his cause, and Bogart – who was hardly the image of a committed freedom-fighter until the final sequences of the film. She had expected to remain with him in Casablanca;

it was he who made the decision to put her on the plane, committing them both to the anti-Nazi struggle ('... the problems of three little people don't amount to a hill of beans in this crazy world; some day you'll understand that').[28]

Most early war espionage cinema was not, however, of such quality. Churned out by Hollywood to meet the national need to stigmatize the enemy, it featured mass-produced sets hung with swastikas or sunbursts, boilerplate plots with standardised chase scenes and predictable dénouements, clichéd characters, and severely rationed humor. In fact, the only memorable anti-Nazi satire among them, *To Be or Not to Be* (1942) was blunted by the tragic death of its star, Carole Lombard, shortly before its release.

Consequently most of the notable Second World War spy films were made near or after the war's end, in some cases well after. Yet they too were heavy propaganda pieces. Two of the most popular were docu-dramas glorifying the war-winning roles of the US's wartime intelligence organizations: the FBI (*The House on 92nd Street* [1945]), and the O.S.S. (*13 Rue Madeleine* [1946]). Aside from their obvious differences in subject matter they were remarkably similar in approach and technique, as their common producer, director, scriptwriter and voice-over might have suggested.

The art of the staged documentary was the brainchild of the producer, Louis de Rochement, whose earlier career as newsreel cameraman, editor, and producer of the popular 'March of Time' newsreel series afforded ample background. Taking its departure from *Confessions of a Nazi Spy* (and *Citizen Kane* [1941]), the genre strove first and foremost for verisimilitude. Both films combined actual and simulated newsreel footage, shot not on studio sets but on outdoor location with grainy film, and introduced by a voice-over which editorialized while presenting factual information. In addition, *The House on 92nd Street* cast unknown actors in starring roles playing characters purposely devoid of individuality and delivering their lines in monotone. (*13 Rue Madeleine*, by contrast, starred James Cagney.)[29]

But it was clear that the de Rochement formula came as a complete package; and that when one or two elements were missing, the results were limp. *The Man Who Never Was* (1956), for instance, attempted merely to combine the same 'now it can be told' format with straight dramatization and understated acting. The film purported to depict faithfully an actual Second World War deception operation, false papers planted on a dead body aimed at convincing the Germans that the 1943 'Husky' invasion was aimed at Greece and Sardinia, and not Sicily.

But while *The House on 92nd Street* and *13 Rue Madeleine* had been written to elevate tension to a rousing climax in the conventional spy thriller fashion, *The Man Who Never Was* suffered from the dual misfortune of having Clifton Webb and a corpse as its leading actors, and of drawing such a lifeless performance from Webb that it was difficult to tell which was the corpse. Various devices not in Ewan Montagu's 1953 book (of the same title) were conjured up to rescue the plot, namely a contrived romance and a cooked-up Nazi spy mission, all to no avail.

An important 1950s film on the same war period, however, was both more sophisticated in its dramatization and successful in making a significant statement about espionage in war. In *Five Fingers* (1952), set in neutral Turkey, James Mason superbly played the role of 'Cicero', the British ambassador's valet-cum-German spy, with all the surface charm and underlying moral ugliness of the original agent.

The film was successful in part because it neatly reflected the heavy ironies lacing the actual story. The real 'Cicero' had sold (1943–44) reams of the ambassador's most secret papers (including summaries of Allied summit conferences and references to 'Overlord') to the Germans. But they had made little use of the intelligence because Hitler had believed 'Cicero' to be a double agent – rightly, as it happened, although exactly when the British caught and turned him is still something of a mystery. In any event the spy died poor, since it turned out that the Germans had all the while paid him with bogus currency.

The importance of the film lay both in its tone and its implied message. Previous spy semi-documentaries had been sober dramas, with voice-overs reminding audiences periodically of the story's authenticity. But *Five Fingers*, although opening with such a narration, quickly 'punctured [the] balloon of solemnity'[30] in favor of a slightly tongue-in-cheek recounting of espionage sting and countersting in a way not a little reminiscent of a Hitchcock thriller. Yet in the mood of sophisticated humor there lay a serious idea:

> Joseph L. Mankiewicz [the director] . . . laced his facile production with an ingenious touch of wry wit, not bitterly pessimistic, but recognising the increasing awareness of moviegoers that in war there are often no purely good sides, and that those who work the middle fence are after all practical individuals with a quicker intelligence than most.[31]

That first filmed hint of the moral ambiguity of espionage would become the dominant theme of a later generation of spy films adapted from the novels of Greene, Deighton and le Carré. *The Eye of the Needle* (1981) might have further developed that theme had it been more faithful to the original (1978) Ken Follett novel (in which the German [not Nazi] spy, Faber, was ambiguously heroic), and had it cast as Faber someone other than the clay-footed Donald Sutherland. Instead, the most that many saw in *The Eye of the Needle* was a backward look to the classic nip-and-tuck chase film, *The 39 Steps*, especially as its fugitive sequences reprised Hannay's flight across the Scottish moors and fleeting sanctuary with the rough farmer and his repressed wife.[32]

THE GREY DAWN OF THE COLD WAR: LABYRINTHS OF BETRAYAL

Just as the moral ambiguity of Second World War espionage was beginning to surface in its early 1950s films, Hollywood was taking a wholly more rigid view of the nature of the foreign threat facing America from the onset of the Cold War in 1946. There were several reasons.

First, the post-war Soviet Communist threat appeared to be far more of clear and present danger to America's shores than even wartime Germany or Japan had been. Stalinist Russia had transformed itself apparently overnight from ally into brutal and fearsome world adversary. Then, beginning in 1946, came the sensational revelations about Soviet espionage activities in North America. President Truman in that year signalled both the onset and the character of the Cold War by demanding a loyalty oath from all government employees.

This poisoned atmosphere helped breathe new life into an old congressional nemesis of the American Left, the House Committee on Un-American Activities (HUAC). During the war the Committee had repeatedly been thwarted in its attempts to hold hearings to uncover evidence of Communist influence in Hollywood. Now, with the outbreak of the Cold War and the return of both houses of Congress to the Republicans in the 1946 election, HUAC turned on Hollywood with a vengeance. Over the next several years it attempted, through a series of dramatic public hearings, to establish a conspiratorial connection between what was being seen on the American screen and world Communism's determination to destroy the American way of life.

Beginning in late 1947 the major Hollywood studios, faced with strong economic pressure from television, turned in full retreat from HUAC's political pressure. First publicly dismissing ten prominent screenwriters and directors for refusing to testify before HUAC, they then proceeded to 'blacklist' unofficially over 150 writers, producers, directors and actors from work in the film industry from then until the early 1960s.[33]

It was in that star chamber atmosphere that one must judge the spy films produced by Hollywood during those years, when virtually all life-signs of an American cinema of the left disappeared. Artists and producers were so intimidated by McCarthyite inquisition that any attempts at nuanced interpretations of the Cold War were doomed to obscurity. What appeared in their stead was a body of anti-Communist spy films so overdrawn and claustrophobic as to caricature their intended purpose.

'Hollywood fired its first shot in the "cold war' against Russia,' *The New*

York Times complained of the first of them, *The Iron Curtain* (1948). It stood 'ready to fight it out . . . to the last sneer'. Derivative of the semi-documentary style of *The House on 92nd Street*, *The Iron Curtain* dramatized the 1945 defection in Ottawa of Soviet embassy code clerk Igor Gouzenko (Dana Andrews) – one of the crucial early Cold War Soviet desertions, since it began the unravelling of the their atomic spy network in North America and later contributed to British Intelligence's self-devouring search for the Soviet mole. But even to contemporary reviewers the bluntness of 'its arraignment of the Russian people and their ideology' diminished the film's effectiveness:

> It . . . seems excessively sensational and dangerous to the dis-ease of our times to dramatise the myrmidons of Russia as so many sinister fiends.[34]

Walk East on Beacon (1952), another docu-dramatised hagiography of J. Edgar Hoover's G-Men, and *Big Jim McClain* (1952), John Wayne's 'tribute to the fine work of the House Un-American Activities Committee',[35] were two of the more egregious period spy films 'that bordered on self-parody with thin intrigues and overly violent flag-waving'.[36] In yet another, the Communist spy (Robert Walker) in *My Son John* (1952), an atheistic homosexual intellectual, was machine-gunned to death near the steps of the Lincoln Memorial.

A 'cinematic armistice' to the paleolithic phase of the Cold War was called none too soon by perhaps the only man who could have, Alfred Hitchcock. His *deus ex machina* was Cary Grant, cast in the classic thriller-comedy about the Cold War, *North by Northwest* (1959), as the victim of mistaken identity. The plot has been described as classic Hitchcock with 'some good new twists on some good old tricks', loosely hung on a CIA scheme to infiltrate a Soviet spy ring. The film's debts to *The 39 Steps* were substantial: Grant, the ordinary man suddenly thrust into extraordinary circumstances, forced to flee from both spies and police (for a murder he had not committed); his encounter with a beautiful blonde (Eva Marie Saint) on a train; his attention-getting performance among an unsuspecting audience; the shooting which did not kill him.

But the film's greater sophistication in detailing the machinations of spymasters, in the chase sequences (the crop-dusting airplane; Mount Rushmore's precipices), and in its exquisite interweaving of comedy and suspense, all made it the ultimate foil of the body of gothic 1950s spy films. '*North by Northwest* was a watershed,' declared Rubenstein:

> Few films after it could treat domestic espionage with half the gravity formerly accorded it. Gun play, car chases and plans for world conquest were the preserve of James Bond, and few directors tried to raise the specter of Soviet spies in the midst of a middle-class

America with any of the melodrama of *My Son John* or *Walk East on Beacon*.[37]

As if to confirm the armistice terms, *North by Northwest* was immediately followed by another film puncturing the seriousness of Cold War intelligence by parodying MI5's efforts against eastern incursion into its Caribbean bailiwick. *Our Man in Havana* (1960) starred Alec Guinness as James Wormold, a vacuum-cleaner salesman who (perhaps fictionalizing the still-secret wartime 'Doublecross' operation against the Germans) conjured up legions of fictitious agents to report on imaginary enemy installations in Cuba, all in order to indulge the extravagant lifestyle of his spoiled daughter, courtesy of British intelligence.

It is worth noting one important difference between *Our Man in Havana* and *North by Northwest*: that while Hitchcock for all his burlesquing never questioned the basic necessity for the silent spy war against the Soviets, *Our Man in Havana*'s underlying message was unambiguously anti-espionage.

THE TWILIGHT OF THE COLD WAR: AMBIGUITIES OF LOYALTY

Hitchcock's genius in extricating the moviegoer from the labyrinths of 1950s' demonology lay in humorously deflating its self-importance. But even light parodies are by nature occasional; and it was changes in the times and tastes which drove the genre in unanticipated new directions.

One might have expected, for instance, the slight warming of the Cold War in the early 1960s to have resulted in a revival of the reflectiveness and sophisticated wit of an earlier era of espionage cinema. But instead the underlying disillusionments and tensions of post-war life in the atomic age prevailed. They evoked both a sense of cynicism and bitterness that the war had not brought relief from uncertainty, and a consequent preoccupation with the compensations of the good life.

The psychology of all that manifested itself in the emergence of two major (and quite opposite) departures to the development of the spy film. The first was the series of James Bond films begun in the early 1960s, phenomenal and enduring in their popularity. The more notable of them were the earlier ones: *Dr. No* (1962); *From Russia, with Love* (1963); *Goldfinger* (1964); and *Thunderball* (1965). They and the others followed the standard plot formula originally laid down by John Buchan in his 1913 novel *The Thirty-Nine Steps*: the hero embarking on his mission; entering enemy territory; entrapped; escaping; and finally defeating the enemy.[38]

As variously played by Sean Connery, George Lazenby, Roger Moore and Timothy Dalton (the films have long since run out of Ian Fleming's original material), Bond was often seen as the revival of the Hitchcockian heroic spy, a sort of armed and tuxedoed Richard Hannay. Both characters were, after all, upper-class British gentlemen, combating foreign conspiracies threatening the British way of life, in exotic regions of an essentially man's world.

But their differences far outweighed those obvious similarities. Bond was a professional spy, ably supported by a superbly equipped British intelligence organization, at first glance the essential 1950s 'organization man'. But, the audience quickly learned, he was more than that. To scratch the corporate Bond was to find the type-hero of male fantasy, the spy straight out of *Playboy*.[39] Fleming's hero pursued a life of adventure and narcissism focused on high consumerism and casual sexual conquest.

Far from being the grey minion of the Secret Service, Bond constantly disobeyed his superiors and followed his own instincts. Yet his questionings were neither ethical nor philosophical, for Bond the hedonist was neither an intellectual nor a political being. His endless toyings with so-available females were larded with suggested perversion and violence. Indeed, the films' portrayals of women in Bond's and his adversaries' hands subtly conveyed the acceptance of both sadism and masochism. And since those adversaries were invariably lesbian women, Jews, Asians, Blacks, or mixtures thereof, it was clear that the cinematic world of James Bond, for all its sophisticated wittiness, was hardly the realm of the many. To the contrary, its perspective was the reductionist view of a world of certainties – 'us' against 'them' – 'us' being unquestionably white, capitalist, Christian, and heterosexual male.

It was precisely because he was a fanciful character that James Bond had instantly become the Cold War's favorite agent. Yet it was the second Cold War spy who came to be seen as the more truly representative of the mood and spirit of the age – and who was Bond's antithesis in every important way. Indeed Alec Leamas (Richard Burton), John le Carré's hero in *The Spy Who Came In From the Cold* (1963), was arguably created in protest against the facile and escapist portrayals of Bond in his various settings. Le Carré denied it, but certainly he never masked his disdain for what that character had represented. 'Bond on his magic carpet [le Carré said in 1966] takes us away from moral doubt, banishes perplexity with action, morality with duty.'[40]

Far from being anti-ethical and escapist, *The Spy Who Came In From the Cold* was all about the ethics of Cold War spying. Leamas was the victim of those ethics, a tired, middle-aged, embittered and cynical spymaster who had mysteriously lost the last and best of his agents to the villainous Mundt of East German intelligence. Called back to London to prepare for one last mission before he was brought permanently 'in from the cold', Leamas was dispatched on a mission to East Germany intended (he was led to believe) to destroy Mundt. But Leamas's true role was in the saving of Mundt's position as a British double agent, which involved, finally, the deaths of Leamas's lover, Nan (Claire Bloom), and himself.

The Spy Who Came In From the Cold has become the classic Cold War allegory, as gothic in tone and message as the Bond films had been romantic. Its mood, as the title suggested, was one of coldness. Filmed in black and white instead of color, its settings were in the classic *film noir* tradition: night or overcast day; bleak landscapes or shadowed rooms; cold winds. The film began and ended with nocturnal scenes of death at that great metaphor of the Cold War, the Berlin Wall. The script was sparing and austere, its only humor ironic or sarcastic.

That gloomy mood effectively conveyed the film's equally dour message, that the sole moral law of Cold War intelligence was 'results', and that in that world of espionage there were no essential differences, methodologically or morally, between East and West. 'The problem of the Cold War', le Carré argued:

> is that . . . we haunt a ruined century. Behind the little flags we wave, there are old faces weeping, and children mutilated by the fatuous conflicts of preachers. . . . there is no victory and no virtue in the Cold War, only a condition of human illness and a political misery.[41]

Leamas, whose only resemblances to James Bond were his anti-intellectualism and physical vigor, was thus made the victim of Cold War espionage, not its hero, cynically betrayed by his own agency to protect in place an ex-Nazi Communist traitor. 'It was a foul, foul operation,' Leamas told Nan as they drove toward the Berlin Wall, still very much out in the cold. 'But it's paid off, and that's the only rule.'

There was a cruel irony in that ghastly contradiction which was lost on neither of them. It was of British intelligence, wholly devoid of morality, sending trusted agents and innocents to their deaths in protection of the supremely evil Mundt, supposedly to uphold the moral principles of God and country in the Cold War. The weight of that irony made Leamas choose death with Nan rather than living on with that awful awareness, leaving them both lying at the foot of the Wall, 'victims of British democracy as much as East German Communism'.[42]

Like *Spione* and *The 39 Steps* before it, *The Spy Who Came In From the Cold* was a hallmark, adding a significant new dimension to the spy film which made it the basis for all that followed. The film questioned not only the fundamental ethics of espionage (which had been done many times before), but more importantly the very moral basis of intelligence establishments. Gone were the glamour of the secret agent, the moral absolutes, the 'us' against 'them' in sharp contrast. Leamas's world was 'a study in gray'.[43] It was Britain's spymasters, not just Communism's, who were morally repugnant. Alec's choice of death with Nan became the supreme protest against the moral expediency of the espionage world, the affirmation of integrity and love.

Thus Leamas became the model of the new Cold War film spy, the anti-hero. He personified the helpless vulnerability of the individual agent caught between rival Cold War spy bureaucracies whose cosy ethics and ruthless methods were, whatever their driving ideologies, interchangeable. His life as a spy had wasted him physically and emotionally; the pessimism and foreboding of his death went unrelieved by any hope of a better world for his having spied. He died, as he had lived, a lost soul out in the cold.

Cinematic spies have never been the same again. Even those who capitalized on the Bond phenomenon were cut largely to Leamas's pattern. If one imagined homogenizing Bond and Leamas, for instance, the product would have resembled the hero of *The Ipcress File* (1965), Harry Palmer (Michael Caine).

Film reviewers made much of Palmer's likeness to Bond (Harry Saltzman, co-producer of many of the Bond films, also produced the Palmer series), but in fact he bore a closer resemblance to Leamas. Trench-coated, bespectacled and flabby, Palmer was working-class chic, a parody of Bond the superhero. While he dined on epicurean foods and Mozart, his accent (like his outlook) was cockney, and his manner insubordinate and indifferent to the larger stakes. He spied not by choice but because the Secret Service had left him no choice – counter-espionage or jail for black-market dealings. Like Leamas, he expended half of his energy bucking the establishment, measuring his own success not so much by destroying his opponent as by finessing him, and surviving to fight again another day.[44]

Others who tried following the 'down-trodden heels of *The Spy Who Came In From the Cold*' did so less convincingly. One was agent Quiller (George Segal), an anti-establishment American spy whose hunt for neo-Nazis in *The Quiller Memorandum* (1966) became a widely imitated theme. The film attempted to imitate le Carré's world, the mundane but perilous existence of the post-war spy manipulated by his controllers. But Segal's Quiller was a hollowed-out Leamas, helped not at all by manufactured crises and the fact that his supporting agents were played by Alec Guinness and Max von Sydow, both destined to become legendary spy actors.[45]

The next major turn in the pattern of the spy film was prompted by American events which evoked dominant moods of suspicion and conspiracy – even paranoia: the assassinations of the Kennedys and King; the Vietnam War; the squalidness of the Watergate affair; the revelations of intelligence agencies run rampant. As each affair was publicized, it was revealed so inadequately and suspiciously that the public mood of mistrust and fear for its democratic institutions became a national obsession. As reflected in espionage cinema, this became the era of the political thriller, in which espionage as the dominant theme gave way to political intrigue, conspiracy and assassination, much of it seemingly pointless.

The film which initiated the trend was also its finest example: *The Manchurian Candidate* (1962). While it became best known for its seemingly eerie premonition of the 1963 Kennedy assassination (it was withdrawn from circulation for over two decades afterwards), it was actually meant to be a seriocomic commentary on 1950s McCarthyism.

In it a bemedalled Korean War veteran and prisoner (Laurence Harvey) had been doubly brainwashed: by his mother (Angela Lansbury), a Freudian android hating men yet aiming at an incestuous relationship with him; and by his Chinese captors. The aims of both (Lansbury was also a Soviet agent) were to turn him into a remote-control assassin to help place their own candidate, a right-wing buffoon (James Gregory) in line for the American presidency. 'In its own hip, flippant mood,' wrote one reviewer, 'its switching between political melodrama, black comedy and Freudian nightmare, it became a harbinger of the 1960s before anyone was sure what the 1960s would be'.[46]

The Manchurian Candidate's mixture of comedy and horror brilliantly portrayed what would become one of the driving paradoxes of political life from that era to the present, that while conspirators might be cretins and buffoons, they were none the less dangerous to the daily lives of ordinary citizens.

That concept, however, was lost on the various assassination conspiracy films which immediately followed (and capitalized on) the Kennedy killings. *Executive Action* (1973) managed to combine (in mid-1940s docudrama form) every conspiracy theory of the presidential assassination with the new Watergate-bred suspicions of government, and still failed to offer any new political or psychological analyses of the crime. *The Parallax View* (1974) depicted the political murders of some Kennedy-like presidential aspirants, masterminded by a giant corporation so devoid of political ideology as to take its victims randomly from both the left and the right.[47]

Relief from this grim, motiveless determinism was to be found in Europe. The best of the espionage-assassination films, *The Day of the Jackal* (1973), made political revenge of French Army officers over the loss of Algeria the basis for the attempted assassination of Charles de Gaulle. More to the point, politics were at the heart of the political thrillers of the 1960s and 1970s directed by Constantin Costa-Gavras. The first, *Z* (1969), was set in Greece. It made the account of the 1963 murder of a leftist professor into a political Greek tragedy symbolizing the death of liberalism in an emerging Fascist state. A second, *State of Siege* (1973), was by contrast the rationalization of an act of terrorism, the 1970 kidnap-murder in Uruguay of an American official whose US foreign aid credentials covered for his real role as a counter-terrorism and torture consultant to the government.[48]

The counterpoints to this *Götterdämmerung* approach to the politics of intelligence were to be found in two quarters. The first was a series of espionage film spoofs, the most notable of which were European. Two French films, *The Tall Blond Man With One Black Shoe* (1973) and *A Pain in the A*** (1975), achieved great popularity in the US in spite of the language obstacle because of their deft parodying of the heavy period fare with essentially visual buffoonery. The first of them spoofed intelligence agencies using a variant of *Our Man in Havana's* plotline, an innocent caught in the midst of a spy intrigue who (through no conscious action of his own) foiled the agency and made off with the vamp. In the second, the 'pain in the a**' was another innocent who hamhandedly thwarted a professional assassin. Both films made essentially the same point: that spy agencies and their operatives were basically nonsensical.[49]

The second cinematic reaction to the Wagnerian spy cinema of the 1970s was a notably successful return to le Carré. But it was a return with a difference. For as le Carré's novels grew in length and complexity after the success of *The Spy Who Came In From the Cold*, it became clear that the standard length of the commercial film was insufficient for their proper cinematic adaptation. The answer was to segment the films into a half-dozen or so hour-long episodes to be presented on television. That innovation became an important contribution to the espionage film genre, and each of the three novels so adapted became a significant cinematic event.

Tinker, Tailor, Soldier, Spy (6 hours, 1980) introduced viewers to a new George Smiley (Alec Guinness) – not the seamy agent of Leamas's betrayal in *The Spy Who Came In From the Cold*, but the colourless yet methodically brilliant counterspy who, even while at odds with the 'Circus' (British intelligence), snared the Soviet mole who had penetrated the agency. In *Smiley's People* (6 hours, 1982), Smiley (Guinness), now back on the inside, lured his Soviet counterpart and nemesis, Karla (Patrick Stewart), into defecting.

Those successes did not prevent the attempt to adapt le Carré's 1983 novel *The Little Drummer Girl* into a two-hour commercial film of the same title (1984). But its disappointing results seemed to reconfirm the conviction that capturing the shadings and complexities of le Carré's fiction required serialization on television.[50]

The most recent adaptation, *A Perfect Spy* (7 hours, 1988), was a return to that medium. It was perhaps the best and certainly the most revealing of the three television films, on several levels. First, it examined the psyche of the spy and the motivations of the double agent. Magnus Pym (Peter Egan) became the 'perfect spy' by virtue of a lifetime's training in deception as expertly taught by his swindling father, Rick (Ray McAnnally). Thus Magnus's doubling into the not-so-perfect spy at the instigation of the insidiously loyal Czech Axel (Rudiger Weigang) was as much another of Rick's confidence tricks as it was anything ideologically inspired.

Equally important, the film was revealing of the author of the book, the most autobiographical of all the le Carré novels. Magnus Pym followed many of the turns which le Carré's own life had, and Rick Pym was le Carré's own father, Ronald Cornwell. Le Carré has said that his writing of *A Perfect Spy* was cathartic, his coming to terms with his own father before he could proceed. But Rick Pym also bore a striking resemblance to another supremely consequential real-life maverick, Harry St. John Philby, the father and role model of Kim.[51]

THE COLD WAR REMEMBERED: SPY AGENCIES' MURDEROUS GAMES

John le Carré has cast as long a shadow over the espionage film as he has over the spy novel. His profound influence continues. As it gradually became evident, even during the 1970s, that the Cold War was coming to resemble more closely a 'long peace', two new themes came to characterize the espionage film.

One had to do with what might be called Cold War nostalgia mixed with Britain's post-war class *angst*. The nostalgia involved the implicit longing for the old days when spies had acted more from conviction than from greed, conviction stemming as much from class guilt as from political ideology.

That combination produced a number of significant films about the Cambridge spy ring (1930s–60s). Aside from *Tinker, Tailor, Soldier, Spy*, which was inspired by Kim Philby's treachery, the two best of them were not about the acts of espionage themselves, but about the systems that produced the spies, and thus about espionage as social betrayal. Taken together the two films bracketed the life of Guy Burgess. *Another Country* (1984) was a condemnation of the public-school system which had produced the young Burgess (Rupert Everett), especially its hypocrisy over schoolboy homosexuality. In the other, *An Englishman Abroad* (1985), Burgess (Alan Bates) became the lonely outcast in Moscow after his defection, balancing his nostalgia for things British with his unrepentance toward his own treason.

The other theme was essentially anti-espionage in tone, harking back to Leamas's relationship with the Circus, but with a new dimension. While *The Spy Who Came In From the Cold* had not queried the basic need for intelligence agencies, the late Cold War films began to cast doubt on their rationale. Whom did the services really serve: governments or themselves? What were their actual functions: to provide objective intelligence or to further their own bureaucratic interests? Whom did they kill: state enemies or threats to themselves? And whom did they protect?

Three Days of the Condor (1975) asked all of those questions and – reflective of the times – provided answers masked in ambiguity. Turner (Robert Redford), a bookish functionary employed by a CIA front, found himself the lone survivor of the mysterious mass murder of his office mates and the fugitive from pursuers whose identities were just as murky. In a further resemblance to *The 39 Steps*, Turner coerced an initially hostile and unbelieving blonde, Kathy (Faye Dunaway), to come to his aid and at the same time assist in foiling the conspiracy. It was that murderous conspiracy which provided the novel departure: a CIA within the CIA, with its own version of 'The Enemy Out There' and with its own foreign policy, the furtherance of which necessitated the killing of its own people.[52]

Costa-Gavras's contribution to the new school, *Missing* (1982), suggested that the State Department was implicated in the 1970 Chilean kidnap-killing of a young American counterculture journalist because he had knowledge of CIA involvement in the overthrow and murder of President Allende. The film sparked a firestorm of controversy (and a $60 million State Department lawsuit against Costa-Gavras and the film), not because it was any more incriminating than *State of Siege*, but because it was an American film, in English, and featured two stars calculated to attract large audiences, Jack Lemmon (Ed Horman), and Sissy Spacek (Beth Horman).

The British made two notable late-1980s contributions to this type of spy film. The first, *The Whistle Blower* (1987), chose as its locus the main theater of spy operations since the 1960s, communications intelligence. It borrowed heavily from *Missing's* plotline of the conservative and initially skeptical father teaming with his dead son's lover to expose the spy agency's murderous conspiracy. Bob Jones (Nigel Havers), a young Russian translator, was murdered by his own cryptographic agency (Britain's GCHQ) to prevent him from threatening the 'Special Relationship' with the Americans by exposing yet another top-level mole in British Intelligence. His father, Frank (Michael Caine), unmasked the agent, Sir Adrian Chapple (John Gielgud),[53] only to be prevented from publicly exposing him by a Cabinet secretary's threats to put him away Soviet-style, and to harm Bob's loved ones.

The other example was the award-winning television drama *A Very British Coup* (3 hours, 1988), which in fictionalizing the attempts of MI5 to discredit and bring down the Wilson government in the 1960s, brought the question of the true functions of agencies very close to the real world of espionage – and to the Official Secrets Act.

The questions raised by *The Whistle Blower* and *A Very British Coup* were both judgemental and anticipatory. What, they asked, were the real effects of intelligence agencies on the democratic institutions of societies which sustained them? And what would be the future results of their continuing unrestrained? The to-be-filmed version of le Carré's *The Russia*

House would (typically of le Carré) carry those queries to the next level, asking what the age of *glasnost* and *perestroika* would hold in store for the intelligence agencies of all the Cold War combatants. The espionage film has always reflected changes in the nature and the politics of espionage. But, strong as the relationship between spy cinema and literature have been, film as a medium has often been slower in its responses than spy novels. This has been partly a matter of timing. Since a number of the great spy films have been adaptations of trend-setting novels, they have sometimes substantially lagged in their production, in the case of *The 39 Steps* by as much as 22 years. Thus while Somerset Maugham's anti-heroic novel *Ashenden; or, The British Agent* pioneered the genre's critical scrutiny of espionage with its publication in 1928, its filmed version, *The Secret Agent*, appeared only in 1936, shortly after two distinctly pro-espionage films, *The 39 Steps* (1935) and *The Scarlet Pimpernel* (1935).

However, both those mid-1930s films exemplified the ways in which spy films could often anticipate changes in the political situation and public mood concerning intelligence activities. Both, responding to the rise of European totalitarianism and anticipating the coming of war, could be seen as muted (even allegorical) justifications of espionage against such threats. So, too, did such later films as *The Manchurian Candidate* (1962), *The Spy Who Came In From the Cold* (1965), and *Three Days of the Condor* (1975) reflect or gloomily portend major changes in the mores and goings-on in the intelligence world. As *The Manchurian Candidate* had anticipated the presidential assassination of John Kennedy by a year, so *Three Days of the Condor* predated by a year or two the damaging revelations about CIA roguery touched off by Watergate and by various presidential and congressional committee hearings.

Throughout the twentieth century the spy film has followed reasonably faithfully the swings in artistic interpretations of spying: from the spy as gentleman hero (1910s and 1920s), to commoner anti-hero or war patriot (1930s and 1940s), to Bondian superhero (1950s and 1960s), to Leamasian anti-hero (1960s and 1970s), and finally to the spy as nostalgic figure or victim (1980s). But two elements of the espionage film have not been as fully developed. First, women have continued to play ancillary, superficial and generally negative roles. A comparison of Greta Garbo's 'Mata Hari', Madeline Carroll's 'Pamela' (*The 39 Steps*) and Diane Keaton's 'Charlie' (*The Little Drummer Girl*) is hardly a study of the progressive development of the understanding or importance of the female spy character.

Second, the cinematic development of the spy agency has been recent phenomenon, little more than a generation old. This is because the general absence of twentieth-century foreign intelligence agencies as established and mature bureaucracies until the end of the Second World War resulted in their being depicted in simplistic terms, until in 1963 *The Spy Who Came*

In From the Cold began to change that interpretation.

Spy agencies during the 1930s and the war years were depicted (if they were depicted at all) as murky entities. The mid-1940s 'now it can be told' hagiographies which followed, *The House on 92nd Street* and *13 Rue Madeleine*, both launched the American agencies from cinematic obscurity and led directly to the era of FBI-fawning, anti-Red crusades such as *Walk East on Beacon* (1952).

Conversely, it was the facile portrayals of the British Secret Service in the James Bond films which John le Carré so historically reversed beginning with his 'Circus' in *The Spy Who Came In From the Cold* (1963). It has been principally the le Carré films which since that time have offered us the most sophisticated and challenging forays into the mind of the agent and the nature of the spy agency. That has been so largely because of their extended lengths and meticulous screen adaptations from the novels. It has also been the result of superior casting and acting, principally of Alec Guinness as George Smiley.

What is most evident from a study of the spy film's development is that it is the British who have initiated its greatest innovations over the years, from the films of Alfred Hitchcock and Leslie Howard in the 1930s to the BBC productions of John le Carré's novels in the 1980s. Consistently many Britain's finest actors and directors have been involved in espionage, just as the first rank of British theatrical talent has produced in the past generation the finest plays about espionage in the world.[54]

It was the British who emphasized and juxtaposed the ambiguities of national and class loyalties so effectively in film. In *The 39 Steps*, for instance, it was Hannay and Annabella, both foreigners, who wanted to save Britain, while the upper-class Professor Jordan preserved establishment appearances while selling out his country. So too in *An Englishman Abroad* it was Coral Browne, the Australian, who confronted the exiled and unrepentant Guy Burgess (Alan Bates) with the awfulness of his treachery ('... you pissed in our soup, and we drank it'). And it was she who, in the film's final scenes, pointed up the hypocrisy of class loyalty (which, along with his country, Burgess had betrayed) in her subsequent transactions with Burgess's London purveyors. His tailor was only too happy to furnish him ('... always getting into such scrapes, Mr Guy . . . we put a little of our souls into our suits, that is our loyalty'); it was his haberdasher – a Hungarian firm – which refused her ('the gentleman is a traitor, Madam . . . as far as we're concerned, Mr Burgess is a client we are well rid of').

It is clear that the British, who are the finest television film-makers, theater producers and actors in the world, have had a mild obsession for some time about espionage as a theme. It may not be coincidental that they have also been the twentieth century's most celebrated spies.[55] Is it because the British, the most dispassionate, understated, undemonstrative and observant of all Westerners, are also the world's greatest dissemblers – at once the legendary actors and the legendary spies of our time?

NOTES

1. The exception to this was the original spy novel, James Fenimore Cooper's *The Spy* (1821).
2. Leonard Rubenstein, *The Great Spy Films* (Secaucus, 1979), p.8; Julian Symons, *Bloody Murder: From the Detective Story to the Crime Novel: A History* (New York, 1985), p.214.
3. Symons, *Bloody Murder*, p.215; John Cawleti and Bruce Rosenberg, *The Spy Story* (Chicago, 1987), pp.39–40.
4. James Parish and Michael Pitts, *The Great Spy Pictures* (1974), p.11.
5. Rubenstein, *Spy Films*, p.11; Parish and Pitts, *Spy Pictures*, pp.11–14.
6. Parish and Pitts, *Spy Pictures*, pp.14–18.
7. The American version, *Spies* (1929), ran only 90 minutes. It was badly reviewed. *Variety*, 6 March 1929, p.29. See also *Variety*, 27 September 1978, p.5.
8. Rubenstein, *Spy Films*, p.13. Haghi was given a distinctly Bolshevik demeanor, his make-up deliberately alluding to Lenin. For an account of the Soviet trade delegation (the All Russian Co-operative Society, 'Arcos Limited') and MI5's 1927 raid on it, see John Costello, *Mask of Treachery* (1988), pp.101–16.
9. *Variety*, 6 March 1929, p.26; Parish and Pitts, *Spy Pictures*, pp.440–41.
10. Rubenstein, *Spy Films*, p.16.
11. Ibid., p.19.
12. A comparably and consistently successful director of spy film classics was Fritz Lang (*Spione* [1928]; *The Ministry of Fear* [1944]; *Cloak and Dagger* [1946]).
13. Gene Phillips, *Alfred Hitchcock* (1984), pp.20, 71–72; Eric Rohmer and Claude Chabrot, *Hitchcock: The First Forty-Four Films* (1979), pp.42–3.
14. Hitchcock often cast tall, debonair and handsome idols as the male leads, most notably Donat, James Stewart, and Cary Grant.
15. Albert LaValley, *Focus on Hitchcock* (1972), p.29.
16. Hitchcock's female leads were invariably cool and beautiful, and often blonde: Carroll, Ingrid Bergman, and Grace Kelly.
17. Hitchcock carried the symbolism of the handcuff one step further: the final scene in the London Palladium ended with a shot of Hannay's hand, handcuff dangling, clutching hold of Pamela's. Rubenstein, *Spy Pictures*, p.21.
18. Lesley Brill, *The Hitchcock Romance* (1988), p.39.
19. Ibid., p.52.
20. *Magill's Survey of Cinema*, Series I, vol.2 (1980), p.933.
21. Ibid., p.937.
22. Parish and Pitts, *Spy Pictures*, p.333. The title of the British film was *Night Train*.
23. Rubenstein, *Spy Films*, p.161.
24. Ibid., pp.131–2.
25. Frank Nugent, 'Confessions of a Nazi Spy,' *New York Times*, 29 April 1939. 'We don't believe,' the review continued, 'Nazi Propaganda Ministers let their mouths twitch evilly whenever they mention our Constitution or Bill of Rights. We thought that school of villainy had gone out with "The Beast of Berlin", made back in '14.'
26. *Magill's Survey of Cinema*, Series I, Vol.4, 1820.
27. Rubenstein, *Spy Films*, p.164; Parish and Pitts, *Spy Pictures*, p.102.
28. Parish and Pitts, *Spy Pictures*, p.103. See also *Magill's Survey of Cinema*, Series I, Vol.1, 305–7; Rubenstein, *Spy Films*, pp.164–5. *Casablanca* won 1943 Academy Awards for Best Screenplay, Best Direction and Best Picture, but Bogart and Bergman were passed over for acting – Bogart bested by Paul Lukas (*Watch on the Rhine*), and Bergman by Jennifer Jones.
29. *The House on 92nd Street* was both a box-office and critical success, receiving an Academy

Award for Best Original Story. *13 Rue Madeleine* was badly reviewed but was carried by its star to commercial success. The docu-drama as a cinematic technique died out in the early 1950s when it was appropriated by television. *Magill's Survey of Cinema*, Series II (1981), Vol.3, 1065–1067.

30. *Magill's Survey of Cinema*, Series II, Vol.2, 786–7.
31. Parish and Pitts, *Spy Pictures*, p.181.
32. James Parish and Michael Pitts, *The Great Spy Pictures II* (1986), p.105.
33. Garth Jowett, *Film: The Democratic Art* (1976), pp.393–6; David Prindle, *The Politics of Glamour: Ideology and Democracy in the Screen Actors Guild* (1988), pp.51–61.
34. Bosley Crowther, 'The Iron Curtain,' *New York Times*, 13 May 1948.
35. Parish and Pitts, *Spy Pictures*, pp.83–85 ('Every decade or so political rightist John Wayne becomes involved in a film project which arouses public indignation').
36. Rubenstein, *Spy Pictures*, pp.44–5.
37. Ibid., pp.46, 49–50; *Magill's Survey of Cinema*, Series II, Vol.4, pp.1742–4.
38. Cawleti and Rosenberg, *Spy Story*, p.50. They further (p.82) attribute Buchan's plot formula to Bunyan's *Pilgrim's Progress*.
39. Cawleti and Rosenberg, *Spy Story*, p.51.
40. Quoted in Peter Lewis, *John le Carré* (1985), p.16. Kim Philby, it was said, admired *The Spy Who Came In From the Cold* for its sophistication after 'all that James Bond idiocy'. Lewis, *le Carré*, p.63.
41. Quoted in Lewis, *le Carré*, p.60.
42. Ibid., p.71, 75–7.
43. *Magill's Survey of Cinema*, Series I, Vol.4, 1605.
44. *Magill's Survey of Cinema*, Series I, Vol.3, 1175–77; Parish and Pitts, *Spy Pictures*, p.241. The subsequent Palmer (Caine) films, *Funeral in Berlin* and *Billion Dollar Brain* (both 1967), were not as successful critically or commercially as *The Ipcress File*.
45. Parish and Pitts, *Spy Pictures*, p.387; Bosley Crowther, 'The Quiller Memorandum', *New York Times*, 16 December 1966.
46. Richard Combs, 'The Possibilities for Perfidy', *Times Literary Supplement*, 5–11 August 1988, p.861.
47. Stephen Farber, 'Conspiracy Movies,' *New York Times*, 11 August 1974; 'Executive Action', *Variety*, 7 November 1973.
48. Vincent Canby, 'Z', *New York Times*, 9 December 1969; *Newsweek*, 15 December 1969, p.105; Vincent Canby, 'State of Siege', *New York Times*, 14 April 1973.
49. Parish and Pitts, *Spy Pictures II*, pp.313–14. Both films generated American imitations which, partly because they relied more heavily on dialogue, were less successful: *The Man With One Red Shoe* (1985), and *Buddy, Buddy* (1983).
50. *The Little Drummer Girl* was also controversial, earning for le Carré criticism that he was anti-Palestinian and anti-feminist, the latter charge stemming from his depiction of Charlie (Diane Keaton) as promiscuous, disingenuous and lacking conviction. Despite its poor reception, the latest le Carré novel, *The Russia House*, was to be made into a commercial film scripted by Tom Stoppard, and starring, interestingly enough, by far the best of the Bonds, Sean Connery.
51. Joseph Lelyveld, 'Le Carré's Toughest Case', *New York Times Magazine*, 16 March 1986, pp.40–91; David Ignatius, 'The Real "Perfect Spy"', *Washington Post*, 15 May 1988. Lengthy TV adaptation was also prone to Wagnerianism, as demonstrated by the 12-part dramatization of the Len Deighton trilogy, *Game, Set & Match* (1989).
52. John le Carré, *The Russia House* (1989), p.231; William F. Buckley, Jr., 'Redford vs. the CIA', *New York Times*, 28 September 1975.
53. Chapple was the characterization of Anthony Blunt, Director of the Courtauld Institute and Surveyor of the Queen's Pictures, who had been publicly exposed as a lifelong Soviet spy in 1979.
54. Representative examples would be: Alan Bennett's *The Old Country* (1977, starring Alec Guinness); Hugh Whitmore's *Breaking the Code* (1986, starring Derek Jacoby); Tom Stoppard's *Hapgood* (1988); and Alan Bennett's *Single Spies* (1989).
55. I am indebted to Samuel Crowl, Professor of English at Ohio University, for the germ of this notion.

Ethics and Spy Fiction

J.J. MACINTOSH

It has been estimated that more than 3,500 spy novels have been published since 1930.[1] I have not read all of these. Nor am I widely read in spy novels written before 1930, many of which are at any rate unreadable: 'Today it takes a determined will and a high tolerance for unrefined and unmitigated twaddle to get through many books by William LeQueux or E. Phillips Oppenheim'.[2] Lacking both, I have read neither. Thus my discussion will be, with respect to the fictional component, selective. Similarly, it will not be possible, within the confines of an essay, to discuss all, or even most, of the moral issues the novels of spy fiction raise. I shall concentrate on a few major authors, and on four main moral issues: the justification of spying itself; the sexism that seems to be an inevitable though unnecessary concomitant of the fictional version of spying; the almost casual acceptance of the other connected immoralities such as murder, torture and deceit; and the morality of writing, selling, buying, and reading literature that is devoted to detailing such activities.

About the last I have little to say, though it lies at the heart of an important point about spy fiction: writers of spy novels have to persuade us, their readers, that the activities about which they are writing are acceptable. This dilemma that faces them is unusual in genre fiction. Writers of romances do not have to persuade us that romance is acceptable, nor do writers of detective stories have to persuade us that murderers should be apprehended.

I suspect, though I have no certainty in the matter, that, as in the similar case of pornography/erotic literature, some spy fiction is harmful, and some of it is not. Spy fiction has been accused, as a genre, of being, or containing, pornography of violence, and, as in the straightforward pornography case, the defence has consisted of four main claims: (a) that in *good* spy fiction there isn't (much) violence; (b) that literature does not affect people anyway; (c) that literature does have an effect, but (as Aristotle thought) the effect in these cases is cathartic or substitutive: the partaker of vicarious violence gets rid of violent impulses by having them thus symbolically relieved; (d) that while admittedly the violence is bad, it is outweighed by the other good features of the work(s) in question, such as their having considerable entertainment value for the reader.

Of course there is more involved here than the mere pornography of violence: there is also a good deal of soft pornography in the genre itself. It is unnecessary, as the works of writers such as le Carré, Deighton, Block, and Lyall show, but it certainly exists.[3] John Gardner, for example, in *Amber Nine*, dwells at length on the torturing of a young woman in a passage which is straightforwardly pornographic in tone.[4]

But raising the question 'Is it immoral to write, or sell, or buy, or read, spy fiction?' presumes that immorality is be found *in* spy fiction, so that question has a certain logical priority, and it is to it that I shall devote the remainder of the essay. We shall, however, find that it leads us full circle to the question with which we began.

THE JUSTIFICATION OF SPYING

It might be as well, before we wade further into the sea of value judgements that surrounds our topic, to say something briefly about what is, and what is not, moral. For the purposes of this essay I shall make some minimal assumptions:

(i)   that causing unnecessary suffering is wrong;

(ii)   that killing is *prima facie* wrong;[5]

(iii) that citizens in a society have certain *prima facie* rights, among them the right to privacy; and

(iv)   that moral justifications (the kind that could be used in particular cases against claims made under points (i)–(iii) to show that, e.g., the suffering was necessary, the killing acceptable, the right inactive in the circumstances) must not make essential reference to particular individuals. Moreover, specifics such as income, nationality, race, sex, and age are not, without further argument, to be taken as morally relevant.

This is not to say that there are not many cases in which they *are* relevant: only that their moral relevance needs demonstration in such cases. In this area morality may differ from the law, which tends to deny such relevance universally: 'the majestic equality of the laws . . . forbid[s] the rich as well as the poor to sleep under bridges, to beg in the streets, and to steal bread', as Anatole France's Chouette remarks,[6] but as St Thomas pointed out long ago, being poor may license people morally to do things which would be forbidden to them were they rich.[7]

Throughout, we shall be talking of real, not conventional, morality:

'. . . She's bad, bad, bad.'
'What makes you think that?' I interrupted.

Isabel looked at me with flashing eyes.

'She's soused from morning till night. She goes to bed with every tough who asks her.'

'That doesn't mean she's bad. Quite a number of highly respected citizens get drunk and have a liking for rough trade. They're bad habits, like biting one's nails, but I don't know that they're worse than that. I call a person bad who lies and cheats and is unkind.'[8]

Although (i)–(iv) provide minimal guidelines they already serve to separate us from the 'fairly orthodox morality' which Kingsley Amis finds in Fleming's Bond novels:

I should have thought that a fairly orthodox moral system, vague perhaps but none the less recognizable through accumulation, per-vades all Bond's adventures. Some things are regarded as good: loyalty, fortitude, a sense of responsibility, a readiness to regard one's safety, even one's life, as less important than the major interests of one's organization and one's country. Other things are regarded as bad: tyranny, readiness to inflict pain on the weak or helpless, the unscrupulous pursuit of money or power. These distinctions aren't excitingly novel, but they are important, and as humanist and/or Christian as the average reader would want. They constitute quite enough in the way of an ethical frame of reference, assuming anybody needs or looks for or ought to have one in adventure fiction at all.

What (if anything) holds this elementary moral system together is belief in England, or at any rate a series of ideas about her.[9]

Elsewhere Amis remarks:

Bond's professionalism is one of the best things about him, both as a moral quality and as a relief from that now defunct and always irritating personage, the gifted amateur who is called, or just happens to wander, in when M.I.5 is baffled and the Cabinet is in despair.[10]

Thus we have a negative attitude towards 'tyranny, readiness to inflict pain on the weak or helpless, [and] the unscrupulous pursuit of money or power', with which surely there can be little quarrel, but on the positive side things are less clear. Why should 'professionalism', whatever exactly that comes to, be accounted morally desirable *tout court*? A professional killer is not, by virtue of being a professional, morally more desirable than an amateur one. And the same is true of professional liars, procurers, card-sharps, and others. Many would hold, indeed, that being paid for performing nefarious activities (and performing them well, if that is part of one's definition of 'professionalism') actually adds to the disvalue we should set on them, and even with morally neutral activities, the addition of 'professional' often diminishes the performance: we contrast genuine mourners with professional ones, and some writers in our genre sneer at 'professional protesters' (phrases like 'rent a riot' have the same intended force).

Similarly with 'loyalty . . . [and] a readiness to regard one's safety, even one's life, as less important than the major interests of one's organization and one's country'. I would not deny that there are (or at any rate could be) organizations, and even countries (though this is surely less clear), whose 'major interests' might be worth setting over and above one's life, but there are not very many of them.[11] Moreover, I have no doubt that the tentative list of such countries or organizations that I might come up with would be very different from that which Amis might produce, and that neither of them would be plausible lists for Bond.[12] Amis himself is willing to wonder whether Bond's choices are wise in this area:

> Bond is quite thrilled by Draco's [private army], and regards Draco himself with respect as 'one of the great professionals of the world!' You and I might fancy a shorter and plainer term in place of 'professional'. Bond must be out of his mind. That helicopter is lent, appropriately, by the French O.A.S. Bond doesn't turn a hair. You or I would, or should, feel that any proceeding even remotely abetted by that lot must be bad.[13]

or again:

> Mr Fleming seems more sold on Blades than on the notion of England, and if Blades is to be the heart and crown of England (for some people that kind of thing undoubtedly is), then Blofeld and Colonel-General Grubozaboyschikov are not altogether on the wrong side.[14]

In Fleming's novels, then, though not in those of, say, Deighton and le Carré, the point of (iv) above – among other things, that proper names (such as 'England') do not carry automatic moral justification – is overlooked, as it often was in the works of earlier writers. Then, in the heyday of the waning of empire, it was assumed that membership in the empire club *was* morally relevant.[15] As Julian Symons points out, there is now a recognition, by some writers at least,[16] that this is *not* a morally justificatory position; unfortunately (he suggests) the awareness is bought at the price of forgetting that *some* moral justification is needed:

'The man's an Englishman, and if he's in with Germany he's a traitor to us, and we Englishmen have a right to expose him. If we can't do it without spying we've a right to spy.' An Englishman spying for Germany, the ingenuous Davies says to the equally unsophisticated Carruthers in *The Riddle of the Sands*, is the vilest creature on God's earth. Davies's views, expressed very early in the twentieth century, were those of his creator Erskine Childers. There is an enormous gap between that simple concept of 'the spy' as patriot or traitor according to his nationality, and the modern intelligence agency. Romantic patriotism drives Davies and Carruthers to become spies in this particular case, but they are aware of engaging in a low sneaking activity unfit for honourable men. Those who work today for American, British, French, Israeli and East European intelligence agencies no doubt see themselves as patriots, but the power that moves them is often that of an egotism so extreme as to be almost pathological.[17]

Symons is right to point out that – in time of peace, at least – spying is normally taken to be dishonourable. Nor is this view new. 'We are true men,' Joseph's brothers tell their unrecognized sibling, 'we are no spies,'[18] and Conan Doyle catches an ideal if not an actuality of high chivalry in the following dialogue:

[Prince:] 'There is this red-bearded nephew of thine, Robert de Duras. See where he stands yonder, counting and prying. Hark hither, young sir! I have been saying to your uncle the Cardinal that it is in my mind that you and your comrades have carried news of our disposition to the French king. How say you?'
The knight turned pale and sank his eyes. 'My lord,' he murmured, 'it may be that I have answered some questions.'
'And how will such answers accord with your honour, seeing that we have trusted you since you came in the train of the cardinal?'[19]

'Honour', however, is not a notion with much moral weight these days, and it has, for all practical purposes, none at all in contemporary spy fiction. It occurs, of course, in one of John le Carré's titles, but the concept itself is brusquely brushed aside in his novels, along with the trappings of empire:

'We'll offer you some kind of guarantee in return,' Haldane said.
'I don't need it,' Leiser replied, explaining quite seriously, 'I'm working for English gentlemen.'[20]

Leiser is, of course, soon shown to have made a grave mistake. Gavin Lyall suggests that the situation is not new:

'There was a time,' Scott-Sobie said, suddenly morose, 'when the word of an Englishman meant something. It meant that, no matter what he'd said, he'd act in his own best interests.'[21]

We might notice at this point that, although we have been talking about spying and spy novels, we all know that, in the real world at least, more is involved. Speaking of the setting for his novel *Portrait of a Spy*, Ian Adams writes

I . . . wanted to populate that landscape with characters who were not only fictional composites of the agents and their victims who I had met, but who would act out in some way the role a spy plays in the public imagination.[22]

In the real world there are not only 'agents', there are also victims. The CIA, for example, is not only actively engaged in gathering information, and thus in committing the crimes incidental to that activity, but is also engaged in, either by way or support for, or straightforward commission of, the crimes of murder, torture, and rape. Its employees indulge in, or actively support, acts of terrorism.[23] The publicity given to its activities is much greater than that attending its British counterpart(s), and partly because of that, though partly too because nowadays it is more imperialistic, the US tends to get harsher treatment than Britain in spy novels:

. . . right in the centre a huge bronze monument by Auguste Rodin, no less, depicting, in allegorical form, the defeat of William Walker, the notorious filibuster, who tried in the 1850s to annex most of Central America aiming to make them slave-owing states in the US of A. Modern Yankee imperialism is no less overt or more subtle – it is more ruthless and efficacious.[24]

It has also been pointed out that there is a correlation between the marital status of fictional spies and their nationality: fictional British spies are typically unmarried, fictional US ones are often married. Bruce Merry, in his *Anatomy of the Spy Thriller*, quotes from Victor Marchetti's *The Rope Dancer*:

'You European intellectuals always make everything so goddam complicated.' Paul shook his head in annoyance. 'Just look at it this way. The cold war isn't important any longer. The tired old international struggles don't have any real meaning in this day and age. There are more important issues now. This is the era of the common man. It's the have-nots against the haves . . . . This doesn't change the primary, the basic things. I loved my wife and children before, and I love them now. Maybe even more than before. They are still very real and very important to me. All I want to do is to take care of them. I couldn't care less about the fucking masses and all their goddam problems.'[25]

and, after some analysis, notes:

. . . the American spy is broken on the twin wheel of financial and family responsibility. Ultimately he is always a small man in a large organisation. The European spy is a large man in a small organisation.[26]

As Merry points out, these ties clearly hamper the activities of the US spy (Deighton's Harvey Newbegin[27] provides another example). This might be no bad thing for, as has already been pointed out, these activities are, *prima facie*, morally undesirable.

Citizens in a society possess the right to expect that, just as their government will work for them, not against them, so too they will be accorded a reasonable amount of privacy. There might be understandable disagreement, in certain cases, about what would count as a 'reasonable' amount, but just as we can recognize the difference between the bald and the hirsute without being able to draw a sharp line between the two, so too we can recognize that some cases of governmental snooping are quite *un*justified. The current reaction[28] in Eastern Europe against the various security police forces makes it clear that citizens there recognize and recognized that their rights were being infringed. The hasty shredding by the Queensland police of some 27,000 files which they were keeping on private citizens when it became obvious that the 1989 elections were going to produce a change of government showed clearly enough their recognition that their behaviour involved an infringement of rights. James Stephens catches the point nicely in *The Crock of Gold*:

Some distance down the road the policemen halted. The night had fallen before they effected their capture, and now, in the gathering darkness, they were not at ease. In the first place, they knew that the occupation upon which they were employed was not a creditable one to a man, whatever it might be to a policeman.[29]

Whether or not these rights are derivable from some more fundamental moral principle is a question of moral theory which, in company with our fictional spies, none of whom, despite their often expensive educations, seem to have read any philosophy, we shall here ignore.[30]

That they have this gap in their knowledge is interesting, for it is not merely that they are unacquainted with moral theory: political theory too seems to be *terra incognita*:

In all my years in Security Services, working on the Soviet and other communist desks, I never once heard any of my superior officers, aside from S, have anything intelligent to say about the capitalist system, much less provide a clear analysis of Marxism. But that is what we were charged with: to block the penetration of our institutions by agents of Marxist governments. Makes you think, doesn't it?[31]

In fact, in this respect, fictional spies mirror the general populace. Anglo-Saxon countries, particularly the US, have managed a staggering feat of negative education: almost no one in these societies knows anything about Marxism. (Except, of course, that it is the epitome of evil.) Students in Germany, workers in Chile, politicians in Italy, can all discuss Marx knowledgeably. But in Anglo-Saxon countries, such knowledge is simply not available. 'Few men think,' said Berkeley's Philonous, 'yet all will have opinions',[32] and the dictum applies strikingly in English-speaking countries in matters of political theory. We need to read only two sentences from Jorge Ibargüengoitia to know that Lidia Reynoso was not educated in the US:

> No sooner was he installed, legs folded under him, than he began to spout stupidities, saying that socialism is a dogma, Marxism should no longer be considered a valid political doctrine since it does not take into account the power drive which is innate in the human being, and so on. . . . Lidia Reynoso, unable to believe her ears, muttered to me, 'But this man is an anti-Marxist!'[33]

One result of this is that it makes the treatment of spying as a game (even if not a 'great' one) much easier. Since the *point* of it is, as lying in the realm of political and moral theory, unknown, it can be treated *simply* as a game. This being so, it is not surprising that the readers of spy novels, like the spectators at football matches, are primarily male.

There is, however, a significant difference between games and spying. The rules and conventions of games don't need justification. They have *historical* antecedents and explanations ('why does the queen in chess have the move it has?'), but not *moral* ones. What justification(s) do we find offered for our fictional spies?

Somewhat surprisingly, what we find is, effectively, nothing, though we do find a range of indications that justifications are required, for our fictional agents tell us time and time again either that there are none, or that none are required: but if they (or their authors) really believed that they would not be tellling us that they believed it. No one 'justifies' writing with black ink rather than blue because that is truly not a moral matter, and just for that reason no one bothers to explain that they do not need to justify it, either.

Throughout the history of the 'great game' genre there has been an awareness that the activities chronicled – not only the incidentals such as torture and murder, but also the central activity of spying itself – stand in need of moral justification. Initially this was thought to be provided by the fact that (a) the spy was working for his or her country, and (b) patriotism was a virtue. Sometimes, with a faint echo of Aristotle's doctrine of the unity of the virtues, it was realized that (b) was not in general adequate but, luckily, it was adequate when the patriotism was for the *right* country, namely England or the US, because they were by definition moral and just.[34]

It does not take a great deal of reflection to find this unsatisfactory, so it is now fashionable *not* to offer this kind of justification. Thus we are left with one of the standing paradoxes of spy fiction: why on earth are these people doing it? They *don't* believe that their country is right; they don't believe that the countries they are spying upon are villainous; they don't, in general, even believe that what they are doing has any value at all. So why on earth are they doing it? Can't they find another job?

Kingsley Amis suggests that:

> What keeps Bond at it may be just concern to do his job, devotion to M and trust in M's judgment, personal obstinacy, plus finally the vaguest patriotism, but the combination is credible.[35]

Well, it *is* credible, but only because Bond does not have the intellectual equipment to think his way out of a wet paper bag. Moreover, as Amis notes, such credibility as it has is credibility *within* the somewhat implausible conventions of the story:

> . . . when the frogman's suit arrives for Bond in *Live and Let Die*. I can join with [Bond] in blessing the efficiency of M's 'Q' Branch, whereas I know full well that given postwar standards of British workmanship, the thing would either choke him or take him straight to the bottom.[36]

John le Carré's Smiley, we are told,

> . . . dreamed of fellowships and a life devoted to the literary obscurities of seventeenth-century Germany. But his own tutor, who knew Smiley better, guided him wisely away from the honours that would undoubtedly have been his.[37]

but why this was such a *wise* piece of guidance is not clear. Is the suggestion that it was better for *Smiley*? Le Carré's novels give us little ground for accepting that answer. Better for the world? For Smiley's country?

The question, 'Why are they doing it?' has occurred to our authors, and it is revealing to see what is on offer. It ranges from

(a) fear and blackmail (e.g., Charlie Muffin in Brian Freemantle's series)
(b) the need for danger (Quiller, Blaise/Garvin in the Peter O'Donnell series)
(c) the desire for money (Oakes)
(d) old-fashioned patriotism (Bond)
(e) being in some not clearly specified way the *best* person to do something that, for some not clearly specified reason, *has* to be done (Smiley)
(f) no reason at all (Deighton's unnamed 'hero').

These reasons do not put our protagonists in a very good light – and yet we are meant to identify with them. And, indeed, we do to some extent.[38] Why? In part, surely, because of the games-playing aspect – we cut off the notion that these are people in the real world and, accepting the clearly artificial nature of the 'rules', treat it as an extended version of the sports pages of our newspapers.

Of course we perform such feats of isolation in all genre fiction. In fantasy, for example, we must both acknowledge scientific laws, for the characters function in 1G gravity wells, and they live and breathe and so on, but despite the presence of the laws of physics and chemistry, the fantasy elements also function. How? Of course we are not told. Science fiction requires that we both use and forget relativity physics. And so on for the others.

In spy fiction we must both acknowledge and forget much of what we already know about human beings. The spy fiction view, like that on offer from some, though not all politicians, military people, and followers of the philosopher Hobbes, is a bleak one which sees human beings as being in constant competition, and nations as being, Platonically, persons writ large. People *can* be Hobbesian under certain conditions; that is why inner-city ghettos have the problems they do, and why people are willing to kill one another in war. But if we were all like that all of the time the human species could not exist: it is a precondition of the existence of the human species that Hobbes is wrong about human nature. Socio-biologists are clearly wrong to argue, as some of the less sophisticated among them do, that because we are the way we are, the things it is 'natural' for us to do must be morally right or at least acceptable. But it is equally true that, in ethics or any other human science, we neglect the biological facts about our species at our peril: we are members of a gregarious species, and moral theories that assume solitariness as the norm from which to begin are built on sand.

Not only must we forget the evolutionary facts about human beings, we must also forget, when reading spy fiction, that espionage is an essentially pointless human activity; we must be willing to pretend that rational adult human beings will accept that it is necessary. Now, we know that in fact many human beings do accept this, and we know too that many of them are intelligent, concerned and moral, but it is hard to convey in fiction why, in that case, these people are willing to treat, in time of peace, another nation or group of nations as the *enemy*. And we must close our eyes to the real world activities of France, Great Britain, the USSR and the USA. Spy novels do not tell us about members of the French Secret Service killing people in New Zealand and getting promoted for their pains. In spy novels there is a pretence of mirroring the real world of spying, but it is not, on inspection, very convincing. There is very little about dictatorships being propped up in the interest of multinational fruit chains.[39]

We have, incidentally, very few genre fictions: romance, including its historical and medical subdivisions; Westerns; science fiction; detective fiction, ranging from the hard-boiled to the semi-cerebral; war; and thrillers, with espionage as a distinct sub-genre. Most of these are recent, and the reason for their arrival, as well as the reason why just these are the ones which have found favour, raises an interesting issue, but not one for which we shall pause here.[40]

What is also interesting is that spy fiction seems to be alone in throwing up so many anti-spy novels. Westerns do not typically give rise to anti-Westerns, and even the satiric films are gentle with the genre; no one to my knowledge has undertaken the perhaps impossible task of parodying Harlequin romances; science fiction has internal parodies, but, significantly, these are almost entirely parodies of *style*: and the parody is usually of a style that is taken to be outmoded. The parodies in this case, as also in the case of detective fiction, are for the purpose of comedy: but the edge is sharper in the spy case. The anti-spy novels do not go in solely for broad humour, and the satire is not only upon the genre, but upon the activity itself: its pointlessness and immorality are often sharply and explicitly portrayed, and this happens too in passing in the non-parodic novels of practitioners such as Deighton and le Carré.

THE INEVITABLE CONCOMITANT: SEXISM

Sexism in spy fiction deserves a section to itself because it is found in almost all spy novels and, unlike the other immoralities involved, has no *internal* justification. The lies, treacheries, thefts, muggings and murders have reasons, however shaky, in terms of the plot, but the sexism is mere gratuitous immorality. I am not suggesting it is unique to the spy novel, it is of course endemic in our society, but it is strikingly present in the spy novel. It appears both overtly and covertly. The overt component is straightforward: it involves the fact that women are typically treated in spy fiction as something less than fully rational adult human beings. This can remain true, even when it is noticed that they are being treated in this way.

Kingsley Amis writes, with reference to a friend of James Bond:

> Darko says he 'consumes a large quantity of women', which sounds
> jolly robust and devil-may-care until you start thinking about what it
> must involve for the large quantity of women.[41]

but what does he mean by '*until* you start thinking'? What took him so
long?[42]

Throughout Ian Fleming's novels we are presented with the same
picture:

> He sighed. Women were for recreation. On a job they got in the way
> and fogged things up with sex and hurt feelings and all the emotional
> baggage they carried around. One had to look out for them and take
> care of them.[43]

The picture could be multiplied with ease. And indeed I take it that the
overt sexism in many spy novels is clear. It might be thought that this is
not the case in the novels of writers such as Deighton and le Carré, whose
female characters are often, if not inevitably, drawn with sympathy.

To see the problem here we need to digress slightly into the realms of
psychology and semantics. Quite apart from other more obvious examples
of sexism it is notable that women in spy fiction are almost always referred
to as *girls*:

> You don't like weak women
> You get bored so quick
> And you don't like strong women
> 'Cause they're hip to your tricks[44]

Yes indeed, and therefore our authors typically take good care that their
heroes never meet any strong women, take good care, indeed, to hide even
the *existence* of strong women from their characters and their readers alike.
(Perhaps, even, from themselves.) There are, it might almost be said, no
women in spy fiction, only 'girls'.[45] Moreover, as Bennett and Wollacott
point out, the sexism is not a separate issue from the ideological one:

> . . . in repositioning Pussy Galore sexually, Bond also repositions
> her ideologically, detaching her from the service of the villain and
> recruiting her in support of his own mission. When Bond orders her
> into bed ('She did as she was told, like an obedient child', p.222),
> she speaks to him 'not in a gangster's voice, or a Lesbian's, but in a
> girl's voice' (p.222) and is thus simultaneously doubly repositioned,
> back 'in place' as a woman and back on the right side in the contest
> between good and evil.[46]

What, exactly, is wrong with calling women 'girls'? Well, there is the obvious fact that women are not girls, and that if they are called girls they will be treated as if their skills and abilities lie within the range of the skills and abilities of girls, not of adult women.[47] There are a host of empirical studies which reveal that our attitudes are directly influenced by sexist language and linguistically conveyed sexist attitudes. Consider the following, based directly on contemporary newspaper reports:

> Buckingham Palace has announced that 19-year old Prince Charles of England, the demure English rose and heir to the throne, has become engaged to Lady Diana Spencer, the 32-year-old, worldly woman who has been seeking the 'right' royal husband for ten years. (It has been stated by reliable sources that Charles is still a virgin. It is acknowledged in royal circles that Lady Diana has had several affairs over the past ten years.) When interviewed, Charles blushed sweetly over his engagement ring, and giggled happily on the TV news. The Queen had happily assented to Lady Diana's request for Charles' hand in marriage. Because of Diana's age and the fact that she is a self-proclaimed opponent of men's liberation, it is expected that the quiet prince will merge his identity with hers.[48]

We can see that there can be sexist uses of language without any clear sexist *terminology*. How does such language affect us? Could we not decide simply to ignore it? Many people, for example, claim, some of them sincerely, to use words like 'he' gender neutrally, and to use 'girl' either neutrally or (save the mark) as a 'compliment'. Are they wrong?

The answer is yes, they are. They are wrong because language is a multi-person game, not a one-person enterprise: there are both speakers and hearers, and if the hearers do not, indeed cannot, hear the language used in a non-sexist way, then it is not non-sexist, no matter what the speakers claim about their intentions. Moreover, initially, we pick up on linguistic cues at a pre-linguistic level.

This is merely a special case of the fact (constantly exploited by Adam Hall in the Quiller novels) that *a great deal* of our information-processing is non- or pre-cognitive. Here's a simple example from the domain of perception. If an object moves past you (and you are looking) you perceive it as moving. If you move your head or eyes past a stationary object you may receive qualitatively similar retinal impressions, but you no longer see the object as moving. The currently accepted view is that the neural centres which initiate the head and eye movements interact with the centre which analyses the information received to allow that system to discount the changes in the retinal images. But notice that this is *not* a matter of *cognitive* analysis, as may be seen by moving the eyeball and hence the retina slightly with your finger: then movement *is* perceived even though you *know* that no movement has occured. *Knowledge* is not what is important here. What is important is the interaction of *this* system with *that*: with that, and no other.

It is worth noting in passing that for an animal that has evolved on this planet two perceptual features are unsurprising. One is that there should not be much cognitive interference with the perceptual process: it is in general much safer to see what is there than what we would like to be there. The second is that we shouldn't be surprised to find a willingness to entertain false positives. Jerry Fodor (whose *Modularity of Mind*[49] I am following closely here) reminds us of Ogden Nash's good advice: 'If you're called by a panther/ Don't anther'. It's better to *mis*take a large number of panther possibilities for a panther, than to *mis*take even one panther actuality for the absence of a panther. (Hall gets this right for Quiller, too.)

We should not be surprised to find that something similar happens in the case of linguistic processing, and so indeed it proves. This is how it goes.

Some linguistic gaps are easier to close than others. You are more likely to hear me if, against an auditory background that makes hearing the final word of my request difficult, I say to you, 'Please pass me the pepper and salt', than if I say, 'Please pass me the pepper and whisky'.

Plausible completions are said to have high Cloze; less plausible ones, low Cloze. Clearly the Cloze value is related to our expectations, and so it's tempting to think that, at some level, we are *attending* to the input, to think, in the jargon, that cognitive penetration is occurring. But in fact the uptake is quite a bit too fast for the process in question to involve our *attending* to what is going on. Additionally, it is quite a bit too stupid. Let me quote Fodor, referring to an experiment of David Swinney's.

> The subject listens to a stimulus sentence along the lines of 'Because he was afraid of electronic surveillance, the spy carefully searched the room for bugs.' Now, we know from previous research that the response latencies for 'bugs' . . . will be faster in this context, where it is relatively predictable, than in a neutral context where it is acceptable but relatively low Cloze. This seems to be – and is traditionally taken to be – the sort of result which demonstrates how expectation based upon an intelligent appreciation of sentential contexts can guide lexical access; the subject predicts 'bugs' before he hears the word. His responses are correspondingly accelerated whenever his prediction proves true. Hence, cognitive penetration of lexical access.
>
> You can, or so it seems, gild this lily. Suppose that, instead of measuring reaction time for word/nonword decisions on 'bugs' you simultaneously present (flashed on a screen that the subject can see) a different word belonging to the same (as one used to

say) 'semantic field' (e.g., 'microphones'). If the top-down story is right in supposing that the subject is using semantic/background information to predict lexical content, then 'microphones' is as good a prediction in the context as 'bugs' is, so you might expect that 'microphones', too, will exhibit facilitation as compared with neutral context. And so it proves to do. Cognitive penetration of lexical access with bells on, or so it would appear. But the appearance is misleading. For Swinney's data show that if you test with 'insects' instead of with 'microphones', you get the same result: facilitation as compared with a neutral context. Consider what this means. 'Bugs' has two paraphrases: 'microphones' and 'insects'. But though only one of these is contextually relevant, *both are contextually facilitated*. This looks a lot less like the intelligent use of contextual/background information to guide lexical access. What it looks like instead is some sort of associative relation among lexical forms . . .; a relation pitched at a level of representation sufficiently superficial to be *in*sensitive to the semantic content of the items involved.[50]

The important thing about all this from our present point of view is that the tuning in of the associative network is pre-conscious. By the time you are *aware* of the word, the associations have *already* been made. And needless to say, the associations with 'he', 'man', etc. are all male-oriented, as a host of further experiments have shown clearly. Similarly, the associations with 'girl' are not those of clear, cool-headed, trustworthy competence.

Of course this point has wider implications. US politicians, for example, are fond of referring to Latin America and the Caribbean as their 'back yard'. But you *own* your back yard and, consequently, you can do pretty much what you like in it.[51] There are all too many examples of this attitude being translated from language into intervention, and similarly, where you find sexist language, you find sexist behaviour. In a wide range of areas, sexist language is being eliminated (it is now rare to find it in academic English), but the language, and the attitudes it embodies, are still with us in spy fiction.

OTHER CONNECTED IMMORALITIES

. . . in this Commandment, not only the Perpetration of Murther, and the actual imbruing our hands in the Bloud of our Brother, is prohibited; but likewise all Causes and Occasions leading to it . . . .[52]

Thus Ezekiel Hopkins in 1692. Here is Adam Hall in 1985:

I went for the one area that will kill without a cry and watched his eyes open very wide before I turned again and went on up the stairs, no excuses, this is the trade we're in and this is the way we ply it.[53]

But as Hopkins might have pointed out, what is wanted in such a situation is not *excuses*, but a *justification*. But this too is conspicuously lacking. Moreover, both Hall and Quiller are aware of this fact:

They'd been uneasy about this at Norfolk when I'd been put through my first psychological evaluation. *Until you can bring yourself to face this aspect of the work, Quiller, you'll be a danger to yourself and to those working with you.* Fowler, with his degree in abnormal psychology and his totally blank eyes and his frightened-looking wife. *During your mission it will occasionally be necessary to take life, and we shall expect you to do it only when the need is vital to the mission or to your own survival but with no hesitation, no compunction, no regret.* Fowler, with his cultivated penchant for the telling phrase. *During your missions you must learn to travel light, and leave your conscience behind.*[54]

This is confused. Either the taking of life when it is 'vital to the mission or to your own survival' is morally justified (which suggests that getting into such a situation is itself justifiable), or it is not. If it is, there is no need to 'leave your conscience behind'. A healthy synderesis can deal with such a situation.[55] On the other hand, if one's conscience is left behind, presumably because the actions are *not* morally justifiable, then the 'vital to your mission' etc. restrictions must have only conditional validity: they are there only because acting otherwise would endanger the mission, which is, itself, unjustified. But whether or not ends can occasionally justify means, if the end is itself unjustifiable, so too, as Hopkins so clearly points out, are whatever means are employed to it, considered simply as means.

Strategically, a main task of the writer of spy stories (which typically involve murder, torture and a host of lesser crimes) is to get the reader to accept these. There is, of course, a sub-genre where such things are not argued for, but simply gloried in:

I shot them in cold blood and enjoyed every minute of it. I pumped slugs into the nastiest bunch of bastards you ever saw, and here I am, calmer than I've ever been and happy too . . . god, but it was fun.[56]

Spillane produces, as Kingsley Amis has remarked, 'a kind of writing in which the reader is – pressingly – invited to enjoy the infliction of cruelty by a character with whom he supposedly identifies'.[57] I think that one would have to be psychologically unwell to enjoy such writing (popular though it is), but I may be simply wrong about this. As John Wisdom said ('with acknowledgements to Henri de Montherlant') the person of 'more experience has had experience of eccentricities in the sane and realizes that since seven people out of ten are monsters they can't be'.[58] That is neat, but it assumes that you cannot have a society in which the majority are psychologically unwell. I am Aristotelian enough not to believe that: societies can be such as to make it impossible for people to flourish in them.

However, leaving this aside, we still have the basic issue: how is the writer to convert the reader? How are we led to accept the more genteel immoralities, given that we would reject the Mickey Spillane version?

There are a number of devices which are, consciously or otherwise, employed. Consciously, no doubt, by the best writers. As Graham Greene remarks:

> These are points a novelist notices, but one can't underestimate what Trollope calls in his autobiography 'the unconscious critical acumen of the reader'. What the novelist notices the reader probably notices too, without realizing it.[59]

Here are some of the manoeuvres employed.

(a) We are, as has already been pointed out, led into a games-playing attitude towards the whole enterprise. The whole question of ethics is simply fudged. As Sauerberg remarks, in his perceptive *Secret Agents in Fiction*, a

> profound analysis of ethics . . . is a liability when it comes to 'efficient' writing. It seems, consequently, that not only is the ethical dilemma a paradox in itself, but its existence as part of a fictional structure forms another paradox: the degree of genuine interest shown in the ethical dilemma may turn out to be in inverse proportion to the reader's sustained interest in the story as a whole.[60]

It should be said that the willingness to ignore the moral issue is not confined to fictional spies and their authors:

> When *Smiles and Songs*, a popular Italian weekly with a circulation of over seven hundred thousand, began to publish an extensive enquiry into espionage, thousands of letters reached the publishers. Housemaids, youths from the provinces, old-age pensioners, eager boys, businessmen, learned physicists, children, clerks, porters and waiters rushed to take up the career of international spy, wanted to know where it was necessary to apply to become a secret agent, and sought all relevant information: how much was earned, was the car supplied, what age must one be, must one know judo, was it necessary to be a bachelor, how much did a course in spying

cost, was it possible to take it by correspondence, was it possible to become a secret agent if one were scared of travelling by air? Among thousands of enquiries of this kind, the only moral question raised was quantitative: 'If I entered the secret service, how many people exactly would I have to kill in a year?'[61]

(b)   we are offered, subtly or directly, the view that the setting of the story is such that reasonable people would behave as the protagonist does: the situation is a difficult and dangerous one; or times are abnormal; or it is a matter of self-defence. Need overrides niceness: *erst kommt das Fressen, dann kommt die Moral*, grub first, then ethics.

(c)   we are offered a distinction between good and bad crimes (e.g., Modesty Blaise and Willie Garvin kill people, but they only kill people who are *nasty*, and they would never, ever, smuggle marijuana).

(d)   the villains are shown to be unacceptable socially by being characterized as non-Caucasian, or otherwise handicapped, and so what is done to them is relatively unimportant, morally.

(e)   we are offered a protagonist who is relatively free to break the rules that bind the rest of us, and we find it possible, in the artificial setting we are offered, to identify with such a character:

> In a society where we are conditioned more and more to believe we have no control or responsibility over and for our own lives, the spy survives as the anima, the fantasy figure licensed to plan and commit all those violent anti-social acts we would like to perform when we are threatened or oppressed by the strain of this life. That the spy can act with such freedom and sanction from the authorities, all under the guise that it is for the protection of our society, makes the role all the more enticing.[62]

This lone wolf characterizing of the spy is an important feature, I think.[63] Associated with it is the portrayal of the spy as *unrecognizable*. This ring of Gyges aspect of the spy (as well as that involving the taking of great pains to learn the art of disguise) can be found before the advent of spy novels. English-speaking readers will think immediately of Sherlock Holmes, but we also have Maurice Leblanc's Arsène Lupin, that 'gentleman-cambrioleur' whose acts were distinctive, but whose person was undiscoverable:

> Son portrait? Comment pourrais-je le faire? Vingt fois j'ai vu Arsène Lupin, et vingt fois c'est un être différent qui m'est apparu . . . ou plutôt, le même être dont vingt miroirs m'auraient renvoyé autant d'images déformées, chacune ayant ses yeux particuliers, sa forme spéciale de figure, son geste propre, sa silhouette et son caractère.

'Moi-même', me dit-il, 'je ne sais plus bien qui je suis. Dans une glace je ne me reconnais plus.'

Boutade, certes, et paradoxe, mais vérité à l'égard de ceux qui le rencontrent et qui ignorent ses ressources infinies, sa patience, son art du maquillage, sa prodigieuse faculté de transformer jusqu'aux proportions de son visage, et d'altérer le rapport même de ses traits entre eux.

'Pourquoi', dit-il encore, 'aurais-je une apparence définie? Pourquoi ne pas éviter ce danger d'une personnalité toujours identique? Mes actes me désignent suffisamment.'[64]

(f)   we have, masked in muddled metaphysics, a piece of total ethical relativism:

In the hotel lobby Fane picked up a message and used an outside line while I looked at a display of dolls in regional costumes and had the odd thought that there actually *were* children like this dancing somewhere on some village square to the music of a pipe band while I stood here living my lies and practising my deceits on the pretext that I was doing my bit to keep the Cold War from hotting up. Which was the real world, those children's or mine? It can only ever be the one we create, the one we have to design for ourselves to give us shelter from confusion and sustenance for our needs. I don't dance so well to a pipe band as to the tune of my own dark drummer.[65]

(g)   finally, as in the le Carré novels, we are presented with a cry of *angst*, with a realization that there is an ethical problem, and with a lengthy failure to resolve it.[66]

None of the above offers a particularly convincing solution. Deighton, the writer whose work I most enjoy, is also one who deals least convincingly with the ethical element.[67] le Carré deals with the ethical issue at greater length, but not to any particularly satisfactory conclusion.[68] And writers such as Hall try to pretend that it is irrelevant.

Thus, it seems that the task of solving the ethical dilemma inherent in the genre has not, to date, been achieved by any of the major writers in the field. And, indeed, that is not surprising: for the correct solution of the dilemma requires an anti-spy novel. We are not offered a convincing rationale for the behaviour of our fictional spies because there is no such justification. So what is required is the novel that shows up spying as an undesirable activity. This we have in the novels of Block and Rathbone, already mentioned, as well as in others (such as Brian Garfield's *Hopscotch*), but of course they are not *typical* spy novels.

This brings us back to the point from which we began: what is the moral status of reading (writing, selling, buying) literature which one comes to see, however reluctantly, as immoral or, at least, as containing immoral elements? On this I shall say nothing further. It is a question for which a separate paper would be required, even if I had a clear-cut answer to it, which I do not.

NOTES

The author acknowledges help in writing this essay by conversations with, and suggestions from, Wesley Wark, Janis Svilpis, Dennis McKerlie and Thomas Hurka.

1. '. . . enough,' remarks David Stafford, 'to kill off the enthusiasm and stamina of the most ardent explorer.' David Stafford, *The Silent Game: The Real World of Imaginary Spies* (Toronto, 1988), p.v.
2. LeRoy L. Panek, *The Special Branch* (Bowling Green, 1981), p.5.
3. Lawrence Block is not, I think, as well known to an English audience as the others. His spy novels, or more properly, spy satires, centre on his rather improbable hero Evan Tanner, who lost the ability (or need) to sleep during the Korean war, and uses his extra time learning languages and involving himself in aiding the activities of a large number of subversive organizations. He was recruited by accident into a US agency which does *not* act in concert with the CIA and spends much of his time achieving (usually) worthwhile ends more or less by chance. Among the titles in this series are *The Thief Who Couldn't Sleep, The Cancelled Czech, Tanner's Twelve Swingers, Two for Tanner, Tanner's Tiger, and Here Comes a Hero*. (Block also writes of the activities of Bernie Rhodenbarr, a New York bookseller and thief in such works as *Burglars Can't be Choosers, The Burglar in the Closet, The Burglar Who Liked to Quote Kipling, The Burglar Who Painted Like Mondrian*, and *The Burglar Who Studied Spinoza*. And in a more serious, or anyway more hard-boiled, vein he writes of Matt Scudder, an ex-New York cop, and ex-(more or less) alcoholic, who solves crimes for his friends and acquaintances.)
4. *Amber Nine* (London, 1967), like the other Boysie Oakes novels, is meant to be humorous, but the torture is dwelt upon too lovingly to be excused as humorous.
5. The notion of a *prima facie* duty (right, etc.) is that of something which can be overridden, but which is such that the overriding requires further moral justification. Such *prima facie* rights, etc., are said to be *defeasible*: but in order to defeat them we must muster *moral* arguments.
6. Anatole France, *The Red Lily*. Ch 7.
7. See, e.g., *Summa Contra Gentiles*. Book 3, Ch. 134; *Summa Theologiae*. $2^a 2^{ae}$, 66.7.resp. It should be said, though, that the basis of Thomas's argument is that poverty can give rise to special *needs* which wealth generally eliminates automatically, so that it is not the poverty, but the accompanying need, which provides the basic moral justification.
8. W.S. Maugham, *The Razor's Edge* (London, 1970), vol.4, pp.205–6.
9. Kingsley Amis, *The James Bond Dossier* (New York, 1965), p.74. (Hereafter Amis. For pagination in the English edition add 10–11 pages.) Not everyone agrees with Amis. Bernard Bergonzi (to whom Amis is directly responding) found 'a total lack of any ethical frame of reference' in the Bond novels ('The Case of Mr Fleming', *Twentieth Century*, March 1958, p.288). In *Casino Royale* Bond argues briefly, fascinatingly and totally implausibly, that good could not *exist* without evil. Sauerberg (Lars Ole Sauerberg, *Secret Agents in Fiction* (London, 1984), p.48) glosses this (as does Amis, in effect) as the assumption that 'evil exists only to make us see the nature of good', but Bond is making a much stronger metaphysical claim. He remarks to Mathis: '[Le Chiffre] was creating a norm of badness by which, and by which alone, an opposite norm of goodness could exist.' Amis remarks, appropriately enough, 'Mathis laughs . . . , as well he might' (p.16).
10. Amis, p.10.
11. Moral intuitions vary sharply here. For some Decatur's 'our country, right or wrong' is simply silly and E.M. Forster's desire (in *What I Believe*) for the courage to choose

friends above country makes eminent sense in many cases if not all, but there are others who sneer at 'Marxist cant about internationalism, and E.M. Forster's high camp dictum about having the guts to betray his country rather than his friend' (Joseph Brodsky, 'A Cambridge Education', *Times Literary Supplement (TLS)*, 30 Jan. 1987, p.100). Brodsky's piece is simply a series of *obiter dicta*. but it is interesting that he finds it necessary to 'strengthen' this one by way of the totally irrelevant reference to Forster's homosexuality. In *The British Spy Novel* (London, 1984), John Atkins suggests that fictional spies are on Forster's side: 'Ostensibly Bond is a patriot. In fact his first loyalty is to himself, the second to his friends . . . and the third to his country' (p.210). 'This,' Atkins goes on to argue, is 'probably true for most agents.'

12. This might be the point to remark that, although I disagree with Amis on a large number of moral and political matters, I find his writing on Bond and Fleming great fun. He is an acute and often highly critical observer of Bond. There are many passages which show that his admiration and liking for the Bond/Fleming combination is combined with a distaste for many of the views implicit in the novels. His defence of Bond is to be explained partly (though only partly, as *Colonel Sun* shows) as a reaction against what he takes to be the over-zealousness of the attacks on Fleming by other writers. What is more, his attacks on people with views he finds unsympathetic are often acute and almost always amusing. He is aware of Bond's immorality but, as people do for their friends, he defends him directly, or offers excuses, or minimizes the offense, or launches an *ad hominem*, or (when all else fails) simply changes the subject. But we don't do any of these things if we think *no* immorality is involved.

13. Amis, p.70.

14. Ibid., p.96.

15. The literature on this point is large: practically all the works in our bibliography make reference to it. Of course the fact that it is *their* country that is involved is still clearly felt to be morally relevant by a number of contemporary US writers. Different empire, same implausible assumption of self-evident moral worth, though it should be said that some US writers combat this fatuity. Lawrence Block's Tanner series provides a case in point, though it is interesting that they are satires, not *pure* spy novels.

16. Though by no means all. Writers such as David Fraser and Robert Ludlum provide, from opposite sides of the Atlantic, contemporary examples of old-fashioned patriotism. Better that, says Kingsley Amis, *à propos* Bond's similar patriotism, than 'the anguished cynicism and the torpid cynicism respectively of Messrs le Carré and Deighton' (Amis, p.83), but on this matter, clearly, opinions may differ.

17. Julian Symons, 'Seen in the distorting mirror', *TLS*, 30 Jan. 1987, p.101.

18. Genesis 42.31, recounting Genesis 42.11, Authorized Version. The *NEB* replaces 'true' with 'honest'.

19. Arthur Conan Doyle, *Sir Nigel*, Ch.24, 'How Nigel was Called to his Master'.

20. John le Carré, *The Looking Glass War* (Toronto, 1966), p.126.

21. Gavin Lyall, *The Crocus List* (London, 1986), p.83.

22. Ian Adams, *S: Portrait of a Spy* (London, 1977; US edition, New Haven and New York, 1982), p.ix.

23. The term 'terrorism' is not mine alone. It was used by Pierre Trudeau, when he was Prime Minister of Canada, to refer to the mining of harbours in Nicaragua. At the time the US government was still in its standard mode of initial denial.

24. Julian Rathbone, *Zdt* (London, 1988), p.241.

25. Bruce Merry, *Anatomy of the Spy Thriller* (Dublin, 1977), p.34; Victor Marchetti, *The Rope Dancer* (London, 1974), pp.83–4.

26. Merry, op. cit., p.36.

27. Most clearly in *The Billion Dollar Brain*.

28. January, 1990.

29. James Stephens, *The Crock of Gold* (London, 1953 [1912]), p.110.

30. There is, however, an extensive literature on the subject. Perhaps the simplest way into the philosophical component of this literature is by way of the anthology, *Philosophical Dimensions of Privacy*, ed. Ferdinand Schoeman (Cambridge, 1984).

31. Adams, op. cit., pp.44–5.

32. George Berkeley, *Three Dialogues . . . in Opposition to Sceptics and Atheists*. Dialogue II.
33. Jorge Ibargüengoitia, *Two Crimes*, trans. Asa Zatz (London, 1984) pp.4–5.
34. Significantly it was *England*, not Great Britain. In the Amis quote above it is England that Bond is meant to base his moral stance on: but Bond, we should note, is Scottish-Swiss (M's obituary notice of Bond, in *You Only Live Twice*). In the case of US writers this unthinking immorality – the acceptance of the view that if *their* country (as opposed to others) requires something it is thereby sanctioned morally – is perhaps unsurprising since it simply mirrors the equally unthinking immorality of the US populace, but it comes oddly from contemporary British writers.
35. Amis, p.83.
36. Ibid.
37. John le Carré, *Call for the Dead* (New York, 1970), p.3.
38. 'We', on the assumption that most readers of this essay enjoy (as I do) reading (some) spy novels.
39. Rathbone's already mentioned *Zdt* provides a welcome exception, as do Lawrence Block's novels. Indeed *Zdt* is a spy thriller with no spies with whom the reader is meant to identify, there is only the Agency as a realistic villain, allied to big business, and prepared with a realism unusual in spy novels to act quite nakedly on the worst of motives.
40. Berger writes:

> Consider the strain on our moral vocabulary if it were asked to produce heroic myths of accountants, computer programmers, and personnel executives. We prefer cowboys, detectives, bull fighters, and sports car racers, *because these types embody the virtues which our moral vocabulary is equipped to celebrate*: individual achievement, exploits and prowess (B. Berger, 'The Sociology of Leisure: Some Suggestions', in *Industrial Relations*, Vol.I, No.2 (1962), p.41, quoted in Merry, op. cit., p.228).

Herbert J. Muller makes a similar point:

> Few have heard of Fra Luca Pacioli, the inventor of double-entry bookkeeping; but he has probably had much more influence on human life than has Dante or Michelangelo (*The Uses of the Past* (Oxford, 1957), p.257.)

For a further discussion of the games-playing aspect of spying see Erving Goffmann, *Strategic Interaction* (University of Pennsylvania Press, 1969). In a brief discussion of the reason for the recentness of spy stories Goffmann retails (from S. Alsop and T. Braden, *Sub Rosa: The OSS and American Espionage* (New York, 1964) the nice story of a French monk, recruited as a spy in the Second World War by American intelligence, who was 'caught when a German officer routinely asked him where he was going, the monk having then felt obliged to say that he was spying, lest he tell a lie'. I suspect, though, that this story is either apocryphal or elliptical. The monk may have had other reasons for saying what he did (for example, he may have been worried about deceit simply), but a monk concerned with *lying* may be expected to have at least some acquaintance with St Augustine or St Thomas, and to know that one is not obliged to *volunteer* the truth in order to avoid lying (silence is not a lie). (Augustine: *Contra Mendacium*, c 10; Aquinas: *Summa Theologiae*, 2ª 2ᵃᵉ, 111.1.ad 4.)
41. Amis, p.71.
42. Part of the answer for Amis is that he was writing in 1965, when sexism was a commonly accepted feature of life. One of the surprising features of spy fiction, though, is how little that has changed.
43. Ian Fleming, *Casino Royale* (London, 1955), p.33. Kingsley Amis, defending Fleming against the charge of sexism, remarks that the 'general sensationalism of *Casino Royale* was greatly toned down in its successors' (Amis, p.40). However, it is in the later *The Spy Who Loved Me* (p.128), of which Amis says, 'Female viewpoint treated with skill and imagination' (Amis, Reference Guide), that we find the following:

> All women love semi-rape. They love to be taken. It was his sweet brutality against my bruised body that made his act of love so piercingly wonderful.

This point of view is not confined to genre fiction, of course. One finds the viewpoint of the typical fictional spy cropping up in the oddest places:

I was still, and must for long remain, in that period of life when one has not yet separated the fact of this sensual pleasure from the various women in whose company one has tasted it, when one has not yet reduced it to a general ideal which makes one regard them thenceforward as the interchangeable instruments of a pleasure that is always the same. (Marcel Proust, *Remembrance of Things Past*. tr. C. K. Scott Moncrieff and Terence Kilmartin (London, 1983), Vol, 1, pp.171–2.)

44. Joni Mitchell, 'You Turn Me On I'm a Radio', *For the Roses*, 1972.
45. This is, perhaps, not quite fair. It turns out that in *some* novels (e.g., in Deighton's *An Expensive Place to Die*) it is possible for a woman to be referred to as a woman if she is over thirty and French: not guaranteed, mind you, but possible.
46. Tony Bennett and Janet Woollacott, *Bond and Beyond* (Basingstoke, 1987), pp.117–8. The references are to Ian Fleming's *Goldfinger*. On this point see further S. Heath, *The Sexual Fix* (London, 1982), and Kingsley Amis's, 'Beautiful Firm Breasts', op. cit., Ch 5. As noted above, Amis, despite his admiration for Fleming, has a very sharp eye for spotting things that are wrong in the Bond novels.
47. The same point applies to the now discredited use of 'boy' to refer to black men. In general we should note that sexist language is, morally, precisely as unacceptable as racist language, and anyone who understands why the second is wrong should not need further argument to understand why the first is.
48. Kathryn Pauly Morgan, 'Women and Moral Madness', in L. Code, S. Mullett and C. Overall (eds.), *Feminist Perspectives, Philosophical Essays on Method and Morals* (Toronto, 1988), p.155. The pastiche was put together by Morgan's students in a Philosophy of Feminism class.
49. J. Fodor, *The Modularity of Mind* (Boston, 1983).
50. Ibid., p.79.
51. In Canada we notice these things: if that's their *back* yard, we can all see what their front yard must be. You own your front yard just as much as you do your back yard, but since it is a more public domain your behaviour there is typically a bit more careful. None the less, it is still *yours*. Something like a fifth of US citizens questioned in a recent survey said they believed Canada was a part of the US; well over half said they believed Canada would like it to be. These figures are not reflected in Canadian surveys. (For an interesting fictional account of the occupation of Canada by US troops for the purpose of safeguarding US business interests see Ian Adams, *The Trudeau Papers* (Toronto/Montreal, 1971).)
52. Ezekiel Hopkins, *An Exposition on the ten commandments: with other sermons* (London, 1692), i, p.13.
53. Adam Hall, *Quiller* (New York, 1985), p.324.
54. Ibid, p.327.
55. *Synderesis* is a notion not much encountered in spy fiction, though it makes an appearance in the novels of Aldous Huxley. The *Oxford English Dictionary* quotes Saint-German's *Fyrst dyaloge in Englisshe betwyxt a doctoure of dyvnyte and a student in the lawes of Englande* (1531): 'Sinderesis is a naturall power of the soule sette in the hyghest parte therof, mouynge and sterrynge it to good, & abhorrynge euyll'.
56. Mickey Spillane, *One Lonely Night*. quoted in Merry, op. cit., p.86.
57. Amis, p.141.
58. John Wisdom, *Other Minds* (Oxford, 1956), p.29.
59. Graham Greene, *Ways of Escape* (London, 1980), pp.200–201.
60. Op. cit., p.72.
61. Lietta Tornabuoni, 'A Popular Phenomenon', in Oreste Del Buono and Umberto Eco (eds.) *The Bond Affair*. trans R.A. Downie (London, 1966), p.22.
62. Adams, op. cit., p.ix.
63. The point is very clearly argued in Jerry Palmer's *Thrillers* (London, 1978), p.25.
64. Maurice Leblanc, 'L'Arrestation d'Arsène Lupin', in *Arsène Lupin gentleman-cambrioleur* (Paris, pbk edn, 1962 [1907]), pp.29–30. For the painstaking preparation aspect see 'L'évasion d'Arsène Lupin', ibid., pp.70–71.

65. Hall, op. cit., 85. We get the same, fairly explicit, rejection of morality in Hall's *The Warsaw Document* (New York, 1972):

    I was fed up with his chocolate-box morality, with his inability to know that in the intelligence services you've got to wrench your sense of values round till they face the other way . . . . (p.209).

    We are, of course, not told *why* this is something you've 'got' to do.
66. For more detail on the ethical content of le Carré's fiction see Harold Bloom (ed.), *John le Carré.* in the Modern Critical Views series (New York, 1987). At the time of writing (January, 1990) le Carré, hitherto fairly diffident about his own views, seems to be becoming much less reserved, not only agreeing to various interviews on his work, but launching out into the real world of ethics with a very strange piece urging that Salman Rushdie's *Satanic Verses* should not be published in paperback. 'Nobody,' writes le Carré, revealing an interesting theological as well as moral standpoint, 'has a God-given right to insult a great religion and be published with impunity' (*Guardian Weekly*, 28 Jan. 1990, 26). I wonder what George Orwell would have made of 'be published with impunity' as a synonym for 'not be killed'.
67. I am driven, reluctantly, to agree with Robert Nye's comment on Len Deighton's espionage stories: 'You begin to see what is lacking . . . It is, putting it simply, a point of view' (quoted, with approval, by Patricia Craig and Mary Cadogan, *The Lady Investigates* (London, 1981, p.217).
68. Le Carré is currently interested in the possibility of writing novels which will allow for the fact that 'we must do without [a traditional] enemy' and write novels with 'new and common enemies' of a non-ideological kind. (Interview, CBC Morningside, 6 June 1989.)

Spy Fiction and Terrorism

PHILIP JENKINS

For most of the history of the genre, spy fiction has tended to describe conflicts between intelligence services which were essentially similar in outlook and methods, however different they appeared in ideology. Smiley is able to understand and defeat Karla precisely because the two men are both professionals employed in the same world. Whether the players are American or British, German or Soviet, traditional spy fiction usually portrays a world of professionals who struggle for influence or information, and who consequently frown on acts of random violence that only provide obstacles to this endeavour. These traditional values need to be stressed because they appear to contrast so sharply with the approaches of the numerous books of the last two decades, where terrorism is a major theme.

The topic of terrorism has now become one of the dominant interests of writers on secret intelligence – largely in consequence of historical accident. From the late 1950s, the work of Ian Fleming had engendered a minor revolution in popular fiction, with a host of imitators adopting the espionage world as their theme. Terrorism did not play a significant role in these novels, chiefly because the image of the revolutionary bomber appeared hopelessly dated. In the Bond books, the closest parallel to a terrorist threat occurs in *Thunderball*, when the fantastic criminal organization SPECTRE blackmails the West with stolen nuclear weapons. But while this spy craze was still in progress – or at least fresh in memory – there began a new upsurge in real-life terrorism in Europe and the Middle East. It was natural for writers on espionage to explore the many new themes and locales offered by terrorism, while thriller writers often adopted the emphasis on international intrigue derived from the Bond novels. By the 1970s, the relatively straightforward violence and heroics of the thriller became increasingly combined with the subtler diplomatic chess of spy fiction.

A novel dealing with both spies and terrorists is thus a hybrid form, often combining different elements that do not entirely fit with each other. Unlike older spy novels, it can no longer be assumed that the enemy shares any common assumptions – we might almost say, the common decencies – of the intelligence world. In particular, the terrorist's lack of professionalism is likely to be manifested in a taste for greater and more destructive violence, often apparently random in character. In literary terms, this can imply a greater tendency towards sensationalism; for writers and publishers, the new subject-matter opened the way to more spectacular action and more extreme violence. In addition, there is the opportunity for the creation of more outrageous villains based on current popular and media stereotypes.

In both cases – violence and villains – the traditional thriller element can overwhelm the influence of the spy story in the terrorist tale, and the result is an enormous potential for melodrama. At its worst, this type of novel has exactly the flaws of the potboiler thriller. For instance, the prolific thriller writer John D. MacDonald published *The Green Ripper*,[1] in many ways an interesting portrayal of a KGB attempt to use terrorist surrogates to destabilize the United States. But this threat is resolved neither by good intelligence or by regular police work. The hero fortuitously contacts the group, and, single-handed, wipes them all out in what he disarmingly refers to as 'one of his John Wayne days'.

SPIES AND TERRORISTS

This is essentially pulp thriller material; but other spy-terrorist novels offer a much richer tradition than might be suggested by such an example. Authors have often explored the overlapping worlds of terrorism and intelligence with real sensitivity, and have drawn on the best aspects of older genres. During the 1980s, several major best-sellers had terrorism as their theme, but derived a great deal of material from the espionage tradition – books such as *The Spike, The Little Drummer Girl, One Police Plaza, Agents of Innocence*, and *Patriot Games*. The emergence of terrorism as a major issue in the spy novel has neither revolutionized nor contaminated the genre, and we find a great many familiar themes. In fact, the best type of terrorism novel often includes some of the best-written and most convincing portraits of intelligence tradecraft, though now directed towards solving problems posed by violent revolutionary groups.[2]

Indeed, it might even be asked whether terrorism fiction is sufficiently different from the mainstream intelligence novel to merit separate attention. The dilemma is well illustrated by one of the most sophisticated fictional studies of both terrorism and counter-terrorism, John le Carré's *The Little Drummer Girl*.[3] This offers extensive material about the processes of the investigation and detection of terrorist activity – everything from the dynamics of interrogation and the problems of interagency conflict to the running of safe houses, ideas for surveillance, and the best means to kidnap a suspect. We are interested in how both Israelis and Palestinians run their networks in le Carré's work, but in both cases the agents employ the same methods as in any spy novel. The Israelis seek to achieve their goal by a classic intelligence tactic, the use of an agent in deep cover to infiltrate a hostile network. It merely happens that the enemy goals involve bombing and assassination rather than the theft or control of information. In this sense, the terrorism novel has exactly the same strengths and weaknesses as much other spy fiction.

While the enemies might be new, the problems to be resolved are often those of the intelligence world in general. In Tom Clancy's best-seller *Patriot Games*, the imaginary terrorist group ULA (the Ulster Liberation Army) gains its strength from the counter-intelligence skills of its leader, a dissident senior member of the Provisional IRA.[4] The plot depends on the unravelling of the ULA's excellent intelligence network, which includes high-level agents in place both in the British government and the Provisionals. The novel provides intricate detail about many different phases of an anti-terrorist operation, including the interrogations of captured militants that allow the authorities to distinguish between the acts of the ULA and those of other groups. Once the existence of leaks has been confirmed, we observe how they are traced by a combination of background investigation and electronic surveillance. This novel is perhaps the first to describe at length the targetting of satellite surveillance against terrorists at their Libyan base-camps. And finally, Clancy depicts the tentative and rather reluctant nature of co-operation between intelligence agencies of different allied countries, a relationship based on the barter of information.

But there are crucial areas where the spy-terrorism genre is in fact a new type, and where it addresses questions very different from those found in the traditional espionage novel. In fact, the writer on terrorism is able to address fundamental intelligence issues that were perhaps underplayed in older spy fiction – above all, in the question of the sponsorship and instigation of political conflict and violence. In older spy stories, there is no serious question about the political motivations of the protagonists. Whatever drives the individual agents, we know that behind them stands the government or national interest of any one of a number of states. A character might be a mole, secretly working for a country other than that which is immediately apparent, but there is no question that he serves one national agency rather than another. In the realm of terrorism, on the other hand, we have no such certainty. The terrorist might be a demented individual, a member of an autonomous group, or the clandestine representative of a government or its intelligence service. In fiction, as in reality, this question of identification is often very difficult to pursue; and the opportunities for intrigue, deception and duplicity are abundant. As we will see, there are many opportunities to use this element of masquerade as the basis for some important political statements.

This means that the spy-terrorism novel can be divided into several fundamental types, depending largely on the significance that the authors attach to the questions of motivation, deception and manipulation. A novel such as *Patriot Games* or *The Little Drummer Girl* concerns the work of intelligence agencies in combating terrorist threats, either within their own countries, or in allied states. This is the simplest form of the genre. But other writers have employed a more complex and perhaps more interesting format, where the role of the intelligence agency is in inciting and instigating the act of violence, again either at home or abroad.

The first type is a version of the police procedural, though usually in more exotic settings, where a hero combats a suitably threatening and alien menace. He does this for the salvation of his country, or at least of his own honour and decency. Unfortunately, this type of novel tends to be predictable, with good very likely to triumph; and the only interest attaches to the particular form of menace devised by the terrorists (nuclear or biological warfare, an elaborate hijacking, and so on.[5] Often, the villains in such works tend to be monolithic, with groups of different causes and political colours ultimately in the employ of the same malevolent ideology. Other writers offer a more elaborate and even byzantine world-view, where individual groups pursue their interests in competition or active enmity against other terrorist organizations. In *Patriot Games*, for example, the ULA is depicted as a violently anti-British group who choose their particular tactics in part to discredit their IRA rivals; while the IRA views sympathetically British attempts to destroy these annoying ultras. The terrorists, in short, are quite as Balkanized as the agencies seeking to destroy them.

Yet another type of terrorist thriller is altogether more complicated in its assumptions. If terrorism is the act of intelligence agencies and states, then the genre enters wholly new political dimensions. This might mean that the hero is now struggling against evil Soviet or Islamic agents in addition to domestic revolutionaries. Alternatively, the source of the evil might be in one's home country, and the villains masterminding the violence would therefore be internal security agencies – CIA, MI6, or other more mysterious forces. This provides a framework for the politically radical spy thriller, a small but interesting type.

In addition, the best writing in this tradition recognizes the many nuances that may characterize the relationship between a terrorist and an intelligence agency or the country which it represents. One excellent example is provided by David Ignatius' *Agents of Innocence*, which is faithfully based on the actual relationship between the CIA and the PLO in the 1970s. The book's two major characters are wholly based on real individuals – respectively the CIA's Bob Ames, and al-Fatah leader Abu Hassan Salameh, who headed the notorious Black September Organization.[6] In the fictional account, as in real life, it is always ambiguous whether Salameh is a directly controlled penetration agent, a mere friendly contact, or a diplomatic channel between Arafat and the Americans. The exact nature of Salameh's primary loyalties is thus a difficult and rather subjective question, which can only be really understood by someone thoroughly conversant with the language and conventions of intelligence. The assertion that X is 'working for' the Americans (or any other power) covers a wide variety of possible relationships that may be open to many interpretations.

The simple choice of terrorists as the villains of an espionage novel therefore leaves many options about the directions that can be taken both by the plot, and by the fundamental political outlook of the work. Curiously, it can be argued that the history of such fiction illustrates not a growth but a decline in political sophistication. Novelists of the early twentieth century often exercised a real critical scepticism in approaching terrorism, made effective use of satire, and were able to describe the role of deception and provocation; while recent writers have often accepted a Manichaean picture of revolutionary violence as a simple attack upon the West and its values. Only in very recent years have authors like le Carré and Ignatius succeeded in portraying the complex intelligence dimensions of terrorism as convincingly as the writers of 80 years ago.

THE FIRST AGE 1900–20

Terrorism in its modern sense originated with the anarchist and nihilist movements of the mid-nineteenth century, and the topic became a literary theme within a very few years. Both Dostoevsky and Zola addressed themselves to the nature of the revolutionary mentality. However, it was the terrorist campaigns at the end of that century that drew the attention of numerous writers to the phenomenon of revolutionary violence, and the complex nature of the movements that were apparently responsible for these acts. In fact, several books written in the first two decades of this century can be seen as the major literary contribution to the study of terrorism.[7]

The first great age of terrorism lasted from about 1890 to 1914, and it involved armed attacks in most of the major European nations, in addition to the United States. The phenomenon gained notoriety from the French campaigns between 1892 and 1894, and within a few years the media had generated a widespread panic. Despite the exaggerations, terrorists did commit many genuine outrages, including several assassinations and numerous bombings. The degree of organization among the activists remains very uncertain, as does the precise political motivation of many of the incidents, but anarchists and radical nationalists attracted most of the blame.

The terrorist campaigns offered writers a number of powerful images that could be explored in either popular novels or in more serious studies. The cases of militants like Ravachol or Vaillant focused public attention on the motivations of the dramatic and rather Nietzschean individuals who undertook the outrages; but there was also excited speculation about the hidden forces that might be orchestrating their deeds. It was the murder in 1900 of King Umberto of Italy that seriously raised the possibility of some kind of Terrorist International. According to contemporary reports, members of an anarchist cell in New Jersey had drawn lots to choose the assassin, and had dispatched the chosen individual to Europe. This idea of an International – perhaps with its 'high command' – has never entirely died, though the villains have been transformed over time from the anarchists of 1900 to the Comintern agents of the 1920s, to the Middle Eastern militants of today. In literature, this was the type of organization portrayed in *The Assassination Bureau, Ltd.*, by Jack London, and *The Power House*, by John Buchan.[8]

The idea of the 'Black International' provided a potent image, but it was by no means the only conspiracy theory which could be used to understand current events. Real terrorism had unquestionably involved manipulation and provocations by police or intelligence agencies, either within their own countries, or else against third parties. The best examples of this occurred in Russia, where the Okhrana infiltrated agents into militant organizations. Penetrated groups were subsequently used to commit outrages in western Europe, or else to discredit the anti-Tsarist movement at home. In one legendary case – of the agent Azev, exposed in 1908 – it seems as if a major part of the Russian counter-subversion enterprise had been dedicated to pursuing actions instigated by other elements of the state apparatus. Russia was notorious for its labyrinthine bureaucracy and its oppressive police system; but might agencies in Western countries have undertaken similar provocations? This was an attractive idea to radical writers anxious to dissociate themselves from violent acts committed by what appeared to be members of the extreme left.

Between 1906 and 1908, there appeared a spate of books inspired by the recent wave of bombing and assassination; and the theme of terrorism as provocation was prominent in the new genre. It is also noteworthy that this theme attracted the attention of such major authors of the day as Conrad, Chesterton and London. In 1907, Jack London published *The Iron Heel*, a widely read fantasy of the forthcoming centuries of savage struggle that would ultimately lead to world liberation in democratic socialism.[9] The hero of the book, Everard, is a dissident leader who creates fighting organizations inpired by those of Russia. However, the real terrorists are to be found elsewhere. As part of its campaign to destroy the left, the imaginary proto-Fascist organization known as the 'Iron Heel' organizes a bombing in the US Congress, which act serves to justify mass arrests of socialist leaders. London takes this opportunity for a polemical digression on the lengthy history of real *provocateur* activities by police, intelligence agencies and employers' organizations. These groups are seen as the main instigators and perpetrators of 'leftist' terrorism in America, from the Haymarket affair through the industrial crises of the opening years of the present century.

The idea that the police might infiltrate and manipulate terrorist groups reached what might be its highest expression in *The Man who was Thursday: A Nightmare*, by G.K. Chesterton.[10] This strange and surreal work is a mixture of comic satire and religious allegory, but it is still said to command much affection among intelligence practitioners. The novel depicts an anarchist group of seven members, drawn from London's bohemian circles. They appear to be serious in their anarchism, as they possess a secret headquarters where bombs are hidden. There is also a clandestine structure, 'the secret conclave of the European dynamiters'. A 'Central Anarchist Council' has seven members, all bearing code-names derived from the days of the week. Gabriel Syme, a police detective, is admitted to the council under the name of Thursday; but he soon discovers that he is not the only police infiltrator. In fact, the whole council is composed of detectives, with the exception of the President, Sunday; and he is no less than God.

It is always wrong to read too much that is serious or specific into Chesterton's writing, but this story contains much that is intriguing and worthy of discussion. Particularly interesting is the description of a counter-terrorist campaign being waged by a New Detective Corps of philosopher-policemen, who are able to prevent assassination and violence by the early detection of subversive and dissident expressions in speech or writing. Suspect organizations can then be infiltrated by police moles; so subversion is repressed by a kind of benevolent Thought Police. As an idea, this might be attractive or repulsive; but Chesterton cannot be accused of creating a simplistic portrait of either the terrorists or their police enemies. This is a kaleidoscopic world of deception and shifting loyalties; which may make it one of the most accurate fictional studies of intelligence ever written.

Conrad's *The Secret Agent* – originally subtitled 'Tales of diplomatic intrigue and anarchist treachery' – also takes as its theme the sub-rosa world of the agent-provocateur.[11] The author did not greatly like the book as an artistic achievement, but the historian must be struck by its accurate analysis of at least a part of the contemporary terrorist wave. The English press had given abundant coverage to the wave of anarchist terror on the Continent, but by the time of the novel's publication (1907), there had been only a handful of incidents in Britain itself. Conrad's fiction portrays an attempt to incite a terrorist campaign in London, but it is not undertaken by any version of the 'Black International'. Instead, the protagonist, Verloc, is a spy in the pay of an unnamed foreign embassy (unquestionably that of Russia). He has respectable revolutionary credentials, and is actually a senior member of the group FP, the 'Future of the Proletariat'; but his diplomatic masters require him to provide a 'jolly good scare' to motivate an international conference on the subject of political crime, to pass sterner measures against exiles and refugees. Specifically, Verloc must create a terrorist scare, 'a series of outrages', in order to combat 'the general leniency of the judicial procedure here, and the utter absence of all repressive measures which are a scandal to Europe. What is wished for just now is the accentuation of the unrest – of the fermentation which undoubtedly exists'.

These words – attributed to a fictional embassy official – give a very accurate representation of the real attitude of the Russian government and Okhrana at this time; and explain the motivation behind the use of *agents provocateurs* to discredit Russian exiles in the west. That the author had given very serious thought to the politics of revolutionary violence is also indicated by the discussion of likely targets. Religious targets, for instance, would be inappropriate in this secular age, while attempts on crowned heads had become mere clichés. In order to shock, an attack on art might be useful – for instance, a bomb in the National Gallery – but the most complete nihilism, the true modern iconoclasm, would be best manifested by a blow against science. Thus the Greenwich Observatory becomes the chosen target. As in the case of Chesterton, Conrad's discussion takes the form of satire, but it offers real insights into the nature of terrorist actions – then as now.

However sophisticated the novels of the early twentieth century, terrorism would for many years be at best a minor theme in the espionage genre. The topic was discussed in works by Buchan, Ambler and Greene, but – as in the real world – the nature of terrorism had changed substantially. Instead of the rather passé anarchist bomber, the typical fictional terrorist of the 1930s was an assassin, in the employ of either a secret society or an intelligence agency; and his cause was likely to be that of the political right. Greene's assassin 'Raven' was in the employ of arms manufacturers,[12] while Buchan's hero Melfort attempted to thwart the terrorist conspiracies of the Nazi Iron Hand.[13]

Not until the 1960s did the general revival of terrorist tactics by revolutionary movements cause a literary rediscovery of the phenomenon. Undoubtedly, the volume of books published now increased enormously, but it is open to question if many of them approached the political subtlety – to say nothing of the literary merit – of their predecessors in the early twentieth century. This is best illustrated by the questions of terrorist motivation and the possibility of provocation, issues about which Conrad and his contemporaries were far more politically sensitive than their literary successors. The themes of provocation and deception exist in modern works, but they are far less common than the idea that terrorists are in fact the anti-social villains that they appear to be. And when contemporary writers see the possibility of terrorist acts being manipulated by outside forces, these are usually identified as the stereotyped evildoers of the 1980s – above all, Communists and Middle Eastern radicals. In short, the 'terrorist novel' has generally become a conservative genre, far removed from its sometimes radical or satirical origins.

MOSCOW GOLD

One common fictional interpretation of terrorism has been that the perpetrators are in fact agents or surrogates of hostile states, usually those of the Soviet bloc. In its simplest form, the terrorist action might be the work of a Soviet spy or agent, who is sent to the West to commit an outrage in order to achieve a specific foreign policy goal. In *The Manchurian Candidate*, a Soviet sleeper is to assassinate a US presidential candidate in order to secure the election of a Communist-controlled candidate; and there have been countless variations of this theme.[14] In Forsyth's *The Fourth Protocol*, a Soviet agent is sent to Britain to detonate a nuclear device, with the aim of creating a political reaction that would win the ensuing election for the left (a plot credited to the personal machinations of Kim Philby). Alternatively, Britain could be detached from its Western allegiance by acts of assassination and terrorism that would be instigated by the KGB, though blamed on the Americans.[15]

In the last decade, novels of terrorism have often discussed a more complex scenario, where the Communists undertake their nefarious work through third parties; and thus, groups like the Palestinian guerrillas or even the IRA are seen as puppets of Moscow. Here, of course, the novelists enter into the very real world of political debate. Especially in the 1980s, the exact role of state sponsorship in terrorism has been the topic of intense debate in many Western countries, especially in the United States. For authors of the political right, like Michael Ledeen or Claire Sterling, terrorism of the post-1968 era has been essentially a tool of the KGB and Cubans to destabilize the West, and the only effective response would be in terms of direct political retaliation against the sponsor states.[16] This theory is reinforced by the Israeli view that Middle Eastern terrorism is sponsored by hostile states such as Syria and Libya.[17]

In contrast, other experts see terrorist movements as independent organizations arising from problems and conditions within the particular countries in which they operate. In this view, contacts between terrorist groups and foreign countries do not indicate state sponsorship of terrorism; instead, they reflect only the opportunism of dissidents in seeking arms and support wherever they can be found. These debates over the nature of terrorism deeply divided the US intelligence community in the Reagan years, and they were also fundamental to the making of American policy in areas like southern Africa and the Middle East. The Ledeen–Sterling school became especially important in 1981, when William Casey became CIA director, and Ledeen was appointed as an aide to the National Security Council.[18] The influence of their ideas was suggested by the 1986 American bombing raid on Libya in retaliation for a bomb attack in Berlin.

In fiction, the state-sponsorship model can be used merely to create a more threatening enemy, based on a host of recognizable stereotypes. In addition to the fanatical Muslim or German terrorist, the hero can also encounter the sinister might of the KGB, providing a clandestine 'hidden hand'. The stereotypes offered by such books often stray into the most extreme McCarthyite propaganda. From many examples, we might consider John D. MacDonald's *Green Ripper*, where a private detective infiltrates a pseudo-religious cult in the Pacific north-west. Here, he encounters a group made up of young American and European radicals of diverse political backgrounds, including former members of the Weather Underground and other domestic revolutionary movements. All had spent time outside the United States, where they had received training from an impressive number of international groups – the Libyans, Soviets, Palestinians, IRA and others. Clearly, the 'Terror International' was still very much in evidence. These young veterans were in training to launch a series of attacks at the 'choke-points' of civilization, through which flow supplies of food and energy, and most essential trade and transport. The result would be 'the new barbarism. There will be plague and poison. And then the new Dark Ages'.

This plot for world conquest is masterminded by the KGB, who dispose of their enemies with sophisticated biological weapons in addition to the more familiar bullets and bombs. MacDonald's thriller presents the view of terrorism that was especially common within the American ultra-right in the 1970s. For example, foreign control of the Weathermen had been a very contentious topic in the Nixon years, and all but the most diehard conservatives had concluded that the movement was little influenced by Communist states. However, a rump remained – especially within the intelligence community – and it was these views that were represented by thriller writers. In *The Green Ripper*, promising recruits are spotted through Communist front groups in the West, and sent for training to reliable allies like the IRA or PLO. They could then be returned to their home countries as fully-fledged terrorists, to begin their surrogate war against Western civilization. Movements like pacifism or student democracy are depicted as indeed the gateways to terrorism. There is also the implication that without the foreign 'hidden hand', there simply would be no terrorism in the West.

Like Robert Ludlum and Frederick Forsyth, John MacDonald uses Soviet enemies as convenient villains, who provide usefully threatening foils for heroic Westerners to combat.[19] The same stereotypes have been equally commonplace in other genres of popular fiction, including science-fiction and even horror fantasy.[20] However, the spy-terrorist thriller has also been used in a much more explicitly political way, above all in novels such as *The Spike* or *Monimbó*, both by Arnauld de Borchgrave and Robert Moss.[21] Here, the idea of the state-sponsorship of terrorism is not merely incidental to the plot, it is the fundamental theme of the book. Fiction is thus used merely as a form to convey an essentially polemical argument. They are manifestos rather than novels, though in fact, these books have enjoyed great commercial success in addition to their propaganda value. The works of de Borchgrave and Moss provide the most sophisticated fictional use of terrorism as a weapon in political and intelligence debates.

Both authors are well-known conservative activists and propagandists, and both have good intelligence ties. *The Spike*, in particular, can be seen as a popular manifestation of the political debates of the late 1970s over the nature of terrorism, and the Soviet role in its instigation. The novel summarizes all the major arguments of the Ledeen–Sterling school of thought, and in fact provides a useful guide to understanding some major themes of the Reagan administration's policies towards terrorism. The greatest perils to the West were twofold: one threat came from Soviet moles and sleepers in Western governments, especially those of the United States and Great Britain. The other menace derived from surrogate terrorist movements, which are controlled by the Soviets, but are directed in the West by a number of apparently liberal front organizations. And although there appeared to be numerous terrorist groups – German, Italian, Japanese – they were all in fact subject to the central command, STAR, under its Russian masters. That the authors intend their work to have immediate political relevance is suggested by the very close identification of fictional villains with real-life radicals and liberals – so close, in fact, as to appear legally perilous. For instance, one of the sinister front-groups bears many resemblances to the real-life Institute for Policy Studies; while one of the KGB agents in the terror network seems to be a barely disguised Philip Agee.

Meanwhile, in this world-view, the West is fatally crippled by the limitations placed on counter-intelligence operations; and the media were in effect serving as Communist tools. The title itself refers to the alleged media tendency to 'spike' or discard stories exposing Communist plots. The hero of the book is a 'reformed' liberal journalist, who investigates and exposes the Soviet plot with the assistance of European and Israeli intelligence agencies. Finally, the novel suggests that the appropriate response to the Soviet manipulation of terrorism would be the creation

of Western-sponsored activists to challenge Communist states – the idea
of a *contra* force, though not yet the actual word. After the West has
defeated the Soviet challenge, a triumphant Vice-President is left to drive
the Soviets away from a perilous Third World confrontation. He warns
his Russian counterpart that 'We've put up with your sort of liberation
movements around the world for quite a few years now . . . It's about time
you learned to put up with pro-Western guerrillas'. The Soviets, naturally,
back down from their threats.[22]

THE MIDDLE EAST

When terrorists are not agents of Moscow, they are often surrogates
for radical Middle Eastern states; and it is these stories that are most
illustrative of changing political attitudes. In the context of the Middle
East, the political ramifications of the spy-terrorist novel become especially
conservative, or at least one-dimensional. There is rarely any doubt of
the evil attributed to Arab guerrilla movements, and consequently of
the rightness of the Israeli cause. At least in the American context, this
becomes a rather simple syllogism: Arab terrorists are evil; Israel fights
Arab terrorists; therefore Israel fights evil. In the cinema, especially, the
1980s have seen the release of numerous films where American agents or
soldiers avenge terrorist atrocities by massacring thoroughly stereotyped
Arab commandos. The alert viewer will note that any Arab character in
such a film is almost certain to be a terrorist, however sympathetically
he or she is portrayed in the early part of the work.[23] In contrast, there
have been fictional works where police or intelligence agencies combat
Irish terrorists, but these never offer the same degree of stereotyping, or
of the unquestionable moral assurance that we find in the Middle Eastern
context.[24]

These conventions also apply to popular literature. Even a cursory
examination of the American bestsellers of the last decade will reveal
many novels on Middle Eastern terrorists, and they vary only in the
degree of psychopathic evil attributed to the Arab or Islamic militants.
(These books can often be identified from their titles alone, by the use
of words or names implying Arab fanaticism and violence – such as Jihad
or Saladin.)[25] It has naturally been difficult for novelists to outdo the
dramatic nature of real-life attacks, and fiction has thus been driven to
imagining ever more outrageous Middle Eastern terrorists committing
increasingly fantastic deeds; and the consequence has been a frequent
element of near-caricature.

It was inevitable that spectacular events like the hijackings of the 1970s
should attract the attention of writers. Given the apparently simple morality
of the conflict, it is equally predictable that novels involving Middle Eastern

terrorism should frequently involve thoroughly evil Arabs, in combat with heroic Israeli agents or spies. Either the Mossad agents combat the Arab or Communist menace, or (more frequently) they assist the hero to destroy a terrorist enemy. In *The Spike*, an Israeli master-spy helps expose the Soviet plot to destroy the West; in *One Police Plaza*, Israeli spies and commandos assist in the destruction of a Libyan terrorist team before it can launch attacks in New York City.[26]

We would naturally expect a far more sophisticated approach to the Middle Eastern conflicts in a work like *The Little Drummer Girl*, and the novel does indeed present the Palestinian case in far more detail than the vast majority of its American thriller counterparts. In addition, there are clear criticisms of Israeli policy. But overall, it is remarkable how far even an author of this quality adheres to the general consensus picture of dedicated Israeli master spies combating brutal and destructive international terrorists, who are loosely modelled on the 'Carlos' network of reality. Kurtz, in particular, is an intelligence genius quite equal to Karla or George Smiley. And though the terrorists are not the mindless psychopaths of other stories, they earn condemnation as frivolous playboys, compared with the dedicated and professional Israelis.

A similar contrast is also found in *Agents of Innocence*, though the Salameh character himself is presented as a sophisticated intelligence professional. It should be said that this book is generally a notable exception to the rather bleak uniformity of most American fictional portraits of the Middle East. Ignatius presents both Palestinian and Israeli viewpoints with great sympathy, and the Arab characters are even allowed to present comparisons between their own revolutionary violence and that of earlier Zionist leaders like Begin. The novel suggests the urgent necessity for Western intelligence agencies to understand the political and intellectual roots of terrorism, but at the same time it implies that such realism will always be defeated by diplomatic and bureaucratic pressures. Ignatius' humane and sympathetic CIA officers are ultimately doomed in their endeavours by their idealistic naïveté: they are agents of innocence.

The general sympathy with the Israeli cause is understandable, but it is astonishing to see how favourably this nation's intelligence apparatus is viewed. Ignatius depicts a Mossad that has penetrated most Western espionage agencies, and which despises amateurish intruders like the CIA. In fact, the sort of novels under discussion often venerate Israeli intelligence and counter-terrorist operations, to the point of making them a regular *deus ex machina* to resolve dificulties in the plot. In *One Police Plaza*, the New York police find no American agency either willing or competent to track a major Israeli operation in the United States; and so they turn to the the only possible alternative, the intelligence facilities of the Roman Catholic Church.

As in the case of the 'Soviet puppet-masters', there are various motives for the near-uniform portrayal of villainous Arabs and Muslims, and Israeli superspies. Most of the writers are simply appealing to familiar stereotypes that already exist in Western cultures, and above all in the United States; but other books are explicitly designed to propound and support the Israeli political view. One example here would be the work of Howard Kaplan in books such as *Chopin Express*, *The Damascus Cover* and, above all, *Bullets of Palestine*, a near-documentary recounting of the misdeeds of the Abu Nidal group. Pro-Israel sentiment here is overt and unabashed.[27]

But there are other explanations of the glorification of the Israeli war on terrorism so often found in American works. Perhaps this reflects the ambiguity felt about covert action conducted by domestic agencies such as the CIA: the public admires such buccaneering behaviour when competently carried out, but they are at the same time aware of the number of crimes and blunders associated with it. In addition, there is a widespread public sense that American intelligence has so often failed to combat terrorism in the real world, a failure most tellingly illustrated by the experience of US armed forces in Lebanon. In the world of anti-terrorism, too, the American failure to rescue hostages at Desert One is frequently contrasted with spectacular successes like the Entebbe raid. The novelist or reader can thus take vicarious pride and pleasure in the Israeli victories that contrast so sharply with what are seen as recurrent American failures.[28]

Moreover, the Israeli successes hold out the hope that the right side can win, given the proper degree of support and training. In terms of the solution to terrorism, many of these stories have essentially similar answers – Western powers need to intervene directly to strike at the states which sponsor anti-Western attacks. This might mean direct military attacks on the lines of the 1986 Libyan bombing raids, or perhaps commando attacks on the Israeli model. *Patriot Games* views approvingly a French commando assault on an *Action Directe* camp in Libya. This novel also suggests that an attack on a Libyan camp would be the appropriate means of preventing an attack in the United States by an ultra-leftist faction of Ulster terrorists. Alternatively, Western powers might well imitate the Israeli policy of assassinating political opponents wherever they are to be found. One curious American book purported to be the actual work of a 'specialist', an agent who killed international terrorists at the behest of American and other intelligence agencies.[29] However, it is at least possible that the book should in fact be counted as part of the fictional genre discussed here.

THE RADICAL TRADITION

If such books are really to be seen as a manifestation of popular wishes and fears, then public attitudes on terrorism appear to be extremely conservative in nature. Indeed, the great majority of fictional treatments explore what might be termed the consensus definition of terrorism – that is, international violence by generally anti-Western groups. However, there are novelists who have attempted other approaches more akin to the tradition begun by earlier writers like London and Chesterton. Either they describe forms of political violence emanating from the political right, or they suggest complicity by Western police and intelligence agencies in 'conventional' terrorism. In so doing, these books are able to suggest the role of deception, provocation and masquerade in both terrorism and intelligence.

Awareness of the potential of provocateur operations is widespread, though the real perpetrators are not necessarily condemned for such activities. In *The Little Drummer Girl*, for example, there are several references to the Israeli campaigns of assassination and sabotage throughout Europe, and le Carré indicates that such acts are often blamed on third parties, either Middle Eastern or European. The suggestion is thus that Arab terrorist groups are often blamed for internecine violence which was in fact the work of their Israeli enemies; and the ever-professional author suggests that this is nothing more than good tradecraft.

On the other hand, it is possible to use the element of provocation to divert blame for terrorist actions away from radical causes. Naturally, the popular fiction of the Soviet Union and its allies uses Western intelligence groups as villains, who are responsible for terrorist actions among other wrongdoing. In *Tass is Authorized to Announce . . .*, the Soviet author Semyonov creates a portrait of CIA agents and their terrorist surrogates quite as sinister as their KGB counterparts in *The Spike*.[30] And while Western conservatives use terrorism to stigmatize liberals and leftists, the Poles and Soviets associate similar violence with Ukrainians and German *revanchistes*. But such an attack on CIA and Western atrocities has not been confined to the Eastern bloc. In fact, the usefulness of terrorism for established authorities is a theme in a number of American or British novels which portray intelligence groups using an act of violence as the cover for growing repression, or even an outright seizure of power. These imaginary provocations have included an assassination of the British politician Enoch Powell; and a Shi'ite suicide attack against the US Congress.[31]

Especially since the mid-1970s, there have also been a number of books associating terrorist actions directly with domestic security agencies. In the United States, political events gave rise to numerous theories about misdeeds by police and intelligence agencies, possibly extending as far as participation in acts of terror and assassination. In fiction, the conspiracy view was reflected in a number of books depicting 'rogue CIA agents' or other intelligence operatives as primarily responsible for political murder and mayhem. The case for such a conspiracy view appeared strengthened by the exposure of Edwin Wilson's Libyan adventures in the late 1970s. In addition, the evidence of bitter divisions within the CIA led authors to portray terrorism as the outcome of such internal politics.[32] The 'Terror International' idea recurs in such books, but in the guise of groups and agencies using violence and assassination to protect the ruling class from liberals like the Kennedys.[33] This idea is chiefly found in American fiction, but by no means exclusively. In Britain, for example, a novel like *Days Like These* portrays MI5 and police connivance in fascist politics and bombing activities.[34]

Many of these books on intelligence conspiracies and assassinations were ephemera, deserving little attention; but one notable exception was Don DeLillo's *Libra*, a bestseller which earned enough critical respect to be seen as part of the literary mainstream.[35] The book focuses on the life of Lee Harvey Oswald, but the assassination of President Kennedy is depicted as the result of rivalries between different sections of the US intelligence community. In fact, the conspiracy is originally intended not to kill the President, but only to scare him into taking seriously the need for intelligence and security. Of particular interest for our purposes are the discussions between the intelligence officials, where we are infallibly reminded of Conrad's diplomatic terrorists.

Libra presents a politically sophisticated and undogmatic view of a terrorist action. Other works in the genre were interesting as radical manifestos, offering a polemic as systematic and thorough as that offered by *The Spike* on the opposing political side. One of the most remarkable was *The Spymaster*, by Donald Freed, who argues for a major intelligence role in most of the acts of political violence in recent American history, including the various assassinations.[36] In this view, the violence grew out of struggles within the American ruling class. Both sides used intelligence factions as their weapons, with leaders who are readily identified with (respectively) William Colby and James Angleton. *The Spymaster* is a compendium of conspiracy theories about the origins of terrorism and political violence, and at every stage, it inverts the assumptions of the mainstream literature. Probably the most striking example occurs when the hero, the liberal 'Spymaster', attempts to avert the murder of President Kennedy by the ultra-rightists within the intelligence community. He is originally warned of the plot by the KGB, who dispatch for this purpose their star agent Kim Philby – assuredly his only appearance as a hero in Western popular fiction.

CONCLUSION

Public concern with terrorism was very much alive at the end of the 1980s, and it seems likely that there will continue to be a significant market for fiction in this area. However, it seems improbable that there can be many more novels that rehash the common themes of the last 20 years; books that simply describe ingenious terrorist plots and the means of thwarting them. For instance, as fictional devices, airline hijackings once had a shocking novelty which they assuredly no longer possess. Equally hackneyed are the popular villains of recent years. There would appear to be little potential for further permutations on either the 'rogue CIA' theme of the 1970s, or on the alleged KGB role in terrorism that so excited writers in 1979 and 1980. It is remarkable that the public appetite for Arab and Soviet terrorist masterminds has endured as long as it has, and it might be hoped that current political changes might lead authors to seek new villains. On the other hand, just as the Palestinians are shedding their status of popular demons for the West, so the Iranians appear to be striving to reinforce popular stereotypes of Middle Eastern terrorism.

If in fact the spy-terrorism genre can no longer continue in the paths that have proved so successful for 20 years, then what directions might it take in the next decade? Certainly one possibility would be to explore conflicts and movements far removed from those that have become so familiar. For example, there would seem to be great potential in moving from the now traditional Middle Eastern setting to examine other terrorist groups – perhaps the Basque ETA or Peru's Sendero Luminoso – who have not hitherto been of great interest to thriller writers.[37]

But the success of authors such as le Carré, DeLillo, Ignatius and Clancy also kindles a hope that there will be increased interest in more carefully crafted books that pay serious attention to the politics of terrorism; and which address the real world of counter-terrorism. Books by these authors differ enormously in tone, theme and subject matter, and yet they have certain things in common. Above all, they demonstrate a much greater focus on the intelligence dimensions of terrorism, and a renewed emphasis on the spy novel roots of the genre. All use a terrorist context to explore what is perhaps the finest contribution of the espionage novel to literature, the closely observed study of individuals attempting to maintain their personal values in the moral 'wilderness of mirrors' that is secret intelligence. This is a world of constantly shifting loyalties where conventional notions of truthfulness and friendship cease to apply; a world in which the 'Perfect Spy' is perhaps the agent whose whole life has been a story of lies and treachery, and whose career culminates in the betrayal of every political and personal loyalty. The heroes of le Carré or Ignatius both attempt to preserve friendships and personal links with terrorists or guerrillas despite the overwhelming pressures to betray them in a higher cause; and the resulting internal conflicts provide a literary theme of considerable interest.

In other words, all these books have achieved critical and commercial success by reaffirming the virtues of the espionage component of the terrorist novel; and in doing so, they have perhaps helped to return the genre to the distinctive qualities that were found in its early twentieth-century roots. It is not certain whether this encouraging trend will continue, but both of Clancy's previous bestsellers[38] inspired a host of imitators of varying quality, and we may naturally expect a future wave of novels that view terrorism from the point of view of the analyst or technician. In other words, the intelligence element in such novels is likely to become ever stronger, and we can reasonably hope both for greater realism and political subtlety in portrayals of terrorists and their enemies. It may be rash to express optimism about trends in popular fiction, but the case of terrorism novels might provide an important exception.

NOTES

1. John D. MacDonald, *The Green Ripper* (New York, 1979).
2. For example, Swedish detective Martin Beck ingeniously manipulates the media in order to deceive terrorists into miscalculating a proposed assassination by time-bomb: Maj Sjöwall and Per Wahlöö, *The Terrorists* (New York, 1976). Frederick Forsyth's *Day of the Jackal* offers a classic account of the ways in which an international terrorist can shift identities in order to cross frontiers.
3. John le Carré, *The Little Drummer Girl* (New York, 1983).
4. Tom Clancy, *Patriot Games* (New York, 1988).
5. These schemes often become wildly elaborate: see for example the use of a blimp to attack the Superbowl crowd in Thomas Harris, *Black Sunday* (New York, 1975).
6. David Ignatius, *Agents of Innocence* (New York, 1987). For the real-life background of the novel and the world of Abu Hassan Salameh, see Steve Posner, *Israel Undercover: Secret Warfare and Hidden Diplomacy in the Middle East* (Syracuse, 1987), pp.277–89; also Michael BarZohar and Eitan Haber, *The Quest for the Red Prince* (London, 1983).
7. This classic age of terrorism has also attracted the attention of modern thriller writers. See especially Ken Follett, *The Man from St Petersburg* (New York, 1982).
8. Jack London, *The Assassination Bureau, Ltd.* (New York, 1963).
9. Jack London, *The Iron Heel* (London, 1974)
10. G.K. Chesterton, *The Man Who Was Thursday* (London, fifth edition 1945).
11. Joseph Conrad, *The Secret Agent* (London, 1974 ed.).
12. In *This Gun For Sale* (1936)
13. John Buchan, *A Prince of the Captivity* (London, 1933).
14. Richard Condon, *The Manchurian Candidate* (New York, 1959).
15. Frederick Forsyth, *The Fourth Protocol* (New York, 1984); Alfred Coppel, *The Hastings Conspiracy* (New York, 1980).
16. Claire Sterling, *The Terror Network* (New York, 1981); Edward Herman, *The Real Terror Network* (Boston, 1982).
17. Uri Ra'anan, *et al.*, *Hydra of Carnage: International Linkages of Terrorism – the Witnesses Speak* (Lexington, MA, 1986); Benjamin Netanyahu (ed.), *Terrorism: How the West can Win* (New York; 1986).
18. Bob Woodward, *Veil: the Secret Wars of the CIA 1981–1987* (New York, 1987).
19. Robert Ludlum, *The Icarus Agenda* (New York, 1988).
20. For a horror theme in the traditional spy novel, see Brian Lumley, *Necroscope* (New York, 1988).
21. Arnauld De Borchgrave and Robert Moss, *The Spike* (New York, 1980); Moss and De Borchgrave, *Monimbó* (New York, 1983).
22. De Borchgrave and Moss, *The Spike*, p.456. Both authors were very active in advocating the same counter-terrorism policies in real life as they suggest in their novels. For

example, De Borchgrave has undertaken journalistic work with Michael Ledeen, and he contributed an essay to Netanyahu (ed.), *Terrorism*; which also featured articles by Ledeen and Sterling. Moss wrote *The Collapse of Democracy* (London, 1977).
23. For example in films like *Half Moon Street*.
24. For the rather ambiguous attitude towards revolutionary violence in Ireland, see for example Bill Granger, *The November Man* (New York, 1979); Clancy, *Patriot Games*.
25. Gordon Stevens, *Do Not Go Gentle* (New York, 1987); John D. Randall, *The Jihad Ultimatum* (New York, 1987).
26. William J. Caunitz, *One Police Plaza* (New York, 1984). The idea of the Israelis as key auxiliaries in the American anti-terrorist struggle found wide credibility. For example, one of the most remarkable fictional works on terrorism is *The Turner Diaries*, by 'Andrew MacDonald', which is notable precisely because it wholly espouses the cause of the terrorists themselves (Arlington, VA, 2nd edition, 1980). This violently anti-Semitic book offers a blueprint for the overthrow of the US government. However, it is interesting that the terrorist characters view their chief opponents not as the bumbling FBI, but as the Israeli agents and spymasters who are seen as the real masters of the country – the 'Zionist Occupation Government'.
27. Howard Kaplan, *Bullets of Palestine* (New York, 1987); Compare Gay Courter, *Code Ezra* (Boston, 1986).
28. Steven Emerson, *Secret Warriors: Inside the Covert Military Operations of the Reagan Era* (New York, 1988). David C. Martin and John Walcott, *Best Laid Plans: the Inside Story of America's War against Terrorism* (New York, 1988).
29. Gayle Rivers, *The Specialist* (New York, 1985).
30. Julian Semyonov, *Tass is Authorized to Announce . . .*, translated by Charles Buxton (New York, 1988). This Soviet riposte to conservative Western views of terrorism was also exemplified in books like Boris Svetov, *et al.*, *International Terrorism and the CIA* (Moscow, 1983); Nikolai Yakovlev, *CIA Target – the USSR* (Moscow, 1984).
31. Arthur Wise, *Who Killed Enoch Powell?* (London, 1972); Margaret Atwood, *The Handmaid's Tale* (New York, 1987).
32. Although most of the 'rogue CIA' stories were politically liberal in tone, the idea was also used by strongly conservative writers. For example, David Atlee Phillips depicted the 'Carlos' group of the 1970s as having been penetrated and taken over by one such renegade American agent (*The Terror Brigade* (New York, 1989)). Phillips is the former CIA officer who was a vigorous opponent of the intelligence exposés of the 1970s.
33. This tradition was well represented in the cinema by films like *The Parallax View* (1974), which is loosely based on the novel of the same name by Loren Singer (New York, 1970). Compare James Grady, *Six Days of the Condor* (New York, 1974); Jim Garrison, *The Star-Spangled Contract* (New York, 1976).
34. Nigel Fountain, *Days Like These* (London, 1985).
35. Don DeLillo, *Libra* (New York, 1988).
36. Donald Freed, *The Spymaster: A Novel of Secret America* (New York, 1980). Freed had earlier published fictionalized accounts of the alleged intelligence conspiracies in the assassinations of John Kennedy (*Executive Action*) and his brother Robert (*The Killing of RFK*).
37. The Philippine New People's Army is the subject of Ross Thomas's *Out on the Rim* (New York, 1987).
38. Respectively *The Hunt for Red October* and *Red Storm Rising*.

Why I Write Spy Fiction

JOHN STARNES

When I was asked by the Editor to write this essay, I agreed, although I am not sure I know why I write spy fiction or, if I do know, that I want to share the knowledge with others. My reluctance to share the secret no doubt is partly due to superstition, an irrational fear that by so doing I may incur the wrath of the gods and have my creative powers destroyed. No doubt there also is an element of sheer laziness involved; a wish to avoid the intellectual exercise of finding out why I write spy fiction and explaining it in a rational, seductive manner.

I have written five spy novels. Four have been published, and the fifth, which I started over four years ago, has yet to be published. The first three are a trilogy, in a Cold War setting, the TV and film rights for which have been sold to David Pictures Incorporated of Toronto. In the summer of 1989 I also concluded a contract with the CBC, giving them the right to make a radio adaptation of the three books to be broadcast by the CBC in two one-hour programs, no later than July 1992. The fourth spy novel is set in North America, in the latter half of the 1700s. It is based largely on a manuscript I first wrote about 1938 while living in Montreal. All four books have been distributed only in Canada.

Born in 1918, I was brought up, like many of my generation, on spy thrillers by authors such as Joseph Conrad, Erskine Childers, E. Phillips Oppenheim, Baroness Orczy, Edgar Wallace, John Buchan, Herman C. McNeile, Somerset Maugham and Compton Mackenzie. Being an only child I had the run of the small but well-stocked library in my parents' house. There was an additional reason for my early interest in books. At the age of about nine or ten, while at a summer camp in New England, I contracted a particularly nasty form of streptococcus blood poisoning. This was before antibiotics were discovered and, apart from nearly having my right arm amputated, I was in and out of Montreal hospitals for nearly a year and invalided for another year. I was out of school for much of this period. Radio was in its infancy and television programs were non-existent. Thus, books became an essential element of my entertainment.

During my long period of convalescence I read omnivorously, not only spy novels but everything I could lay my hands on. My tastes were eclectic. I was as fascinated with spy fiction as I was with Charles Kingsley's *Westward Ho*, Jane Austen's *Pride and Prejudice* or Alexander Dumas' marvellous tales of adventure, to mention only a few of the books I recall having read during this period. I remember having been strongly influenced by stories of the First World War: for example, stories about British 'Q' boats which, disguised as fishing and merchant vessels, successfully stalked German submarines and other German naval vessels.

Spy fiction, therefore, was something I learned to appreciate from an early age and an urge to write seems to have been with me for many years. During the Second World War I served for a time in the Canadian Intelligence Corps headquarters overseas, acquiring some practical knowledge about the real world of spies, and some time after joining the Department of External Affairs, I headed the organization from 1958 to 1962 in that department which dealt with security and intelligence matters. At the same time I was chairman of the Canadian Joint Intelligence Committee. In 1970 I left the Department of External Affairs to become the first civilian Director-General of the Security Service of the Royal Canadian Mounted Police, until I resigned in 1973.

Thus, by the time I began to write my first spy novel, about 1979, I had acquired a good deal of knowledge about espionage and counter-espionage and many other security and intelligence activities. More important, during the periods 1958–62 and 1970–73 I acquired a first-hand, intimate knowledge of the close-knit international community of security and intelligence, how it worked or failed to work, and some of the extraordinary personalities involved. I learned that often spy fiction is but a pale shadow of reality. Many of the real spy cases of which I had knowledge were more bizarre than even the most lurid spy fiction. One or two were sheer farce. Some recent books, such as Peter Wright's *Spycatcher*, illustrate the point. Despite its gross exaggerations, inaccuracies and several boring chapters, Wright's book about the real world of counter-espionage and counter-subversion beats most invented stories by a country mile.

I decided early in 1972 to take early retirement but I was unable to give effect to my decision until April 1973, when I felt I could do so without harming the Security Service's work or incurring too heavy a financial penalty in the form of a reduced pension. I resigned at the relatively early age of 55 out of sheer frustration; frustration with the evident lack of interest of ministers and senior officials in the very serious problems of the Security Service and frustration with the unwillingness of the Commissioner of the RCMP to make the Security Service 'more civilian and more separate in character', a key feature of my appointment.

In April 1973, for the first time in my adult life I was completely free of the stultifying restrictions imposed by working in any bureaucracy. I was, of course, bound by the undertakings of one kind and another not to disclose classified information acquired in one's work which anyone dealing with security and intelligence questions is required to observe. For the first few months I simply revelled in no longer having to obey someone else's orders. But during this time I began to think about resurrecting a novel of adventure I had partly finished in the late 1930s. Entitled *Captain Quanide*, it dealt with the life of a soldier of fortune during the American War of Independence. Eventually it formed the basis for my fourth novel to be published, *The Cornish Hug*.

My literary ambitions were shelved when I was approached at different times by the Department of Justice, the Treasury Board and the Department of Manpower and Immigration to work under contract on various projects. This work occupied a good deal of my time until about 1977 when whatever plans I had to write were swept aside by the establishment of the Keable Commission by the Parti Québecois in Quebec, and the McDonald Commission by the Federal government to inquire into 'certain activities of the Royal Canadian Mounted Police'. Since most of the 'activities' in question had been carried out by the Security Service of the RCMP, which I had headed, I was called upon to testify, at length, in public and in camera. In all I had about 130 hours under oath, leaving little time for writing novels.

As the work of the two very different commissions unfolded I became increasingly disheartened and disgusted by the hypocrisy, political maneuvering and patent unfairness involved. Eventually, the Keable Commission was shut down, but the McDonald Commission continued its work until the summer of 1981 when it was wound down, more than four years after its establishment on 6 July 1977. I attempted to work off some of my frustrations by writing a non-fiction book entitled 'Operation Orestes'. Explaining the purpose of the book in the introduction I wrote:

> There can be no question that the maintenance of internal security involves difficult, sometimes distasteful decisions. As is the case in so many matters of public policy, ideal solutions are hard to find, and the issues involved cannot always be portrayed and perceived in black and white terms. The truth often seems to lie outside all popular political perceptions, whether they be right-wing or left-wing in character. Yet, in matters affecting the nation's security it is necessary to eschew political expediency and finally to deal with reality rather than appearances; to be declarative rather than equivocal. . . .

I added:

> Not least among the reasons for wishing to write such a book is the fact that the Security Service is not merely some disembodied bureaucratic concept; it is people. Men and women who are prepared to dedicate

a good part of their lives to their job. These human assets are worth more in the end than any organization, even an agency as unusual as a security service. Hopefully, some of what I have written may contribute to a better public understanding of what those men and women have chosen to do.

After I had finished this work I made no attempt to have it published. The draft manuscript gathers dust on a shelf. Instead, I began to turn over in my mind the idea of writing a novel about espionage which could deal with some of the unpleasant realities behind the existence of an organization such as the RCMP Security Service. The idea for my first novel to be published, *Deep Sleepers*, began to take shape.

I have been asked whether the book had a didactic purpose. I believe it did, in that the discussions about the work of a security service which took place in public and in camera convinced me that Canadians generally were uninformed, uninterested and hypocritical about security and intelligence matters. Using the novel form, I hoped, perhaps naively, that I might be able to change Canadian attitudes in some slight measure. I do not think I have succeeded.

The book does illustrate some of the hidden, unpleasant realities of espionage and counter-espionage, but it was not long before I began to forget my didactic purpose and telling the story became a more worthwhile and satisfying end in itself. Among other things it became a love story. The various characters took over and became real people with whom I lived each day, and sometimes part of the night and early morning as well. As the plot and the characters developed I became more and more absorbed. I began to forget the frustrations of the activities surrounding the McDonald Commission and to enjoy the sheer pleasure of creating something.

At the outset I was concerned that knowledge of real espionage cases of which I had knowledge might inadvertently creep into the story. I was also concerned to avoid mentioning some of the more exotic and secret methods of espionage and counter-espionage to which I might have become privy as head of the RCMP Security Service. However, the concerns I had on this score, and particularly insofar as tradecraft was involved, were quickly dispelled as I started to do the necessary research for the book.

I soon discovered that many matters which had been classified 'top secret', or even higher, in the early 1970s, by the early 1980s were in the public domain, having been published in numerous magazine and newspaper articles in Europe and North America. Even more astonishing to me was to discover how much detailed information had been published in book form: for example, John Barron's book, *KGB* (1974), R.V. Jones's

Most Secret War (1978), Stevenson's book about Sir William Stephenson, *A Man Called Intrepid* (1976), Ray Cline's *Secrets, Spies and Scholars* (1976), *The Espionage Establishment* (1967) by David Wise and Thomas Ross and James Bamford's *The Puzzle Palace* (1982) and the seminal work *British Intelligence in the Second World War* (1979) by F. H. Hinsley and three collaborators, to mention only a few.

By the time my third spy novel, *Orion's Belt*, was published in 1983 I can honestly say the principal reason for writing had become the sheer pleasure of doing so. I discovered I liked telling a story, the intricacies of developing a plot and creating characters to fit into it. No doubt there are always other reasons for writing spy novels, but whatever these may have been for me they took second place to the fun (and the agony) of writing fiction.

The fourth novel, *The Cornish Hug*, although dealing with espionage, did so in an historical setting, using much of the research I had done 40 years earlier for a novel dealing with the American War of Independence. The new manuscript suffered from lack of additional research and editorial guidance and the fact that at the time I was still deeply involved in the aftermath of the McDonald Commission hearings and court cases being held in Montreal, where I appeared as a witness for the defence.

There are those, such as Frederick Forsyth (*The Day of the Jackal* and *The Fourth Protocol*), who suggest that a relaxation of the Cold War may adversely affect the appetite of the reading public for espionage thrillers. Perhaps the suggestion is right; readers are a fickle lot and, if there is a public perception (however mistaken) that spy fiction is out of date then books of that genre simply will not sell. However, while spy novels could fall out of fashion, I'm inclined to think that any such development would be short-lived. In my view spy thrillers will continue to attract readers as new spying techniques, targets and twists are discovered and developed. Even if the Americans and the Russians no longer have each other as their principal targets they will continue to perceive threats to their security which can only be met by espionage, and old conflicts, such as the Arab–Israeli confrontation, will continue to provide spy novelists with fresh material and a reading audience. Espionage and literature about spies have existed for centuries, and even should *glasnost* lead to a genuine rapprochement between the Soviet Union and Western nations they will not cease to spy on one another. Even the best of friends and the closest of allies carry out espionage against one another.

If I am wrong, however, and spy fiction ceases to attract readers, I for one will be genuinely sorry since I enjoy reading it, and enjoy creating it even more. To me the writing of spy fiction presents a special kind of challenge; the invention of plausible plots, settings and characters to be woven into a story which titillates readers and to which they can relate easily.

In a certain sense the fifth story, entitled *Albric's Cloak*, which I began writing about four years ago, has become a victim of *glasnost*. Although the *leitmotiv* is co-operation between the KGB, the CIA and the British SIS in defeating a powerful, ruthless group of international crooks who have become the possessors of a economically viable means of turning base metals to gold, much of the story is in a pre-Gorbachev setting with strong overtones of Cold War espionage. I am going to have to rewrite it because, even if readers have not yet turned away from Cold War spy thrillers (the latest bestseller lists certainly suggest spy novels are still among the top ten), a number of Canadian publishers, editors and literary agents appear to have done so. At least, that was the impression I received from several publishing houses (including one US and one British publisher) to whom I sent the manuscript after my former publisher went out of business.

From my rather limited experience in trying to find a Canadian publisher for *Albric's Cloak* I find it hard to make a judgement about how difficult it is to have spy fiction published in Canada. I approached four well-known Canadian publishing houses and three eminently successful literary agents with discouraging results. One publisher was kind enough to send me a copy of one of their readers' reports which concluded: 'A great read. The book moves at a nice pace, with a few interesting plot twists. The characters are dynamic and the writing is solid'. In writing to me the senior editor said, 'The book received positive comments from both readers and were we actively seeking to establish a stronger presence in this genre, the outcome might have been different'.

Another publisher wrote: 'Spy thrillers have not been a particular specialty of ours in the past, and it appears that for the foreseeable future we will not be expanding in that area'. A third wrote: 'Your manuscript was read with interest by several readers and although there is much good in it, we felt there was insufficient enthusiasm and commitment to allow us to make a positive decision regarding the publication of your book'.

On the basis of my brief experience it would appear that spy fiction may not be a top priority with some of the better known Canadian publishing houses and literary agents. However, even during the short space of time involved, I discovered there was a high rate of turnover among the senior editors and staff of some of the publishing houses I approached, leaving the impression that their policies on such questions as whether to publish spy fiction are in a state of flux and subject to quick change.

A senior editor associated with a large, well-known British publishing house, to whom I sent the manuscript of *Albric's Cloak* and copies of my published books, wrote early in 1989:

> Thank you very much indeed for letting me read your stories. I am afraid I don't think I can offer to act for you. The spy diplomatic backgrounds are well done in two of them and the background of Canada is well done too. But I just didn't find the atmosphere strong enough or the stories exciting enough to know how to place them effectively for you. I do apologize for writing such a disappointing letter. I fear this is more a reflection on the market place not the quality of your writing.

While the latter comment no doubt was intended to let me down gently it also may indicate that some English publishers perceive there is a waning market for spy literature.

If there is a lack of interest by Canadian publishers in spy literature, in part perhaps, this can be attributed to the absence of a Canadian literary tradition of spy thrillers. At least, there seems to be no literary tradition of spy literature of the kind that has existed in England for so many years. That is not to say that there are not a number of good Canadian authors such as Anthony Hyde (*Red Fox*), Heather Robertson (*Igor: A Novel of Intrigue*) and William Deverell (*Mindfield*) who have successfully written spy literature, and I have no doubt there are many others. However, whether there will ever exist in Canada a unique genre of spy fiction based on Canadian themes, history and politics remains to be seen. One difficulty in developing such a body of literature may lie in the rather limited appeal such books are likely to have outside Canada.

I have been encouraged by the responses of readers, many of whom have offered worthwhile suggestions which have guided me in further writing. I am always astonished (and embarrassed) at the number of readers who spot typographical, grammatical and other errors and take the trouble to write about them. Since the Public Lending Rights Commission came into being I have had a rough measure of the extent of the public's continued interest in the books. I am happy to say the financial reimbursement I have received from them has continued unabated, and even increased in 1988/89, suggesting the books continue to be in demand.

Reviews of their works are, of course, a matter of importance to authors. On the whole I believe I have been fairly treated by those reviewing my books in publications and on TV and radio, with the possible exception of one reviewer who was unnecessarily unkind in writing about *The Cornish Hug*, regarding it, mistakenly I think, as an unwarranted intrusion by a rank amateur into the serious business of the professional historian. Yet *The Cornish Hug* was never intended as anything more than a spy novel, an adventure story set in North America in the 1770s. I have no pretensions to being an historian or an academic and I am the first to admit that my historical research was hurried and lacking in professional experience.

I have mentioned some spy novelists who may have had an early influence on me. I have, of course, tried to keep pace with contemporary spy fiction. In particular, I enjoy reading books written by Len Deighton, John le Carré and Ken Follett, although none of them has had any special influence on my own writing. I have been invited to review a number of such books, for example, le Carré's *The Little Drummer Girl* and *The Russia House*. While I admire le Carré's writing, the complicated plots he develops and the extraordinary characters he creates, I would find it impossible to emulate his style and his literary skills. However, I find that a number of the recent non-fiction books about espionage, such as John Costello's *Mask of Treachery*, Robin W. Winks' *Cloak and Gown*, Phillip Knightley's *The Second Oldest Profession* and Nigel West's *Games of Intelligence*, while not influencing me as such, nevertheless have provided me with new ideas and fresh insights for future spy novels I may write.

Critical Afterthoughts and Alternative Historico-Literary Theories

D. CAMERON WATT

The essays that have preceded this epilogue have dealt, in some detail, with the development of spy fiction and films in the twentieth century and their relationship with real intelligence. Several essays, most notably those of Professors MacIntosh and Jenkins, have gone much further, discussing in detail the relationship between spy fiction and ethics, and the use of mainly American fiction as a tool in the political debate over terrorism in recent years.

The authors come from three rather different cultures and reflect the different development of the study of intelligence in those three cultures. The writers from Britain attack their themes mainly from a historical basis, the distinctive mark of the British school, as I have pointed out elsewhere.[1] The Americans are mainly concerned with the moral issues involved in reconciling clandestine organizations, or rather organizations whose activities are by their nature rendered ineffective if they cease to be clandestine, with the principles of democratic control and the division of powers established in the American constitution, with its particular emphasis on the role given to the legislature of review and scrutiny of the actions of the administration. The Canadians, as with the Canadian people today, balance uneasily between the British and American examples, a balance reflected in the programme of activities of the Canadian Association of Security and Intelligence Studies, as reflected in their admirable newsletter. Mr Starnes, a former director-general of the Security Service of the RCMP turned writer of spy fiction, laments the apparent lack of interest among Canadian publishers (and, therefore, among the Canadian reading public) in spy fiction.

Common to all the authors, however, seems to be the acceptance of spy-fiction as what the French would call *un don*, as a given collection of undifferentiated data. This is perhaps a pity. For the examples they discuss seem to me, as a lifelong reader of spy-fiction, to cover at least four different groups of phenomena. The first is comprised of fiction in which spies play a part, one which would be very much enlarged if one added to it fiction in which secret associations, secret societies and so on play a part. The second group constitute straight spy adventure stories, stories about spies, secret services, in which the hero, or more rarely the heroine, is the employee of some more secret than secret branch of a country's clandestine services. This is very often a sub-branch of the thriller. James Bond spent much of his time dealing with international criminal organizations, despite the fact that he worked for the SIS; Modesty Blaise works very closely with the British head of SIS, and there is a political angle to the enterprises on which she engages to help him. But her opponents are usually professional criminals, not the KGB or its equivalents.

The third category is the spy novel as a branch of the political novel, especially the political conspiracy novel (which is not quite the same thing). Many of William Haggard's novels[2] turn on this type of theme which also covers novels about political conspiracies thwarted, usually by individual maverick agents who are as much at odds with their own bureaucratic heads as they are with the high-up politicos who are plotting to subvert democracy or whatever. The most extreme example of this must be Brian Freemantle's Charlie Muffin, with his smelly feet, cheap clothes and ultimate ratlike ability to survive.

The last category is the spy novel as moral tale, the genre of Graham Greene, much of Ted Allbeury's work, and of John le Carré. Haggard (whose morality is not one of which one would presume Mr le Carré would approve, or *vice versa*, for that matter) writes with a strong moral tone of disapproval of the world in which his hero finds himself. His villains are slippery politicians, including at least one Labour prime minister with superficial parallels with Lord Wilson, diplomatists who, under stress,reveal a lack of integrity and so on. Incidentally, his hero gets on very, very well with his Soviet counterpart, and even accepts an invitation to go bear-shooting with him.

These categories are so very different from one another that it is extremely misleading to take examples from one and make them the basis for generalization; still more to lump together examples taken from two or more and make them the basis for some generalization. The second group are, after all, basically a development of the hero-based adventure story. The changes which the works of this genre have gone through since the days of the *Boy's Own Paper* reflect the changes in the contemporary environment in which adventure is credible. Apart from deserted valleys in the inner recesses of the Hindu Kush from which a piratical coup d'état was to have been launched against Kuwait, had it not been thwarted by Modesty Blaise, adventure in the unexplored parts of the globe of the Rider Haggard/ Jack London kind has not an awful lot left unexplored to draw on. Hence the popularity of adventure science fiction of the Robert Henlein genre. Spy fiction does, after all, cater for a very wide range of audiences (like detective fiction with its range from Mike Hammer to Ruth Rendell).

Which brings one to the motives of those who write about spies and spy fiction. It is difficult to avoid the impression, even where some of

the contributors to this volume are concerned, that for some the basic
motive is condemnatory. Like Calvin Coolidge's preacher on Sin, they are
'agin it'. Their greatest approval is given to writers of the Graham Greene/
Ted Allbeury/le Carré variety, for whom the whole range of covert and
clandestine activities represent a political equivalent of commercialized sex,
joyless, repetitive sin, in which innocence is corrupted, and the only end is
a degraded obscure death. Allbeury has permitted redemption to only two
of his heroes. In each one it took the form of escape, to a home in Somalia
with one of the sexiest heroines in any spy novel written since the war, or to
the life of a truck farmer in Vermont selling his produce by the roadside. Le
Carré has, so far, shown no such signs of belief in redemption. His attitude,
even to the unfortunate Smiley, is that of the Scots Calvinist minister, 'Ye're
all damned; damned; damned'. James Bond, by contrast, the target of so
much condemnation, has the almighty gall to enjoy it. Unforgivable.

The other attraction of the study of espionage and of its fiction is the
lure of the secret, the seduction of the 'inside story', the belief that
there is always a secret behind the façade. To know is to be oneself an
insider, to belong to the arcane innermost ring, to partake of real power.
From the secret societies of little boys to TV faction, journalism and the
airport bookstall school of espionage history with their interminable cries
of 'cover-up', the lure of 'knowledge' is irresistible. In its extreme form
this impulse leads to the conspiratorial school of historiography – in
the espionage fiction analyst it seems to lead to the investigation of an
endless regression of Chinese boxes or Russian *Matrushka* dolls; but like
schoolchildren's secret societies there is nothing in the end but the activity
itself.

Which brings one to the story itself. The structure of the spy story needs
more investigation before any developments in the genre (or, as argued
here, different genres) can be analysed. It is obvious, but important when
comparisons are being drawn between reality and fiction, to remark that a
story needs an inception and a dénouement. Reality, on the other hand,
knows no beginning save that arbitrarily selected by the historian, and very
few dénouements that can be defined as such. There is no end to the work
of real intelligence agencies any more than there is an end to history. And
it is only in retrospect that the historian, like any creative artist, can discern
the edges to the historical canvas, the opening and closing chords and the
leit-motiv to the historical opera, and whether it is a tragedy or a comedy
or in which proportions the two elements are mixed.

Fiction needs an end. Reality denies it. That is the first difference. Spy
fiction needs a success, a danger thwarted, a secret exposed or recovered,
an enemy robbed or deceived. Spy fiction needs an enemy; it needs too a
manichean approach, our side, their side, good versus evil. The enemy,
external or within, must be plausible in the eyes of the contemporary

audience or readership. One of the odder notes of the public debate in the 1980s over the openness of the media and its freedom from legal restraint (save where the privacy of the individual and any aspect of 'inter-ethnic' relations is involved) was the apparent conviction of opponents of the new official secrets legislation that there was no external enemy, no internal subversion, and therefore no need for any secrets legislation whatever. Their outcry, it must be said, did much to prevent, if not silence, any serious debate as to whether the new legislation had struck an appropriate balance between liberty and its protection.

The choice of the enemy has been made much of in discussion since the collapse of the Warsaw Pact in the last six months of 1989. But the most well-equipped and prepared of authors have changed their villains and their locale from book to book with an inventiveness to match that of Dick Francis, the writer of racetrack crime novels, who equips himself with a new hero, a new locale, a new crime, a new set of villains, and a complete change of cast every year. An excellent example is Eric Ambler who after a shaky start with a mad Balkan nuclear scientist (a story brilliantly redeemed by his hero, a mousy nobody transformed by concussion into a pulp fiction hero of Sexton Blake simplicity) ran through a whole gamut of left-wing defined villains, international arms traders, Italian Fascists, Balkan professional freelance agents (though never a Nazi), Indonesian colonels, up to his most brilliant device, the anonymous intelligence agencies of various great powers, made the subject of blackmail through an intelligence news sheet by the intelligence chiefs of two minor NATO powers in search of adequate funds on which to retire.[3] Not for him the boring predictability of endless KGB hitmen or conspirators (something which seems to have eroded the brilliance even of Anthony Price, whose obsession with a new generation of moles has reduced one of his most recent novels, *Here be Monsters* [1985], to little more than straight conversation).

But besides an enemy, spy fiction needs a device, a secret, a McGuffin, as Alfred Hitchcock termed it. Without a McGuffin there can be no threatened Apocalypse from which the hero will in due time (and possibly at the expense of his soul, if one is dealing with the Calvinists) save whatever he, or his readers, holds dear. In Conan Doyle's introduction of spies into Sherlock Holmes' range of consultancy, it was the plans of the latest British submarine. In real life in the years 1942–48, it was vital parts of American solutions to the engineering problems of developing a nuclear device that worked. In Adam Hall's latest novel, *Quiller KGB* (1989), there were two McGuffins, a plot to murder Mr Gorbachev, and a Gorbachev-approved plot to bomb the Berlin Wall open. Without a McGuffin there is no point around which the story can revolve and no threatened dénouement to keep the attention of the reader. Gavin Lyall's *The Secret Servant* (1986), perhaps the most original play on the hero as man of integrity in a very dodgy world, had as its McGuffin a letter revealing that Britain's answer to Henry Kissinger, a kind of amalgam of Sir Michael Howard, the late Hedley Bull and Professor Lawrence Freedman, had, in the course of service with a Long-Range Desert Group in North Africa in 1942 kept himself and the survivors of his group alive by killing and eating a French *poilu*. Even by Hitchcock's standard, this was a McGuffin and a half; Mr Lyall has wisely made no effort to top it. But there is a good deal to be said for historians of spy fiction suiting themselves to chart changes in the nature of the McGuffin, along with changes in the enemy as one of the indicators of whatever socio-literary developments they are investigating.

With this there are two other developments to be noticed. The first is the rise and fall of the innocent bystander as hero, the man (it has, I think, always been a man) who falls through the facade into the other side of the mirror. Richard Hannay in *The Thirty-Nine Steps* is one of the archetypes of this form of hero, one brought to an advanced state of development by Eric Ambler, even to the point in *The Intercom Conspiracy*, noted above, of killing off an earlier hero (for the sin, presumably, of having become an incompetent know-it-all) while introducing in his place a trio of innocents, the editor of the *Intercom* newsletter, his daughter and the Swiss psychiatrist who eventually becomes his son-in-law. Anthony Price recruits three of his innocent bystanders into his intelligence agency.

The second, to be true, has yet to happen; that is the development of the spy novel as game on the lines of the Dungeons and Dragons games so beloved of the computer-bewitched fantasists of the new generation. Their games, with the continuous interpolation of the need to choose between different actions, each of which unleashes new scenes of danger and new consequences, have been translated into newstore pulp fiction where the choice propels the reader backwards or forwards to different sections of the book. Such a development would go far to accommodate spy fiction to reality.

The essays in this collection have mainly concentrated on the spy-novel as a branch of the political novel. Here it must be said that, since the writings of John Buchan, with their increasingly easily chartable relationships with his levels of political knowledge and ethos, there has been a considerable deterioration. The political novel, at its best, as with, for example, Joyce Cary's portrait of Lloyd George's war-time Cabinet in *Prisoner of Grace* (1952) (a portrait based on Cary's conversations with L-G's surviving brother), can recreate atmosphere in a manner most historians envy. Even when pedestrian, as with Allen Drury's *Advise and Consent* (1966), the political novel can greatly enhance and enlighten our understanding of the political processes on which it turns. Le Carré's *Tinker, Tailor, Soldier, Spy* (1974) is very much that kind of book, depicting an élite of the 1930s, deprived of their empire, turning to treason. The trouble is that its central character, the mole, fails to match any of the 'moles' whose discovery made this kind of book so popular, having little in his make-up of Philby or Maclean, a little of Burgess, a little of Tom Driberg and little else, since on discovery his personality disappears and it becomes clear that le Carré's main targets of hostility are those who survived. What has been lost is any connection between the world of high politics as Buchan saw it, and the world in which his agents operated. One is tempted to comment that writers of spy fiction today do not seem to move in the same circles as they used to.

Instead, one has to see the spy-novel as an artefact in our understanding of the social history of the era in which it is written. In that connection it is perhaps worth relating the genre not only to the realities of contemporary espionage but also to changes in the literary fiction of which it is part. It is tempting in this context to see the emergence of 'working-class' anti-heroes of the kind evidenced by the hero of Len Deighton's early novels, *The Ipcress File*, *Horse under Water*, *Funeral in Berlin*, *Billion-Dollar Brain* and so on, engaged as he is in a constant class war with the gentlemen officers with their Brigade of Guards ties and Establishment connections, as the equivalent of the picaresque provincial heroes of the early novels of John Wain, Kingley Amis and John Braine, the hero of John Osborne's *Look Back in Anger* and the emergence of the 'kitchen sink' school of English painting. It should, of course, be noted that in no sense were Deighton's heroes actually working-class. Like the university students of the early 1950s, they were lower middle-class products of the grammar schools of the 1930s and 1940s, scholarship boys now enabled to 'stay on' past their sixteenth birthday and go to university on the wave of post-conscription further education and training grants and the 1944 Education Act. For the real working class, one had to turn to the novels of James Mitchell and his television series, *Callan* and *When the Boat Came In*, laid in the period between 1918 and 1938 in his native Tyneside.

Callan was a gaolbird, done for theft and GBH, who had bettered himself. The hero of Mitchell's MI5 style novels,[4] John Craig, was a working-class, battlefield-promoted, Geordie veteran of the Mediterranean Special Boats Squadron, who had gentrified himself and made money as the real brains behind a broken-down shipping company smuggling arms to the FLN as a development from smuggling cigarettes via Tangiers, who was recruited to MI5 as a result of being targeted by OAS terrorists. He, like Modesty Blaise, became a kind of classless James Bond, rougher than tough, international in his feeding habits (very Philhellene as a result of his SBS background, he had a hideout in Cyprus) a wine-drinker as much as a beer-boozer, a karate expert with a Black belt and with his own master in a much more knowledgeable vein than James Bond, but as infallible with the opposite sex, save for the book and a half (or to be more accurate, the latter half of one and the first half of another) when, as a result of having been tortured by electrodes attached to his genitals, he was rendered impotent.

Since Mitchell, we have had laid-back hippy agents, as in Adam Diment's novels, Yuppie agents as in Martin Woodhouse and the psychologically inward directed professional of the Quiller novels,[5] living for the adrenalin flow that the ultimate risks bring with them. Deighton, too, has turned to the professional classless agent whose job, like that of Smiley's assistant in *Tinker, Tailor, Soldier, Spy* and the following spy novels, is as much one of family predilection as that of any officer in the military, naval or diplomatic services. (Detectives, on the other hand, rarely seem to follow in their father's footsteps. In this they differ from professional criminals.) Perhaps this reflects a downturn in the growth of the intelligence services which was so marked a feature – in fiction at least – of the first two decades of the Cold War, as was the multiplication of little sub-branches akin to and often at odds with the mainstream intelligence services such as MI5 or MI6.

One of the effects of this professionalization of the agent-hero has been the disappearance from much of the more recent fiction of the moral issues which loomed so large in their predecessors. It is this which makes Professor MacIntosh's opening comment that 'writers of spy novels have to persuade us, their readers, that the activities about which they are writing are acceptable' so unfortunate and so distortive. It may very well be true of his own approach; but like so much writing today about issues of public morality in literature, unless it is backed by a very considerable body of sociological research, such a statement is normative, rather than, as it purports to be, descriptive. On sales alone, the evidence is against Professor MacIntosh; as it is on popular acceptance of vigilante-style films of the Charles Bronson *Death Wish* variety or girlie magazines of the top shelf of the newsagent's display kind. These, like hard-core porn films, may be driven from the market by police or legal action, or by heavy moral pressure on monopoly wholesalers such as W.H. Smith. But they do not have to persuade their own markets that they are acceptable, only the self-appointed censor-guardians of public morality. Ethical values, like everything else in plural societies, are themselves plural, and multi-cultural in multi-cultural societies, as the case of Salman Rushdie has reminded us.

This approach (and Professor MacIntosh is nothing if not Calvinist in his approach to spy-fiction) has largely vitiated what could have been the most valuable in this collection of essays. For spy fiction raises often in an extreme form a whole series of ethical and moral conflicts and dilemmas including that of a virtue Professor MacIntosh fails entirely even to mention, loyalty. 'Loyalty', said the Scot in C.S. Lewis's novel, *That Hideous Strength* (1945), 'is too important a virtue to be given to individuals'. In this he was raising in an acute form the whole series of problems of loyalty to a government or a whole series of governments of which one as a citizen or a public servant disapproves, problems which led the French military under the Third Republic to distinguish between the *pays légal* and the *pays réel*, and which so exercised the German generals and their staffs under Hitler, driving some into *Nursoldatentum*, others into varying degrees of conspiratorial opposition, others into varying degrees of 'fellow-travelling'. The deep agent, the sleeper, the mole, all are continuously involved in such conflicts. The double agent who can no longer remember to which side his real loyalties are given, with whom he really identifies, is as common a figure in spy-fiction as we are told he is or was in reality. Even before he got stuck in his Debrecen groove, Anthony Price showed signs of becoming obsessed with this theme with his young Russian agent murdered before he could actually defect to the Oxbridge culture with which he had come to identify in *Colonel Butler's Wolf* (1972), and the British intelligence officer entrapped in Korea into working for the Soviets who decides finally that he will *Soldier No More* (1981).

There is too the age-old problem of ends and means. Mr Starnes, himself a practitioner, has put the dilemma in one form in the lengthy passage from his unpublished book he quoted on p.206. The problem is, of course, as old as that of sin itself; though I do not know myself of a spy-novel version of James Hogg's *Confessions of a Justified Sinner* (1824), there are elements in James Angleton's justification of his methods or in Noel Behn's *The Kremlin Letter* (1966) which much resemble this. Indeed, Professor MacIntosh holds that 'espionage is essentially pointless human activity . . . and that it is hard to convey in fiction why . . . there are people willing to treat, in time of peace, another nation or group of nations as the *enemy*'. Here again the historian must express surprise at the absolute opposition of 'war' and 'peace' as states which, whatever the legal position, are so different from one another that in the real world there is no gradation; that intelligence, like insurance, crime-prevention, or the maintenance of at least a minimal effective response to the threat of force or blackmail, is not a legitimate, if not an essential factor in the maintenance of peace. One suspects that Professor MacIntosh has been misled by the spy counter-spy element in so much of modern spy fiction and faction, and has never considered the role that intelligence assessment plays in policy-making.

In the end one is left feeling that the many lures which have attracted and continue to attract readers to the very wide range of themes embodied in spy-fiction have never stirred in Professor MacIntosh's breast. (Few if any of the points made on pp.177–8 of his essay are relevant to Eric Ambler's novels, and it would be an interesting exercise to apply them to Anthony Price's *Our Man in Camelot* [1975].) This is a pity because it puts him in much the same class as the colour-blind criticizing Turner or the tone-deaf Richard Strauss. To concentrate only on the mindless thuggery of the drug-store adventure story, and to drag in the usual accusations of sexism and racism is morally uplifting only to those who enjoy a good prayer meeting condemning sin.[6]

It is interesting to turn from Professor MacIntosh's essay to that of Professor Jenkins, the only one to mention that fascinating version of the police-secret-society spy story, G.K. Chesterton's *The Man Who Was Thursday* (1908). There is a good deal more to Chesterton's book than fits into Professor Jenkins's thesis, most particularly in the chase which follows the revelation that (just as Stalin's purge trials revealed all but Lenin, Stalin and Molotov of Lenin's original politburo to have been capitalist agents), all the members of the secret society's inner circle but Thursday himself were police agents whom Thursday himself as head of the police as well as the secret society had recruited. But Jenkins's main theme is the American bookstall brand of the anti-terrorist novel. Again it is a pity he is not familiar with any English treatments of this theme apart from le Carré's *Little Drummer Girl*. The real paradox, which the kind of novel he is concerned to denounce cannot face, is that so-called 'terrorism' is the instrument of the small state or the nation *manqué*, where it is not an expression of civil war. It is the nature of the small state or the conspiratorial arm of the nation *manqué* that it will seek external allies; as it is and has been for most of this century the weapon of the major state unwilling or unable to risk a major conflict to turn to subversion and destabilization and to look for allies in the *IMRO* or the *Ustachi*, the Bretons, the Dashnaks displaced from Soviet Transcaucasia, as Italy, Hungary, Poland and Germany did between the wars. Mussolini subsidized the *émigré* Arab nationalist journal *La nation arabe*, Bari radio broadcast subversion throughout the Middle East, Italian and German arms reached the Arab rebels in Palestine, and in 1938 Britain had more military forces locked up in Palestine than it could have put at France's disposal in the event of a German attack on Czechoslovakia. But it is in the nature of such organizations that they are neither efficient nor amenable to direction from their paymasters. It is very doubtful that Mussolini authorized the assassination of King Alexander of Yugoslavia or Hitler that of Dolfuss. Terrorism itself walks the most uneasy of lines between crime and warfare: what is odd is that the British media – and Professor MacIntosh – cannot see that the political use of murder and explosives against British targets is a form of warfare and that those who choose to direct such usages are enemies. It is this which is perhaps the most significant change in moral attitudes among a significant section of the British élites since 1969, a change largely unmatched in America where foreign terrorism against American targets on American soil, as opposed to US aircraft or other targets outside the US, has not been known since Robert Kennedy's assassination.

Here again the differences between the three political cultures are apparent, something which makes the collection of voices in this book itself a fascinating contrast. Outside Northern Ireland, few British writers are concerned with Britain's use of force against overseas supporters of terrorism, though, in that curious transatlantic echo-effect that is itself one of the few phenomena that actually support the notion of a special relationship, British commentators waxed unbelievably critical of American actions against the same country which only the previous year had shot an unarmed policewoman in central London and got away with the murder unscathed and unpunished. But the kind of novel at which Professor Jenkins's criticism is directed has not found much of an audience in Britain and British attitudes to Israel are far more ambivalent at certain levels than are American. IRA terrorism in Britain itself, has, so far, proved containable; the general public remain unexcited save by the intermittent and well publicized outrage.

Philip Jenkins's essay can, however, call attention to what has perhaps been the major development in the general body of spy fiction since the war, the disappearance of the novel which focuses on the figure of the spy himself (or herself) operating within all the dangers and double loyalties faced by the classic agent in place, and, apart from Anthony Price's novels, of the role of intelligence assessment, in favour of the counter-intelligence and security aspects of covert activities. From Michael Gilbert's pair of 'elderly cut-throats', Mr Calder and Mr Behrens,[7] to Smiley's entrapment of Karla, and Len Deighton's latest trilogy,[8] only the Quiller novels among British best-sellers have dealt with the problems of agents operating in a hostile alien environment; and Quiller is an 'in-and-out' man, based on a safe base in London, now in a counter-intelligence role, now in a more positive rescue operation in that confusion of positive and defensive intelligence which is so marked a feature of contemporary spy-fiction.

There have, of course, always been novels of counter-espionage from Le Queux onwards; and the vast bulk of political thrillers have always taken as their theme the defence of democracy rather than the overthrow of tyranny. Buchan's *Courts of the Morning*, a translation of T.E. Lawrence's doctrine of guerrilla warfare into a Latin American context, is the outstanding exception. To that extent, perhaps, the writers of spy fiction have been operating within conventions of the kind laid down by Professor MacIntosh, even though they would not satisfy him as to the acceptability of their work.

Perhaps what has been lost is the early twentieth-century sense of advancing civilization, of the threat to everyday order voiced by Buchan's Scudder in *The Thirty-Nine Steps* cited earlier. In the Manichean world supposed by early Soviet attitudes to international law, an attitude parall-eled, as has frequently been pointed out, by the classic writings of Islamic international law, in which the world is divided into opposed segments, the abode of peace and the abode of war, between which any but the most short-term agreements are impossible, counter-espionage becomes synonymous with counter-subversion, treason becomes ideological rather than corrupt, and the price of freedom becomes not only eternal vigilance but, to the nervous and more excitable, eternal vigilantism. In such an atmosphere the Republic often seems in danger as much from its defenders as its enemies.

The record of the covert services in Britain in recent years has not been such as to inspire confidence in the judgement and good sense of its leadership. A school of writers was allowed to spring up who could carry its internal feuds on to the airport bookstalls, while memoir-writing or genuine historical work was discouraged. How far individual members of the covert services began to model themselves on the CIA is a matter of dispute. But there can be little doubt that the era of revelations in the history of the CIA fired a generation of British journalists with the desire to emulate the Pulitzer Prize winners on the other side of the Atlantic. They were fed with the stories spread by the CIA's defectors, the Agees and others, and helped by the political leg-work of men such as Duncan Campbell (a frequent contributor on such matters to the *New Statesman*), who had his own profoundly political reasons for wishing to reveal and discredit the secrecy surrounding the activities of Britain's covert services and its allies.

The development of this climate of opinion has gone *pari passu* with the rise to influence of the le Carré–Allbeury school and has been accompanied both by an increasingly critical attitude in the media towards the methods allegedly used by the covert services, including (shades of James Bond returning to roost) increasingly common allegations of 'shoot-to-kill' policies followed by the security forces against the IRA both in the cases subject to the Stalker investigation in Ireland and in the deaths of the three members of the IRA active unit in Gibraltar in 1989. Television has enhanced this effect by a series of dramas in which the covert services have, to varying degrees, been depicted as trigger-happy enemies of libertarians and of the rule of a law in which the death penalty has been abolished. One school of spy-fiction, the adventure fiction of the 1940s, of Calder and Behrens and of James Bond, has so much become part of the public image of the covert services that the liberal establishment and its favoured fiction and television writers are now in reaction against it, equating it with the better publicized activities of the CIA and the French security services in very different cultures with different traditions of the military role, different attitudes to violence and in France's case a recent clandestine civil war of extreme violence in which the President himself was the target of several assassination attempts. Literature reacts to its own perceptions of reality, perceptions profoundly influenced by uncritical transnational and transcultural importations.

There is, of course, one other quite different possible explanation for these historical changes in the manner, direction and theme of spy-fiction in Britain. It is suggested by two items of observable fact. The first is the enormous advantage gained by the British Secret Intelligence Service from its literary reputation at a time when it was at its lowest ebb facing the threat of Nazi Germany, unable to equip its agents in place properly for lack of funds, deeply penetrated by the German *Abwehr* and the Gestapo, unable to break the ciphers either of Soviet Russia or Germany and run by the most extraordinary collection of military-political weirdos. The second is the series of connections between the leaders of the Secret Intelligence Service and prominent British literary figures from Le Queux through Somerset Maugham and Compton Mackenzie to Geoffrey Household, Robert Harling, Ian Fleming, William Haggard, Ted Allbeury and the great le Carré himself, in whose Smiley novels the *cognoscenti* can recognize leading figures from the covert establishment. Everyone who has served in British intelligence in any role is bound by the Official Secrets Act to clear with the authorities any piece of writing which may use information which has come their way as a result of their experience in His/Her Majesty's Service. It follows, therefore, that the changes in literary fashion observable in spy fiction over the years, especially as regards the image of the covert services conveyed in them, must be at the dictation of the intelligence authorities themselves.

If this hypothesis is to be entertained it must follow that somewhere in the recesses of Century House and its successors, there is an office (call it DI 101(L)) with various sub-desks for film, radio, television, etc., tasked with the evolution of guidance to the stable of writers of spy-fiction. There must, of course, be, in addition, a committee, PIAM(O) Projection of Intelligence Activities in the Media (Official), on which sit representatives of the Joint Chiefs of Staff, the Cabinet Office, the Home Office, the intelligence branches of the three armed services, of DI_5 and DI_6, of GCHQ, of Special Branch, the SAS under the chairmanship of the appropriate official of the Foreign and Commonwealth Office, whose claims to literary pre-eminence among the non-military branches of the public services have never been questioned. There is, of course a PIAM(M) at the ministerial level, which never meets, but membership of which, carrying as it does the right to free personal copies of any book a minister feels it is in the public interest that he or she should read, is much sought after.

It is this machinery, originating as it did in the discovery by Mansfield Cummings that the small share of royalties which would accrue to the SIS (in secret, of course) would reconcile the Treasury to the establishment of a post for an aged officer for whose pension Cummings had omitted to arrange, which is responsible for the changes in the literary projection of

the services from the legendary work of Le Queux and Buchan through the
outré portrait of C himself painted by Willie Maugham, one calculated to
strike fear into the most stolid of Prussian breasts, to the macho licensed-
to-kill image of James Bond, before which even Kim Philby trembled, and
at the mere thought of whom Burgess and Maclean took to their heels and
fled. Rebecca West did her bit to order with her picture in *The Meaning of
Treason* (1949) of the implacable interrogator, William Skardon, charming
the most resolute of enemy agents or nuclear physicists into confessions.

Fleming's Bond, however, turned out, like Frankenstein's monster, to
have got a little out of hand. Innocent Britons abroad were being picked
up merely because they shared James Bond's taste in tea or cigarettes. The
Foreign Office chairman of PAIM(O) was moved to protest on behalf of the
overworked members of the Consular Service. The old-fashioned efficiency
of William Haggard's Colonel Russell, experienced as he was both with
high-class Italian houses of assignment and Russian bear-shoots, was not
enough. And so the great decision was reached, to unleash the debunkers.
It began with Graham Greene's bedside book, continued with *Our Man
in Havana*, and then, on one never-to-be-forgotten occasion when the
chairman was ill and a junior with an exaggerated sense of social guilt
and/or a depraved sense of humour (explanations vary) stood in for him,
the decision was taken. Not only would there be anti-Establishment agents
(Haggard had already been conceded a Jamaican deputy, to spite the South
Africans) including a hash-smoking hippy (the Home Office representative,
outvoted, resigned and the Special Branch representative, who had been
asleep during that meeting of the Committee, was posted to liaison work
on port-control on St. Helena); but there would be a school of debunkers.
Step forward, le Carré.

Rumour has it that the Committee now realizes it has another Frankenstein's monster on its hands. Various remedies have been proposed,
including Jeffrey Archer; but all to no avail. SIS has unfortunately not been
recruiting literary men for years. No new writer has come forward; and its
members, increasingly harried from No. 10, are getting a little desperate.
Watch the best-seller lists. Of course, there is always Douglas Hurd; he does
seem for the moment to be too well entrenched in the Foreign Office, where
he breathes a little too critically down the neck of PAIM(O)'s chairman. So
far, the Prime Minister has not persuaded him to make the great sacrifice
and resign to devote himself to writing. Time will tell.

The readers can choose which of the two explanations, the socio-
historical or the conspiratorial, they prefer. As a historian myself, I like
the flavour of the conspiratorial cock-up. But then I too served, long ago,
in intelligence. I have even been prosecuted successfully under the Official
Secrets Act before being positively vetted . . . so my lips are sealed.

NOTES

1. D. Cameron Watt, 'Intelligence Studies: The Emergence of the British School', *Intelligence and National Security*, Vol. 3, No. 2 (April 1988), pp. 338–41.
2. These include: *Slow Burner* (1958), *The Telemann Touch* (1958), *The Unquiet Sleep* (1962), *The High Wire* (1963), *The Antagonists* (1964) and *The Powder Barrel* (1965).
3. Eric Ambler, *The Intercom Conspiracy* (London, 1970).
4. Written under the pen-name of James Munro, these included: *The Man Who Sold Death*, *The Money that Money Cannot Buy* and *Innocent Bystanders*.
5. Adam Diment's novels, *The Bang Bang Birds*, *The Great Spy Race* and *Think Inc.*, appeared in the 1960s. Martin Woodhouse's *Tree Frog, Moon Hill, Blue Bone* and *Mama Doll*, appeared between 1965 and 1974. Adam Hall's long-running Quiller saga began with *The Berlin Memorandum* (1964).
6. J.J. MacIntosh replies to these criticisms in *Intelligence and National Security*, Vol. 6, No. 1 (January 1991).
7. Featured in two collections of short stories, *Game Without Rules* (1977) and *Mr Calder and Mr Behrens* (1982). Gilbert's novel, *After the Fine Weather* (1963), about a terrorist take-over in the Tyrol, is also worthy of attention.
8. *Hook, Line and Sinker* (1990) followed the successful *Game, Set and Match* (1986).